"Bryan Mercurio's book breaks new ground in making the link between international legal obligations and domestic policymaking in the field of pharmaceutical patent law. Demonstrating a solid understanding of the fundamentals and nuances of these complex areas, Mercurio's clearly written book offers expert analysis and recommendations which will garner attention from both scholars and policymakers. With the publication of this book, Professor Mercurio further cements his place as the world's leading international economic law scholar researching on intellectual property rights."

– Lorand Bartels, University of Cambridge

"Professor Bryan Mercurio once again demonstrates his expertise in both international economic law and intellectual property law . . . The book is a must-read for any scholar interested in this important topic, and in general. The book is innovative in approach, significantly advances the literature and should be engaged with not only by the academic community but also by policy-makers in Hong Kong and elsewhere. Page after page, the book demonstrates how few, if any, scholars possess Professor Mercurio's ability to expertly understand the details of the patent regime and the pharmaceutical industry, and with it offers clear and practical recommendations as a way forward in this important area of the law and policy . . . I deeply enjoyed [the book] and found it to be a superb piece of scholarship and one that is much needed in the legal literature."

– Professor Irene Calboli, Singapore Management University

"This timely, well-written and carefully analyzed book provides a definitive study of the pharmaceutical patent system in Hong Kong. More broadly, it reveals the far-reaching impacts new international trade and intellectual property standards can have on local health systems. The book strikes a rare but appropriate balance between a global perspective and local contextual analyses. It is a must-read for anybody interested in intellectual property, public health and international trade."

– Peter K. Yu, Professor and Director, Center for Law and Intellectual Property, Texas A&M University

"Professor Mercurio has written the definitive book on this important topic. Innovative, well researched and argued, it will have a significant impact on policy not only in Hong Kong but internationally. It is a must-read for academics, policy-makers and practitioners involved in the area."

– Professor Andrew Mitchell, University of Melbourne

T0381622

DRUGS, PATENTS AND POLICY

In pharmaceutical patent law, the problem of lack of policy direction and inappropriate legal framework is widespread – particularly among jurisdictions with little to no pharmaceutical research or manufacturing. This book aims to inform public policy and influence debate through a comprehensive review of Hong Kong's pharmaceutical patent law. By demonstrating the need for a holistic review of pharmaceutical patent laws and evaluating Hong Kong's system in light of health policy and economic and social factors, Bryan Mercurio recommends changes to the legal framework and constructs a more efficient and effective system for Hong Kong. He thoroughly evaluates the international framework and best practice models to offer a global perspective to each issue before providing local context in the analysis. While the focus of the book is Hong Kong, the analysis on pharmaceutical patent law and policy extends to other jurisdictions facing issues on reforming their national system.

BRYAN MERCURIO is Professor of Law, Associate Dean (Research) and Vice Chancellor's Outstanding Fellow of the Faculty of Law at the Chinese University of Hong Kong. He is a leading expert in the intersection between international economic law and intellectual property rights.

DRUGS, PATENTS AND POLICY

A Contextual Study of Hong Kong

BRYAN MERCURIO

The Chinese University of Hong Kong

CAMBRIDGE
UNIVERSITY PRESS

University Printing House, Cambridge CB2 8BS, United Kingdom

One Liberty Plaza, 20th Floor, New York, NY 10006, USA

477 Williamstown Road, Port Melbourne, VIC 3207, Australia

314-321, 3rd Floor, Plot 3, Splendor Forum, Jasola District Centre, New Delhi - 110025, India

79 Anson Road, #06-04/06, Singapore 079906

Cambridge University Press is part of the University of Cambridge.

It furthers the University's mission by disseminating knowledge in the pursuit of education, learning and research at the highest international levels of excellence.

www.cambridge.org
Information on this title: www.cambridge.org/9781108796125
DOI: 10.1017/9781108615235

© Bryan Mercurio 2018

First published 2018
First paperback edition 2019

A catalogue record for this publication is available from the British Library

ISBN 978-1-316-51234-0 Hardback
ISBN 978-1-108-79612-5 Paperback

CONTENTS

FOREWORD

ANTONY TAUBMAN[1]

The law of patents of invention has, for centuries, been shaped by vigorous policy debate and by the development and refinement of the law through contentious proceedings in court. The Anglo patent law tradition, which has partly shaped the law of Hong Kong, is conventionally viewed as being founded on the 1623 Statute of Monopolies; this law was itself passed by the English Parliament amid a roiling political debate about trade and commercial policy and the prerogative of the sovereign to grant monopolies – it therefore sets out the essence of the law of patents of invention in the form of a specific exception to an overarching abolition of monopolies. The more elaborated principles of patent law today can largely be sourced to the jurisprudence developed through historic judicial decisions, by definition in the context of commercial disputes. Contentious policy debate and adversarial judicial proceedings have not only accompanied the evolution of patent law over the centuries, they have in critical ways help to shape the modern law and its practical application.

And this is for good reason. There is much at stake, and the modern patent of invention is a conscious, policy-driven creation of the legislature, not a fundamental artefact of natural law. To be sure, many would share the sense that, in principle, an inventor is entitled to due recognition for the contribution to society of a beneficial new technology – a sense by no means limited to the domain of Western cultures, finding also expression in the Universal Declaration of Human Rights.[2] Yet the modern system of patent law is a more specific, more complex contrivance, crafted and refined as a utilitarian mechanism for producing public knowledge goods, in the form of usable and transmissible new technologies. At first blush, its

---

[1] Director, Intellectual Property, Government Procurement and Competition Division, WTO. Any views or analysis presented in this Foreword are the writer's own and do not represent the position of the WTO, its Secretariat or its Members. This Foreword does not endorse or support any of the views, recommendations or criticisms set out in this volume.
[2] Article 15, International Covenant on Economic, Social and Cultural Rights (1966).

normative logic is counterintuitive – using exclusive private rights to produce inclusive public goods – and reconciling this apparent paradox is the very essence of patent policymaking.[3] Ensuring that exclusive rights are such as to promote public welfare was the thrust of the Statute of Monopolies nearly four centuries ago, and remains the central task of the contemporary policy maker in this domain. Technologies, forms of innovation, and means of developing and disseminating new technologies evolve by their very nature, and patent law – while remaining true to certain core principles – has to adapt if it is to continue to serve creators and beneficiaries of new technologies. Informed policy debate, grounded in empirical research, is an invaluable foundation for the necessary elaboration and refinement of patent law.

When it comes to patents on medicines, the policy debate is all the more intense, and the public welfare interests are fundamental. It is self-evident that pharmaceutical innovation and equitable access to the fruits of such innovation are vital for both human well-being and social welfare. And we have strong expectations that policy mechanisms to enable innovation of, and access to, new medicines should deliver in practice – underscored by the articulation of specific targets for 2030 in the 2015 United Nations Sustainable Development Goals (SDG).

The entry into force, more than two decades ago, of the WTO Agreement on Trade-Related Aspects of Intellectual Property Rights (TRIPS) established a new principle at the level of international law that patents should be available for pharmaceutical inventions. This principle was contentious during the negotiations on TRIPS,[4] and the adoption and implementation of the principle has hardly stilled policy debate in this area. To the contrary – the implementation of TRIPS in more than 130 distinct jurisdictions[5] has sharpened and focused debate; equally, it has produced a rich trove of empirical data – in the form of distinct legislative

---

[3] Articulated in the TRIPS Agreement itself (Article 7) in notably positive-sum terms: "the promotion of technological innovation and to the transfer and dissemination of technology, to the mutual advantage of producers and users of technological knowledge and in a manner conducive to social and economic welfare, and to a balance of rights and obligations."

[4] Jayashree Watal, "Patents: An Indian Perspective," in Watal and Taubman (eds.), *The Making of the TRIPS Agreement: Personal Insights from the Uruguay Round Negotiations*, WTO, 1995.

[5] See TRIPS Article 66 Least-Developed Country Members, providing that "LDC members shall not be required to apply the provisions of this agreement . . . for a period of 10 years from the date of application." The transitional period was first extended in 2005, IP/L/40 (30 November 2005). In 2015, the Council for TRIPS extended the application of the transitional period until 1 January 2033, IP/L/73, 6 November 2015.

approaches, patent examination guidelines and judicial decisions – from numerous established and emerging patent law jurisdictions seeking to apply the same broad principles in diverse economic, technological and social contexts. This dynamism and diversity opens up new prospects for informed policy debate, despite the formidable challenges of analyzing the data available from numerous national and regional systems. The experience of implementation has also underscored a practical reality that was not well reflected in early debate over TRIPS and public health – that TRIPS articulates general principles to be adhered to, but leaves open considerable latitude at the domestic level on a host of legal and procedural matters that are, in turn, vital for the successful attainment of the ambitious goals set for the patent system in this area.

The 2001 Doha Declaration on the TRIPS Agreement and Public Health responded to the intensification of policy debate over patents and medicines that had been spurred by the implementation of TRIPS in national laws; it has, since then, helped to frame that debate, making clear that the objectives of intellectual property systems (the patent system in particular) and of public health policy are not inherently at odds, but that the TRIPS Agreement must "be part of the wider national and international action to address" the public health problems afflicting developing countries and least developed countries (LDCs), and that it "does not and should not prevent members from taking measures to protect public health." Further, while the principles of TRIPS are essentially technology neutral, there is a certain recognition that – because of policy and regulatory dimension – pharmaceuticals do require distinct treatment: hence, the TRIPS provisions for protection of clinical trial data, the extended exception in this domain (to at least 2033, reaching beyond the SDG target date) for LDCs (and an earlier extended implementation period for patent protection of pharmaceuticals in developing countries in general), the amendment to the Agreement itself, which created an additional pathway for access to generic medicines for countries particularly reliant on international trade for their pharmaceutical needs, and the broader framing of TRIPS and public health policy articulated in the Doha Declaration.

Professor Mercurio's past scholarly work has contributed extensively to the literature on intellectual property law in its international legal and policy context, and especially as it is framed by the TRIPS Agreement and subsequent regional and bilateral trade agreements. The present volume helpfully distills and builds upon this work to yield a monograph that is focused, systematic and closely informed on the central choices that confront policy makers today as they seek to adapt the patent system to the demands of today in the pharmaceutical sector in particular. In doing so, Professor Mercurio has mapped out the current policy choices generally presented to the practical policy maker in a national jurisdiction in a comprehensive and structured manner. He has effectively distilled the developments – often challenging for analysts to follow – in bilateral and regional trade agreements that have significantly altered the legal and regulatory landscape for many national jurisdictions. This work can therefore be abstracted from the individual jurisdiction it discusses and can serve as a practical taxonomy of policy choices faced by many countries – and can serve, also, as a selective guide to the background literature in this inherently complex and necessarily difficult domain of policymaking.

While the present writer would differ – respectfully, collegially and productively – with some of the lines of analysis, policy assumptions and conclusions presented in this volume, he has already benefited from the privilege of reading through the manuscript, an illuminating reading which has precipitated new insights in response, and will continue to refer to the book to assist in understanding the evolving context, and content, of law and policy in relation to patents and public health. Coming as it does from the perspective of an international civil servant, this Foreword is appropriately silent on the specific context of Hong Kong and does not venture to suggest that reform is necessary or called for in any of the areas discussed, or to advocate that the specific recommendations in this book are appropriate or optimal for this or any other jurisdiction. However, in the light especially of continuing practical experience with technical assistance and outreach undertaken in partnership within the multilateral system and with regional and national counterparts, it is clear that attaining improved outcomes for innovation and access to medicines requires situating patent law and related areas (such as test data protection) within their broader policy context: the changing, and diversifying, innovation landscape (including, with relevance for Hong Kong, the recognition of traditions of medical knowledge other than Western pharmacology), the interaction of the patent system with international trade (considering, for instance, the potential role of Hong Kong as an exporter of medicines, including under the system established by the TRIPS public health amendment), and the specifics of national medicines policy (procurement and innovation strategies, the regulatory system, pricing and other market policies, the application of competition policy in this domain, and statistics on actual access to medicines as well as projections of the future disease burden). An optimal, coherent set of policies requires a comprehensive grasp of each of these policy domains and their interaction with one another.[6]

The following work therefore provides the policy maker with a critical and informed guide to navigation through a demanding policy landscape; its elaboration and analysis of the legal and policy issues lay out the contours and central features of the landscape, and to engage with its advocacy of certain lines of approach through this journey provides for a rich and informative dialogue about the appropriate path to take.

[6] Zafar Mirza et al., "Policy Coherence for Improved Medical Innovation and Access" (2013) 91 *Bulletin of the World Health Organization* 315–315A.

ACKNOWLEDGMENTS

This book is the product of more than fifteen years of studying, examining and questioning the linkages between international trade law and pharmaceutical patents and has benefited from numerous conversations with individuals from all walks of life. The idea to write such a book came long ago, but it would not have been possible if not for the Hong Kong University Grants Committee awarding me a General Research Fund (GRF) (No. CUHK450012) for the project entitled "Intellectual Property Rights and the Pharmaceutical Industry: Evaluating Hong Kong's Regulatory Framework." The funding has been much appreciated.

There are so many people to thank for their assistance with this manuscript. The Dean of the Faculty of Law at the Chinese University of Hong Kong, Professor Christopher Gane, deserves recognition for his support, friendship and leadership. Non-work-related meetings over the last few years at the Tin Tin Bar (which inevitably turned into work-related meetings) were a welcome and enjoyable distraction, which ironically led to increased focus and determination. Enjoy retirement, boss, whenever it finally comes! I also thank my former dean at the Faculty of Law at the University of New South Wales, Professor Leon Trakman, and the current dean at that same institution, Professor George Williams, for their unwavering belief and support since day one. Without them, I would not be in academia. I owe them both a debt of gratitude.

I also thank Cambridge University Press, with whom I have cultivated a deep relationship over the last decade. Finola O'Sullivan and Kim Hughes have been supportive, good natured and professional throughout our many projects, and Joe Ng incredibly helpful in the production of this book. I look forward to working with all of them again in the not too distant future.

I would be remiss in not specifically mentioning Dr. Danny Friedmann, my former PhD student and research associate, for his passion for everything to do with intellectual property rights and for the enthusiasm and willingness he showed in agreeing to assist with two chapters in this book during a difficult time of transition in his life. I also thank Dr. Antoine Martin, my current research associate, and PhD student Dini Sejko for reviewing an earlier draft and assisting with the notes. The task can appear tedious and unimportant, but the details matter.

Last, but perhaps most important, I owe a debt of gratitude to Daria Kim. Daria served for two years as my trusty senior research associate on this project, and her diligence and dedication really kept this book on track. Her meticulousness and detail-oriented approach was needed and will not be forgotten. She is incredibly talented and it is not an exaggeration to say that without her this book may not have happened. Watching her talent blossom in front of my eyes has been one of the highlights of my career to date. It is just a shame she couldn't take the summer heat in Hong Kong and returned to Europe. She will soon complete her PhD and there really is no limit to how far she can go in her career.

ABBREVIATIONS

ANDA	Abbreviated New Drug Application
AUSFTA	Australia-United States Free Trade Agreement
CAFTA–DR–US	Dominican Republic-Central America FTA
CETA	Comprehensive Economic and Trade Agreement
CIPR	UK Commission on Intellectual Property Rights
CPC	Community Patent Convention
CPP	Certificate of Pharmaceutical Product
Doha Declaration	Doha Declaration on the TRIPs Agreement and Public Health
DSB	Dispute Settlement Body (WTO)
DSU	Dispute Settlement Understanding (WTO)
EPC	European Patent Convention
EPO	European Patent Office
EU	European Union
FDA	Food and Drug Administration (US)
FDI	foreign direct investment
FTA	free trade agreement
GDP	gross domestic product
GMP	good manufacturing practice
HA	Hospital Authority (HA)
HIV/AIDS	human immunodeficiency virus/acquired immunodeficiency syndrome
HKAPI	Hong Kong Association of Pharmaceutical Industry
HK-EFTA FTA	Hong Kong-European Free Trade Association Free Trade Agreement
ICH	International Conference on Harmonisation of Technical Requirements for Registration of Pharmaceuticals for Human Use
IP	intellectual property
IPD	Intellectual Property Department (HK)
IPO	Intellectual Property Office (UK)
IPR	intellectual property right
ISDS	investor-state dispute settlement

ITB	Innovation and Technology Bureau (HK)
ITF	Innovation and Technology Fund
KORUS	Korea-United States Free Trade Agreement
LDC	least developed country
NAFTA	North American Free Trade Agreement
NDA	New Drug Application
NOA	notice of allegation
PCT	Patent Cooperation Treaty
PHOSITA	person having ordinary skill in the art
PPB	Pharmacy and Poisons Board (HK)
PTE	patent term extension
PTO	Patent and Trademark Office (US)
R&D	research and development
SCP	Standing Committee of the Law of Patents
SIPO	State Intellectual Property Office (China)
SPC	supplementary protection certificate
TPA	Trade Promotion Agreement
TPP	Trans-Pacific Partnership
TRIPS Agreement	Agreement on Trade-Related Aspects of Intellectual Property
UK	United Kingdom
UPC	Unified Patent Court
US	United States
VCLT	Vienna Convention on the Law of Treaties
WHO	World Health Organization
WIPO	World Intellectual Property Organization
WTO	World Trade Organization

1

Introduction

Questions relating to pharmaceuticals sit at the intersection of social, economic and technological issues and force policy and law makers into taking difficult decisions that balance the needs and interests of multiple (and often competing) stakeholders. The subject of this book, pharmaceutical patent law, is merely a subset of the wider field of pharmaceutical law but just as complex, and with all of the same policy considerations. Most notable among these are how to provide the populace with access to a wide range of medicines within the confines of a finite budget, promote national innovation/industry development and comply with obligations under international agreements.

Until the advent of the World Trade Organization's (WTO) Agreement on Trade-Related Aspects of Intellectual Property (TRIPS Agreement) in 1995,[1] international intellectual property (IP) law – of which pharmaceutical patent law is also a subset – could be characterized as decentralized and lacking in any meaningful and substantive harmonization. This is not to suggest that the TRIPS Agreement is the first international IP effort. To the contrary, the multilateralization of IP began in the latter part of the nineteenth century through the negotiation and adoption of two important treaties[2] – the Paris Convention for the Protection of Industrial Property (1883)[3] and the Berne Convention for the Protection of Literary and Artistic Works (1886)[4] – which, inter alia, introduced the principle

---

[1] Agreement on Trade-Related Aspects of Intellectual Property Rights, 15 April 1994, 1869 U.N.T.S. 299, 33 I.L.M. 1197 (1994).

[2] It could even be suggested that the internationalization of IP law, regulation and policy began even earlier when IP-related issues appeared in Friendship, Commerce and Navigation (FCN) treaties, the first of which is reputed to be a 1778 treaty between France and the United States. See M. Sornarajah, *The International Law on Foreign Investment*, 3rd edition (Cambridge University Press, 2010) 180, note 41.

[3] Paris Convention for the Protection of Industrial Property of 1883, 21 UST 1583, 828 UNTS 305 (as revised at Stockholm on 14 July 1967, and as amended on 28 September 1979).

[4] Berne Convention for the Protection of Literary and Artistic Works, 9 September 1886, revised in Paris on 24 July 1971 and amended in 1979, S. Treaty Doc. No. 99–27 (1986)

of national treatment into international IP law. Without denigrating the advancements of these treaties, it is fair to say that they mostly focused on procedural aspects of IP law and merely serve as a structure for developing IP policy and a framework for enhanced international cooperation.

As such, signatory countries retained almost unlimited latitude to craft and shape substantive domestic norms. Even the term of patent protection varied widely, with protection in many countries ranging from fifteen to seventeen years from the date of filing or date of the grant of the patent and some countries granting protection for as little as five to seven years (Article 33 of the TRIPS Agreement now requires that patent rights be granted for a period of twenty years from the date a patent application is filed). In such a setting, experimentation became the norm and countries developed and maintained widely differing practices in almost all forms of IP. Substantive norms in relation to pharmaceutical patent law were no different, and became quite divergent. For example, while Article 27.1 of the TRIPS Agreement now requires Members to provide patent protection for both processes and products, in all fields of technology, the situation prior to the TRIPS Agreement widely varied. As many as fifty countries provided patent protection for processes but not products – meaning that while the countries protected the technology and process/method used to manufacture generic products, companies in those jurisdictions could still "reverse engineer" the product to develop a different process or method to create an equivalent product. Patents over the final products, therefore, provide for more complete protection to the patent holder and significantly weaken the position of generic pharmaceutical manufacturers.

Binding on all WTO Members and enforceable through the dispute settlement mechanism, the TRIPS Agreement became the new standard for international intellectual property law and did so by not simply mirroring the standards of the existing IP agreements but by building on them with the addition of substantive standards, rights and norms. With WTO membership at that time encompassing 127 Members (Membership now includes over 160 countries and accounts for nearly 98 percent of world trade),[5] the TRIPS Agreement became the first international agreement to attempt some harmonization of substantive IP law.

(the 1979 amended version does not appear in UNTS or ILM, but the 1971 Paris revision is available at 1161 UNTS 30 (1971)).

[5] See WTO, "Accessions," www.wto.org/english/thewto_e/acc_e/acc_e.htm, accessed 20 February 2017; WTO, International Trade Statistics 2014, www.wto.org/english/res_e/ statis_e/its2014_e/its14_toc_e.htm, accessed 20 February 2017.

That being said, while the TRIPS Agreement is fairly prescriptive and shapes the IP laws of every WTO Member, it does not mandate complete harmonization. That is, Members retain *some* ability to tailor domestic legislation to reflect the local socioeconomic context and development priorities. For instance, even when prescriptive the TRIPS Agreement merely requires that Members meet certain minimum standards – Members retain wide latitude to exceed the standards when desirable so long as the laws and regulations remain consistent with the TRIPS Agreement.[6] In addition, a number of provisions contained in the TRIPS Agreement are vaguely drafted or allow for wide interpretation, thus providing Members with sufficient policy space. Moreover, the TRIPS Agreement also contains certain "flexibilities" that allow Members to tailor laws and regulations in an attempt at minimizing the negative impact of intellectual property rights (IPRs) on domestic needs and priorities. As this book will demonstrate, flexibilities are particularly relevant and readily available for pharmaceutical patent laws and regulations.

Therefore, despite setting out minimum standards in a fairly prescriptive manner, the TRIPS Agreement nevertheless affords Members some, albeit circumscribed, scope to craft laws and regulations in a manner consistent with domestic policy and in line with developmental objectives.

1.1 The International Framework

Before undertaking a jurisdictional analysis, as this book does, it is necessary to first understand the requirements, limits and boundaries of the international framework. It is therefore worthwhile to more fully explain the background, objectives and contours of the TRIPS Agreement before proceeding to discuss the aims and objectives of this book.

The impact of the TRIPS Agreement cannot be understated – its creation brought about a "tectonic shift" in the protection and enforcement of IPRs.[7] As mentioned above, the TRIPS Agreement incorporates the substantive parts of Paris and Berne but it is unlike any previous international

---

[6] TRIPS Agreement, Article 1(1), states: "Members shall give effect to the provisions of this Agreement. Members may, but shall not be obliged to, implement in their law more extensive protection than is required by this Agreement, provided that such protection does not contravene the provisions of this Agreement."

[7] Charles R. McManis, "Teaching Current Trends and Future Developments in Intellectual Property" (2008) 52 *Saint Louis University Law Journal* 855, 856.

IP agreement in a number of ways: It is comprehensive in scope in addressing procedural, substantive and administrative aspects of IP, broad in coverage with the addition of several new topical areas, includes most-favored nation and national treatment as cornerstone principles and provides for minimum levels of protection and enforcement.

Arriving at the same time as several new technologies (i.e., biotechnology, widespread use of the internet and e-commerce), the TRIPs Agreement changed the landscape and dramatically altered thinking about international IP. The norms established in the TRIPS Agreement are unquestionably the international standard and starting point for any further development of international IP rules (such as free trade agreements (FTAs) or stand-alone agreements administered by the World Intellectual Property Organization (WIPO)).

Negotiations for the TRIPS Agreement were long and arduous. The United States and other developed countries sought to gain multilateral backing to their unilateral efforts to enforce IPRs by directly linking IP to international trade by arguing that a country with weak or otherwise insufficient IP protection engages in unfair competition as it can benefit through the cheap production and sale of counterfeit goods and drive the costlier original goods out of the market.[8] These countries also argued that effective protection of IPRs would lead to increased investment, employment, technology and balance of payment issues.[9] In contrast, developing countries saw the proposed link as a way to transfer health from the poor to the rich and initially flatly rejected the idea of including IPRs into the multilateral trading system, arguing that WIPO was the appropriate forum to discuss IPRs.[10]

The United States and others ultimately convinced developing countries to negotiate for the inclusion of IPRs into the multilateral system by offering "carrots" and "sticks." The stick came as a threat of continued unilateral action against what could be seen as "unfair trade" and implicitly a threat to the continuation of trade assistance and aid from developed

---

[8] See, e.g., Marshall A. Leaffer, "Protecting United States Intellectual Property Abroad: Toward a New Multilateralism" (1991) 76 *Iowa Law Review* 273; Max Baucus, "A New Trade Strategy: The Case for Bilateral Agreements" (1989) 22 *Cornell International Law Journal* 1; Hans Peter Kunz-Hallstein, "United States Proposal for a GATT Agreement on Intellectual Property and the Paris Convention for the Protection of Industrial Property" (1989) 22 *Vanderbilt Journal of Transnational Law* 265.

[9] See sources in note 8.

[10] Duncan Matthews, *Globalising Intellectual Property Rights: The TRIPs Agreement* (Routledge, 2002) 33.

countries to the developing world.[11] The carrot came in the form of concessions in other trade areas, notably increased market access to developed countries in the areas of agriculture and textiles as well as several important TRIPs-related concessions such as promises of technology transfer, technical assistance and deferred implementation of the substantial portions of the TRIPS Agreement. After initial hesitation, the carrots and sticks proved too much to resist and developing countries agreed to negotiate measures aimed at eliminating trade in counterfeit goods. This limitation soon faded and developing countries were eventually persuaded to negotiate a more ambitious agreement regulating a broad range of IP-related interests.[12]

When developing the procedural and substantive standards, rules and principles of the TRIPS Agreement the drafters sought to balance several differing and at times competing interests. This balance is reflected in the objectives and principles of IPRs, represented in Articles 7 and 8 of the TRIPs Agreement, and include the promotion of the transfer of technology, the prevention of abuse of IPRs and the promotion of public health.

---

[11] The United States first began unilaterally enforcing IPRs by virtue of the authority of the US Trade Representative (USTR) under Section 301 US Trade Act of 1974 and Special 301 in 1988. More specifically, the United States initiated litigation against other countries in the US Court of International Trade (USITC) under its domestic unfair trade practices laws, even though the respondent countries had not violated any international agreement. The United States filed cases against several developing countries, most notably Brazil, Argentina, India, China and Taiwan, and extracted concessions from the respondents in a number of cases. In doing so, the United States effectively promoted the linkage of IP and international trade. See Jasper Womach, "Agriculture: A Glossary of Terms, Programs, and Laws, Congressional Research Service Report for Congress," (2005), p. 230, available at https://digital.library.unt.edu/ark:/67531/metacrs7246/m1/1/high_res_d/97-905_2005Jun16.pdf, accessed 21 December 2017.; Alan O. Sykes, "Constructive Unilateral Threats in International Commercial Relations: The Limited Case for Section 301" (1992) 23 *Law & Policy in International Business* 263, 318–19; Michael Blakeley, *Trade-Related Aspects of Intellectual Property Rights: A Concise Guide to the TRIPs Agreement* (Sweet & Maxwell, 1996) 6. See also Report of the Panel, *United States – Section 301–310 of the Trade Act of 1974*, WT/DS152/R (22 December 1999). Likewise, the European Union adopted Council Regulation 2641/84 to counter "illicit" trade practices against European exporters. For more information, see Wolfgang W. Leirer, "Retaliatory Action in United States and European Union Trade Law: A Comparison of Section 301 of the Trade Act of 1974 and Council Regulation 2641/84" (1994–95) 20 *North Carolina Journal of International Law & Commercial Regulation* 41.

[12] For a succinct history of the origins of the TRIPs Agreement and its negotiating process, see Matthews, Globalising Intellectual Property Rights, Chapter 1 (origins) and Chapter 2 (negotiations). For more detailed background on the TRIPs Agreement, see Susan K. Sell, *Power and Ideas: North-South Politics of Intellectual Property and Antitrust* (State University of New York Press, 1998).

But one should not be under any illusions regarding the inclusion of IPRs into the WTO framework – the TRIPS Agreement was negotiated to promote the protection and enforcement of IPRs, and other interests (including the promotion of innovation and transfer of technology) are decidedly secondary.[13]

The balance struck in the TRIPS Agreement may therefore not be ideal for some (or even most) Members. However harsh this may be, in many respects the debate about the suitability of the aims, objectives and consequences of the TRIPS Agreement is academic; the TRIPS Agreement is *the* international framework and is not going to disappear (much less be amended in any meaningful manner). In some ways, for patents this is disappointing as more evidence surfaces that questions the link between ever-stronger protection and innovation.[14] And while most commentators view pharmaceuticals as a special industry wholly reliant on IPRs for its survival (and the continued development of medicines),[15] others are less enthusiastic and point out several alternative paths.

Thus, countries are left to navigate within the confines of the present system and restricted to legislating in a manner consistent with the international framework. Recently, a number of countries have attempted to

---

[13] See Bryan Mercurio, "TRIPS and innovation: a necessary reappraisal?," paper commissioned by the International Centre for Trade and Sustainable Development (ICTSD) and World Economic Forum, November 2014, http://e15initiative.org/publications/trips-patents-and-innovation-a-necessary-reappraisal/, accessed 20 February 2017.

[14] Ibid., citing numerous economic studies. See also Chamber of Deputies, Center for Strategic Studies and Debates, "Brazil's Patent Reform: Innovation Towards National Competitiveness" (2013), p. 20, http://infojustice.org/wp-content/uploads/2013/09/Brazilian_Patent_Reform.pdf, accessed 20 February 2017.

[15] For studies evaluating the impact of patent protection on the pharmaceutical sector, see, e.g., Henry Grabowski, "Patents, Innovation and Access to New Pharmaceuticals" (2002) 5(4) *Journal of International Economic Law* 849, 851 (concluding that the "explanation for why patents are more important to pharmaceutical firms in appropriating the benefits from innovation follows directly from the characteristics of the pharmaceutical R&D process ... In essence, imitation costs in pharmaceuticals are extremely low relative to the innovator's costs for discovering and developing a new compound."); Wesley M. Cohen et al., "Protecting Their Intellectual Assets: Appropriability Conditions and Why U.S. Manufacturing Firms Patent (Or Not)" 2 (National Bureau of Economic Research, Working Paper No. 7552, 2000) (stating that patent protection "is important in only a few industries, most notably pharmaceuticals"), www.nber.org/papers/w7552, accessed 20 February 2017. See also Neel U. Sukhatme and Judd N.L. Cramer, "Who Cares about Patent Term? Cross-Industry Differences in Term Sensitivity," 2014, https://scholar.princeton.edu/sites/default/files/sukhatme/files/sukhatme_who_cares_about_patent_term_0.pdf, accessed 20 February 2017.

work within the system to effectuate a recalibration that ensures the proper balance between the encouragement of innovation in the form of exclusive rights and user interests and competition. The most public displays of such attempts revolve around action taken in what the country deems is in accordance with the "flexibilities" existing in the TRIPS Agreement, with the most notable of these being the issuance of compulsory licenses for a pharmaceutical products in Brazil, India, Taiwan, Thailand, Zimbabwe, Rwanda (where Canada issued a compulsory license in order to export a generic medicine to Rwanda under the 2003 Waiver of Article 31(f)) and a handful of other countries. Other countries, most notably India and more recently Argentina, have attempted to limit the influence of IPRs on the domestic pharmaceutical market, increase the availability of generic medicines and protect domestic generic producer interests by adopting stringent standards for the granting of a patent.[16] These efforts are in concurrence with the United Nations Human Rights Council, which in 2013 adopted a resolution reinforcing the right of WTO Members "to use [flexibilities provided in the TRIPS Agreement] to the full ... to protect public health and, in particular, to promote access to medicines."[17]

At the same time, a number of developed and developing countries have recently initiated major reviews of their pharmaceutical patent systems – including Brazil, South Africa and Australia – with a view to ensuring the system works in harmony with the needs, priorities and level of development of the jurisdiction.[18] Even more recently, negotiations of so-called

[16] While the compatibility of some of these measures with the TRIPS Agreement may be questionable, the point here is simply to illustrate attempts at rebalancing the system away from the rights holder and in favor of user interests.

[17] Human Rights Council, *The Access to Medicines in the Context of the Right of Everyone to the Enjoyment of the Highest Attainable Standard of Physical and Mental Health*, at statement 2, A/HRC/23/L.10/Rev.1 (11 June 2013). The resolution also stressed "the responsibility of States to ensure the highest attainable level of health for all, including through access [to] essential medicines, that are affordable, safe, efficacious and of quality," and urged governments to "promote a range of incentive schemes for research and development, including addressing, where appropriate, the delinkage of the costs of research and development and the price of health products." Id. statement 3 and 5(n).

[18] See Brazil's Patent Reform, above n. 14; Chan Park, Achal Prabhala, Jonathan Berger et al., "Using Law to Accelerate Treatment Access in South Africa: An Analysis of Patent, Competition and Medicines Law," A Study Commissioned by the United Nations Development Programme, Programme Regional Service Centre for Eastern and Southern Africa (2013), www.undp.org/content/dam/undp/library/hivaids/English/using_law_to_accelerate_treatment_access_in_south_africa_undp_2013.pdf, accessed 20 February 2017; Tony Harris, Dianne Nicol and Nicholas Gruen, "2013 Pharmaceutical Patents

mega-regional FTAs awakened a skeptical public to the effects of TRIPS-plus provisions on the price and availability of medicines.

1.2   The Raison d'Être: Inform and Influence Public Policy in Hong Kong

Unlike other countries that have recently made use of the TRIPS flexibilities or reviewed the suitability and appropriateness of their pharmaceutical patent system, the Hong Kong Special Administrative Region is not seeking to amend its regime in order to support and promote public and industrial policy. This is curious, as Hong Kong has long viewed itself as "an innovation-led, technology-intensive economy in the 21st century…a world centre for the development of health food and pharmaceuticals…and the marketplace for technology transfer"[19] and continues to assert its strong belief that "sound intellectual property rights protection [is one of the] drivers for technological innovation in Hong Kong."[20] One would think that a government that sees the prosperity of its jurisdiction dependent on innovation and IP would periodically review its IP system to ascertain whether it matches the needs and priorities of the jurisdiction. Instead, IP policy has focused on service-oriented and procedural considerations that could lead to the employment of highly skilled talent, such as the idea of marketing Hong Kong as an IP "Trading Hub" and the impending shift from a registration-based patent regime to an examination/original grant system.

Neither has the government elaborated any strategy of how the IP system can contribute to any desired policy goals. Factors such as stimulating local innovation and promoting local production of branded or generic pharmaceuticals, which are at the core of many other jurisdictional reviews, appear to be distinctly secondary considerations in Hong Kong. Instead, Hong Kong's overarching interest seems to be that of controlling

Review Report" Commissioned by the Australian Government (2013), www.ipaustralia
.gov.au/pdfs/2013–05–27_PPR_Final_Report.pdf, accessed 20 February 2017.

[19] Hong Kong SAR Legislative Council, Official Record of Proceedings, 7679 (2013), (Mar. 20, 2013), www.legco.gov.hk/yr12–13/english/counmtg/hansard/cm0320-translate-e .pdf, accessed 20 February 2017 (Council Member Ng Leung-Sing quoted the report of the Commission on Innovation and Technology (1998) and called on the government to "set forth a vision of making Hong Kong an innovation centre for the Asia Pacific Region").

[20] Hong Kong SAR 2013 Policy Address: Seek Change, Maintain Stability, Serve the People with Pragmatism, The Government of the Hong Kong SAR §105 (2013), www .policyaddress.gov.hk/2013/eng/pdf/PA2013.pdf, accessed 20 February 2017.

the cost of medicines and pharmaceutical products. Even here, however, the government has not demonstrated awareness of the impact of patents on healthcare costs (or even willingness to evaluate such impact) or clearly set out a medicine procurement policy that aims to reduce costs.[21]

Given its reputation as a free market mecca, it is unsurprising that Hong Kong has not availed itself of flexibilities such as the issuance of compulsory licenses for medicines. More surprising, however, is that it has not attempted to tailor its pharmaceutical patent system to match its needs, interests and priorities or perceived level of development. Hong Kong's patent law effectively remains the 1997 version of its then former master, the United Kingdom[22] – drafted in the United Kingdom, presumably with British interests and stakeholders in mind. While sovereignty over Hong Kong passed from the United Kingdom to China in 1997, the substance of the law remained intact.[23] In fact, Hong Kong has not even contemplated a systemic review of the pharmaceutical patent system despite the fact that it recently initiated two "comprehensive" reviews related to the topic of this inquiry.[24] The most recent review, carried out by the Hong Kong Intellectual Property Department in 2011, primarily focused on the merits and implementation of an original grant patent system in Hong Kong,[25] while the earlier review, undertaken by the Food and Health Bureau and Department of Health in 2009, concentrated on the issue of

---

[21] See Hong Kong SAR Legislative Council, Official Record of Proceedings, at 10130, (2011), www.legco.gov.hk/yr10–11/english/counmtg/hansard/cm0511-translate-e.pdf, accessed 20 February 2017.

[22] The People's Republic of China resumed sovereignty over Hong Kong in 1997 under the Joint Declaration of the Government of the United Kingdom of Great Britain and Northern Ireland and the Government of the People's Republic of China on the Question of Hong Kong, 1984.

[23] Hong Kong patent law comprises Patents Ordinance (Cap. 514); Patents (Designation of Patent Offices) Notices (Cap. 514A); Patents (Transitional Arrangements) Rules (Cap. 514B); Patents (General) Rules (Cap. 514C). The substantive norms are provided in Hong Kong Patents Ordinance (1997, last amended 2009) O.H.K., Cap. 514.

[24] See *Official Record of Proceedings* (6 July 2011), Hong Kong SAR Legislative Council 13830 (2011), www.legco.gov.hk/yr10–11/english/counmtg/hansard/cm0706-translate-e .pdf, accessed 20 February 2017 (stating "[t]he Government considers that it is now high time to take a comprehensive review of the patent system, so as to ensure that our patent system can keep abreast of the times and promote local creative industries").

[25] See generally, Hong Kong SAR, Commerce and Economic Bureau, Intellectual Property Department, Review of the Patent System in Hong Kong: Consultation Paper, (2011), www.ipd.gov.hk/chi/pub_press/press_releases/2011/paper_20111004_c.pdf, accessed 20 February 2017.

pharmaceutical product safety.[26] Remarkably, neither review mentioned, much less evaluated, Hong Kong's legal framework for pharmaceutical patent protection. Pharmacologist Benjamin T.Y. Chan succinctly summarized the situation: "Hong Kong is not concerned with issues of regulating the pharmaceutical industry, pharmaceutical R&D and patent protection, and state reimbursement of pharmaceutical payments which are characteristic priorities of policymaking in advanced economies."[27]

Perhaps even more remarkable is the near absence of scholarship on Hong Kong's pharmaceutical patent regime (or on pharmaceutical policy more generally), with no existing literature before this project analyzing linkages between pharmaceutical patents and policy areas such as public health, innovation and pharmaceutical industry development. The relevant literature is sparse, and even then barely touches on the relevant issues. For instance, in a study looking at the biotechnology sector, Professor Yahong Li found that patent laws in Hong Kong were a significant reason for Hong Kong lagging behind in patenting biotechnology.[28] Likewise, Professors Sharif and Baark, in a study assessing Hong Kong's innovation system and innovation policies, pointed to insufficient programs and IP laws for supporting what could be a stronger technology market in Hong Kong.[29] Similarly, Chib and Chan argued that Hong Kong must reconsider patent and drug registration issues in order to remain competitive.[30] Thus, while there is some literature criticizing the current approach, there does not seem to be any relevant literature assessing what specifically would

---

[26] See Hong Kong SAR, Food and Health Bureau and the Department of Health, *The Report of the Review Committee on Regulation of Pharmaceutical Products in Hong Kong*, (2009), www.ppbhk.org.hk/eng/files/Report_of_Review_Committee_eng.pdf, accessed 20 February 2017.

[27] Benjamin TY Chan, "Pharmaceutical Policy in Hong Kong: Defining an Evolving Area of Study" (First Conference on Pharmaceutical Policy Analysis, Zeist, Netherlands, 19–21 September 2007).

[28] Yahong Li, "An Overview of Patent Protection for Biotechnology in Hong Kong," in Felix Chan and Richard Wu (eds.), *Law for Practitioners Series 2003* (Sweet & Maxwell 2004).

[29] Naubahar Sharif and Erik Baark, "The Tamest of Tigers? Understanding Hong Kong's Innovation System and Innovation Policies" (2005) 1(3–4) *International Journal of Technology and Globalization* 462. See also Joseph Wong, "Biotechnology in Hong Kong: Prospects and Challenges," Hong Kong Innovation Project Report No. 9, www.savantas.org/wp-content/uploads/2014/06/9_JWong.pdf, accessed 20 February 2017.

[30] Bindu Chib, "Hong Kong Pharmaceutical Patents: Breaking the Ranks?" (October 2004), Asia Law, www.asialaw.com/Article/1972094/Hong-Kong-Pharmaceutical-Patents-Breaking-the-Ranks.html?Print=true&Single=true, accessed 20 February 2017; Kitty Tsz Ki Chan, "Evaluation of the Drug Regulatory Systems in Hong Kong, Singapore, Taiwan, United States and European Union," submission for Master of Public Health, University of Hong Kong, February 2013 (on file with author).

need amending in the Hong Kong patent regime or otherwise providing solutions to the problems identified.[31]

The government's benign neglect results in outdated, vaguely drafted legislation that in places may even be contradictory. This creates uncertainties for all the major stakeholders, including both the branded and generic pharmaceutical industry, who would be better served with clear rules and regulations. The full extent of the impact of an inappropriate legislative framework on innovation, health, employment and other societal and policy interests is simply unknown, and without a comprehensive and systemic review the knowledge gap forms a lacuna and prevents informed policy deliberation and debate. With no signs of governmental movement in this regard, this research project undertook a review of the system. This monograph, the result of a three-year comprehensive review, will assist in filling the gap. Through an evaluation of the pharmaceutical patent system in Hong Kong, this monograph seeks to make recommendations that will recalibrate the legal system in order to maximize the benefits of innovation and better address the needs, priorities and interests of Hong Kong and all relevant stakeholders.

The aim of the book is chiefly to inform public policy and influence debate through a comprehensive review of Hong Kong's pharmaceutical patent law. For each substantive pharmaceutical patent issue, the international framework and current law in Hong Kong is reviewed before an assessment of whether the pharmaceutical patent law is in line with and beneficial to the needs, interests and priorities of Hong Kong and other relevant stakeholders. Unlike much of the existing literature on pharmaceutical patents and international IP, the study did not approach the topic with a preexisting view of whether IPRs and the patent system is "good" or "bad" either as a whole or for a particular sector. Instead, the starting point is that IPRs and the patent system cannot be viewed as "good" or "bad" in the abstract but rather any value, benefit, determent or harm entirely depends on how the systems work in a particular setting and time period. What may be beneficial or innocuous in one setting may be detrimental

---

[31] Other publications associated with this project notwithstanding, which include Bryan Mercurio and Daria Kim, "Patently Lacking: An Analysis and Call for Systemic Review of Pharmaceutical Law and Policy – A Case Study of in Hong Kong" (2014) 9 *Asian Journal of WTO & International Health Law and Policy* 63; Bryan Mercurio and Daria Kim, "Foreign Direct Investment in the Pharmaceutical Industry – What Are the Key Determinants? A Case Study of Singapore and Hong Kong" (2015) 10 *Asian Journal of Comparative Law* 235; Bryan Mercurio and Daria Kim (eds.), *Contemporary Issues in Pharmaceutical Patent Law and Policy* (Routledge, 2017).

or harmful in another setting. This book, therefore, particularly draws on comparative law and law in context methodologies to formulate feasible options suitable for Hong Kong.

To this end, this monograph will evaluate the pharmaceutical patent system in light of policy, economic and social factors relevant to Hong Kong. The ultimate aim is to use the information and data collected to recommend changes to the legal framework in order to construct a more efficient and effective system for Hong Kong. The views of the author have been shaped by information and data collected through various methods, including literature reviews, interviews and survey data. The project did not attempt to conduct a large-scale economic study,[32] and opinions have been shaped (and in some way limited) by available data and resources. Therefore, while the author firmly believes the recommendations made throughout this book are sound, he is nevertheless resolute in the opinion that the government must undertake a systemic review of the entire pharmaceutical patent system, including how it is affected by broader governmental initiatives such as policies on innovation, healthcare, employment and the like. As will be demonstrated in Chapter 2 and throughout the remainder of the book, governmental policy and guidance in the area of pharmaceutical law is unclear and underdeveloped. Therefore, if the government desires to improve the system, it must undertake a systemic review. Only then can it truly reshape the system in line with clear aims and objectives.

While the focus of the book is on Hong Kong and the purpose is to inform and influence domestic public policy, Hong Kong is not unique in its approach to pharmaceutical patent law. Indeed, many if not most jurisdictions have failed to undertake a systemic review of their system to ensure that it meets domestic needs and priorities and/or is in line with the state of development.[33] In this regard, while there is a limited jurisdictional focus of the book the underlying issues, principles and arguments are universally applicable – by contrast, domestic situations inevitably are varied and thus priorities and recommendations are jurisdictionally specific.

---

[32] But see Aidan Hollis and Paul Grootendorst, "The Cost of Potential Pharmaceutical IP Provisions in Hong Kong," in Mercurio and Kim (eds.), *Contemporary Issues in Pharmaceutical Patent Law and Policy*, chapter 9.

[33] See Phil Thorpe, "Study on the Implementation of the TRIPs Agreement by Developing Countries," Commission on Intellectual Property Rights, Study Paper 7, www.cipr.org.uk/papers/pdfs/study_papers/sp7_thorpe_study.pdf, accessed 20 February 2017.

1.3   Limitations and Challenges

Researching pharmaceutical patent law and policy in Hong Kong has been a challenge, and while most obstacles have been overcome (whether directly or indirectly), some difficulties proved insurmountable. Information and statistics that are widely available or easily accessible in most other advanced economics are simply not available or publicly disclosed in Hong Kong. Government databases are both sparse and opaque and industry information closely guarded. This has made economic forecasting difficult, and forced the economic portion of the research to rely on relatively small sample sizes to make projections. While easier and more complete access to statistics and data would undoubtedly have been useful, enough information was gathered to enable robust analysis, conclusions and recommendations.

1.4   Structure of the Book

Following this chapter, Chapter 2 introduces the array of complex considerations involved in pharmaceutical patent policy and law-making. More specifically, the chapter will introduce the "bundle" of interests and policies that influence the pharmaceutical patent regime, including interests relating to legal/IP, health, industrial and innovation policy. The chapter will also review the government's stated policy aims and objectives in each of these areas in order to provide necessary context and insight for the remainder of book.

Although government policy direction is often unclear and underdeveloped, this in itself is useful information and assists in drawing conclusions and separating unrealistic ambition from realistic alternatives. Hong Kong is a small, relatively wealthy jurisdiction with an aging population and rising health expenditures (which are forecast to continue rising). Hong Kong views itself as a hub for economic liberalism and places great importance on the rule of law and respect for private property rights; in some ways, these make up its comparative advantage in a region replete with economic competitors for trade, finance and investment. While there is a purported push toward the cultivation of innovative research and development in Hong Kong in general, including in the pharmaceutical sector, there is little evidence to suggest this will be successful. There is also no evidence suggesting that Hong Kong's small pharmaceutical manufacturing sector has the desire or capacity to expand. In short, while it would seem that the government would like to encourage the development of a thriving pharmaceutical sector, it is highly unlikely to come to fruition in the near to medium term (or long term without a significant change in policy direction). The objective of any reform to the pharmaceutical patent regime must therefore be to reduce costs and increase access to medicines for the population while at the same time maintaining Hong Kong's reputation as a jurisdiction that fully respects law and order and property rights.

Chapter 3 discusses the underexplored (in Hong Kong) but extremely important topic of the standards for patentability, such as novelty, inventive step and utility, as well as exclusions from patentability and the protection for biologics. In so doing, the chapter explores the policy space available to tailor one's law around subissues such as new use of known substances. Drawing heavily on the experience of other nations, this chapter will ultimately recommend a more detailed and predictable standard than exists in the current law.

Chapter 4 relates to term extensions, which are not currently available in Hong Kong. The chapter draws on international experience and while questioning the merits of term extensions for delays in the granting of patents and delays in granting marketing approval of pharmaceutical products, the chapter recommends a course of action that provides principles and safeguards should the jurisdiction follow the trend and adopt such a mechanism.

Chapter 5 focuses on exceptions to patent rights. The chapter reviews the major flexibilities allowed under the TRIPS Agreement and explores their implementation and use in other jurisdictions before evaluating Hong Kong's legislative framework. Finding Hong Kong's laws in regard to a general exception (including a regulatory review or "bolar" exception) insufficient and opaque, the chapter recommends amendments to the current legislation that are clearer, more precise and more in line with Hong Kong's priorities. In regard to compulsory licensing, Hong Kong's laws are rather flexible and although unlikely ever to be utilized, do not require immediate attention.

Chapter 6 discusses the quasi-patent rights of protection for undisclosed test data. While not fully addressed in the TRIPS Agreement (Article 39 on undisclosed test data notwithstanding) test data exclusivity is a sui generis right that has become commonplace in the developed countries and spread in numerous FTAs to developing countries. Hong Kong offers a lengthy period of test data protection with minimal safeguards, which is curious given the state of the pharmaceutical industry in Hong Kong and its constructed policy objective. This chapter offers amendments to safeguard the system through the addition of several legislative and treaty-based amendments.

Chapter 7 focuses on patent linkage – that is, the linking of marketing approval for pharmaceutical products with patent status. Hong Kong does not currently link patent status to the issuance of marketing approval, and this chapter recommends that Hong Kong maintain this position. However, given that patent linkage is spreading quickly via FTAs, the chapter recommends some ways to safeguard the system, minimize impact and avoid the most onerous aspects of patent linkage should it be implemented in Hong Kong.

Chapter 8 offers concluding comments on the need for Hong Kong (and almost every other nation) to undertake a systemic review of the pharmaceutical patent system to ensure it is operating efficiently, as intended and in line with the needs and priorities of the jurisdiction. In the case of Hong Kong, this research concludes that the law is not operating in harmony with governmental policy or in line with the needs of the population. Clearer governmental policy objectives are a necessary step toward resolving the disharmony. This research seeks to influence the public policy debate by first deducing Hong Kong's objectives and then by offering recommendations to reform the pharmaceutical patent framework.

2

The Contextual Framework of Hong Kong's Pharmaceutical Patent Laws and Policy

Pharmaceutical patent laws and policy cannot be developed in the abstract. Instead, they involve an array of multifaceted policy considerations. Influenced and shaped by a multitude of sometimes contradictory interests, pharmaceutical patent laws and policy both are a product of and at the same time impact on a host of sectors, most notably health, industrial, intellectual property and innovation. The final product is policymaking at its most delicate and complex and laws that attempt to balance the competing interests.

The objective of this chapter is to provide contextual background information to the remainder of the monograph by mapping out policy areas that affect (and are affected by) the patent system. Possession of this information is critical before proceeding to evaluate and recommend changes to the current system. Stated more simply, one cannot assess the workings of the current system unless and until the policy objectives that lie behind the system are fully understood. In this regard, this chapter will seek to ascertain the objectives that drive pharmaceutical patent laws and policy in Hong Kong.

Lacking clear direction from the government, this chapter will review the government's policy aims and objectives in the health, industrial, intellectual property and innovation sectors in order to form the basis of information from which to ascertain and/or construct the objectives that drive the government's pharmaceutical patent policy. While clear policy direction is of course the preferred course of action, government policy in a number of areas is often unclear, underdeveloped and even conflicting. This is problematic, of course, but the lack of clear pharmaceutical policy objectives and direction is in itself useful information and plays a substantial role in drawing conclusions and separating unrealistic ambition from realistic options.

The analysis of interests and policies in this chapter reveals several important considerations that must be taken into account when shaping pharmaceutical patent policy. First, Hong Kong is a small, relatively wealthy jurisdiction with an aging population and rising health expenditures (both of which are forecast to continue rising). Second, Hong Kong is not a leader in innovation in any sector, and the jurisdiction hosts little to no research and development (R&D) in the pharmaceutical sector and possesses limited manufacturing capacity. While the government has in recent times discussed the possibility of transforming Hong Kong into a regional pharmaceutical center, the discussions are preliminary in nature and appear rather half-hearted; there is little evidence to suggest the discussion will result in any tangible plan of action. The final consideration is that Hong Kong is a hub for economic liberalism and places great importance on its stability, friendly business climate, the rule of law and respect for private property rights (including IPRs) for its survival. In many respects, these overarching policy objectives are its comparative advantage in a region awash with competitors for trade, finance and investment opportunities.

Taking these factors into account, the chapter concludes by constructing a jurisdiction-specific policy objective for pharmaceutical patents: The objective of the pharmaceutical patent regime should be to reduce costs and increase access to medicines for the population while at the same time maintaining Hong Kong's reputation as a jurisdiction that fully respects law, order and property rights.

2.1   General Landscape

This section provides necessary context through a brief description of Hong Kong's economic and legal pharmaceutical landscape, public healthcare system and the pharmaceutical industry. Each will be addressed in turn.

2.1.1   The Economic and Legal Climate

Hong Kong is a small, technologically advanced jurisdiction that is heavily reliant on services for its economic prosperity. With over 90 percent of its gross domestic product (GDP) in the services sector, Hong Kong hosts little manufacturing, industry or agriculture. The government of Hong Kong thus actively promotes the territory as a hub for innovation and technological development with some success. For instance, *Forbes* magazine recently placed Hong Kong among the top technology hubs with a "compelling prospect in the near future"[1] and the 2016 Global

---

[1] Karsten Strauss, "The World's Top 4 Tech Capitals to Watch (after Silicon Valley and New York)," *Forbes*, 20 March 2013, www.forbes.com/sites/karstenstrauss/2013/03/20/the-

Innovation Index Report ranks Hong Kong fourteenth among 128 countries (down from eleventh out of 142 in 2015 and fourth in 2011, it must be noted).[2] Moreover, Ernst & Young's 2012 Globalization Index places Hong Kong first among the sixty largest countries measured by GDP according to degree of globalization.[3] Other estimates are slightly less complimentary or bullish,[4] but nevertheless find Hong Kong possesses potential for innovation development.[5]

---

worlds-top-4-tech-capitals-to-watch-after-silicon-valley-and-new-york/#37bf60a4552e, accessed 20 February 2017.

[2] See Soumitra Dutta, Bruno Lanvin and Sacha Wunsch-Vincent (eds.), "The Globalization Index 2016: Winning with Global Innovation," www.globalinnovationindex .org/gii-2016-report; Soumitra Dutta, Bruno Lanvin and Sacha Wunsch-Vincent (eds.), "The Globalization Index 2015: Effective Innovation Policies for Development," www .globalinnovationindex.org/userfiles/file/reportpdf/GII-2015-v5.pdf; Soumitra Dutta (ed.), "The Globalization Index 2011: Accelerating Growth and Development," www.wipo .int/edocs/pubdocs/en/economics/gii/gii_2011.pdf. Links accessed 20 February 2017.

[3] See "Country Profiles: A Further Look into the Top 10 Performing Economies in the 2012 Globalization Index," Ernst & Young's Annual Globalization Index, (2012) at 4 (finding that Hong Kong "does best in cultural integration [and] its main strength lies in exchange of technology and ideas" and predicting that it will "remain on top of the Globalization Index . . . on the back of its forecasted increased trade and capital flows as well as improvements in technology and culture"), www.ey.com/Publication/vwLUAssets/Country_profile_of_ Top_10_globalized_countries/$FILE/Country-profiles_top10_globalization.pdf. accessed 20 February 2017. It should be noted that although the report includes "technology and ideas" as one of the five main pillars and "drivers for globalization" (together with factors such as "openness to trade, capital flows, labor movements, and cultural integration"), the Index does not provide a detailed explanation of these indicators/factors or of the scoring system.

[4] More moderate estimates are cited in the Global Competitiveness Reports, which ranks Hong Kong ninth out of 138 economies on a competitiveness indicator but twenty-seventh in regard to innovation: "[Hong Kong] remain[s] far behind the world's innovation Powerhouse . . . [I]nnovation remains the weakest aspect of Hong Kong's performance and the business community consistently cites the capacity to innovate as their biggest concern." See Klaus Schwab, "Global Competitiveness Report 2016–2017," the World Economic Forum (2016), p. 16, 27 and 196, www3.weforum.org/docs/GCR2016–2017/ 05FullReport/TheGlobalCompetitivenessReport2016–2017_FINAL.pdf. accessed 6 March 2017.

[5] See, i.e., Naubahar Sharif and Erik Baark, "From Trade Hub to Innovation Hub: Hong Kong," in Charles Edquist and Leif Hommen (eds.), *Small Country Innovation Systems: Globalization, Change and Policy in Asia and Europe* (Elgar, 2008), questioning Hong Kong's desire to move from facilitator between China and the world to innovator. ("Hong Kong has a weak [national system of innovation], particularly if innovation is defined . . . in terms of knowledge creation through R&D inputs and patentable technology as output. This weakness is chiefly a result of Hong Kong's historical place as a trade hub vis-à-vis China . . . In evaluating past innovation policies in Hong Kong, the most conspicuous point to be made is how 'late' the policies have been in their introduction.") Although the authors find that "Hong Kong has made progress in transforming its role from that of an unrivalled trade hub

At present, however, Hong Kong has not formulated a strategy or implementation/action plan for innovation and technology. The only tangible results of the government's interest in innovation have been the establishment of the Innovation and Technology Fund (ITF) to provide support to applied projects initiated by the industrial and R&D sectors[6] and the recent establishment of the Innovation and Technology Bureau, which is now responsible for policy matters on the development of innovation and technology in Hong Kong.[7]

The simple point is nonetheless that Hong Kong is a globalized society that has all of the ingredients necessary to facilitate innovation and technological development. In particular, the government understands that multiple factors account for Hong Kong's standing and readiness to embrace innovative technologies, and has consistently emphasized the rule of law and strong protection of IPRs. In this regard, the 2013 Policy Address states:

> We attach great importance to the significant contribution of innovation and technology to the development of the economy and industries. There are a number of drivers for technological innovation in Hong Kong, including our rule of law, internationally acclaimed universities and sound intellectual property rights protection.[8]

This point is important because it sends a strong policy message that the rule of law and the protection of IPRs are key characteristics of Hong Kong's business climate and play a role in the territory's comparative advantage in the region. It is also clear that the government understands the interrelation between innovation and IPRs. For example, recognition

---

into that of an innovation hub," they forecast that in areas "such as automotive parts, Chinese medicine and integrated circuit design, Hong Kong is looking to exploit its 'traditional' role as a facilitator between China and global networks." Ibid. at 226–31.

[6] The ITF R&D projects for the manufacture of Western drugs and proprietary Chinese medicines are covered under the category of biotechnology. As of October 2017, the ITF has allocated more than HK$13.092 billion to support 6,709 projects – with 2,523 Innovation and Technology projects receiving funding of more than HK$10.281 billion, of which only 441 projects totaling HK$849 million went to the biotechnology sector. Biotechnology projects include funding for the development of new drugs, modernization of traditional Chinese medicines, improvement of drug formulas, development of new drug delivery systems, conduct of clinical trials, development of drug manufacturing processes and quality control methods. See "Innovation and Technology Fund Statistics" at www.itf.gov.hk/l-eng/statistic.asp, accessed 21 December 2017.

[7] See generally the Innovation and Technology Bureau, www.itb.gov.hk/en/.

[8] The Government of the Hong Kong SAR, "The 2013 Policy Address: Seek Change, Maintain Stability, Serve the People with Pragmatism," at 43, www.policyaddress.gov.hk/2013/eng/p43.html, accessed 20 February 2017.

of the linkage between innovation and IPRs was behind the key objective of the patent system review in 2011, which was undertaken with a view to "develop Hong Kong into a regional innovation and technology hub."[9]

Beyond the basics, however, the cultivation of an innovation hub requires a deeper understanding of both the special relationship between patent protection and innovation and a thorough understanding of the sector-specific regulatory framework. Such an understanding would ideally be based on particular indicators and characteristics to measure and qualify the scale of innovation, technological capacity and expertise in local industry, including the maturity of the research infrastructure, the number of establishments in the local researched-based sector, and public and private investments into drug development activities.[10] Thus far, the government does not seem interested in delving deeply into the issue or attempting to map the landscape of, inter alia, research capabilities, existing strengths and weaknesses.

Without such governmental action, we are forced to turn to secondary studies and anecdotal evidence. Even here, there are limited studies focusing on Hong Kong, and essentially none in the pharmaceutical sector. The only directly on-point pharmaceutical-specific study is of limited value as it is small scale and conducted by the Hong Kong Association of Pharmaceutical Industry (HKAPI), an industry association for branded companies. In this 2010 study, the HKAPI sought to evaluate Hong Kong's potential to attract R&D for local clinical trials and to "develop into a regional hub for clinical trials."[11] Of note, the study found it was necessary for the government to establish a dedicated team to assist in the development of specific human resources in clinical studies and to establish a reliable patient-recruitment mechanism in relation to specific diseases in order to be successful – both of which would require coherent and sustained planning and development. The study, however, did not focus on

---

[9] "Policy Agenda of Commerce," Industry and Tourism Branch and Innovation and Technology Commission, Commerce and Economic Development Bureau, Hong Kong SAR Legislative Council Panel on Commerce and Industry 4 (2011), www.legco.gov.hk/yr11–12/english/panels/ci/papers/ci1018cb1–37–3-e.pdf, accessed 20 February 2017.

[10] See generally Yi Qian, "Do National Patent Laws Stimulate Domestic Innovation in a Global Patenting Environment? A Cross-Country Analysis of Pharmaceutical Patent Protection" 1978–2002 (2007) 89 *Review of Economics and Statistics*, 436.

[11] See Hong Kong Association of Pharmaceutical Industry, "To Enhance the Clinical Trial Capacity in Hong Kong," (2010), especially 2–4, www.legco.gov.hk/yr11–12/english/panels/ci/papers/ci0515cb1–1820–2-e.pdf, accessed 20 February 2017 (forwarding recommendations based on the respondents' submissions; the recommendations mostly address administrative matters and did touch on the regulatory issues).

pharmaceutical developments as considered for the purpose of this chapter, and although many respondents positively evaluated Hong Kong's potential for the discovery segment of the pharmaceutical value chain (including medical research infrastructure, equipment and laboratories of the clinical trial sites, expertise of local investigators and the "friendliness" of the regulatory framework), the study was based on the responses of 26 of 44 HKAPI members and conducted in response to the government's stated desire to expand local clinical trials.[12]

From a legal point of view, Hong Kong maintains a strong commitment to the protection of the rule of law and preservation of IPRs. This commitment is more than legislative with Articles 118 and 139 of the Constitution, respectively, providing that the Hong Kong government "shall provide an economic and legal environment for encouraging investments, technological progress and the development of new industries" and "shall, on its own, formulate policies on science and technology and protect by law achievements in scientific and technological research, patents, discoveries and inventions." Additionally, Article 139 makes clear that the Hong Kong government, and not the central government in Beijing, "shall, on its own, decide on the scientific and technological standards and specifications applicable in Hong Kong."[13]

With a transparent system based on English common law that provides for predictable laws, regulations and enforcement, Hong Kong consistently ranks well in the World Bank's Worldwide Governance Indicators Reports as well as in the World Justice Project's Rule of Law Index. For example, the 2016 World Justice Project ranks Hong Kong sixteenth globally (among 113) and as fifth in the East Asia and Pacific region, with particularly high scores in relation to due process of law (and respect for due process), law and government data transparency and the reliability of complaint mechanisms. In all these factors, Hong Kong ranks far better than the average of regional countries and even above the average high-income countries.[14]

Hong Kong is also a committed member of the international law community. Hong Kong became a member to the WIPO Paris Convention for

---

[12] In particular, nineteen members of the HKAPI reported conducting 436 clinical trials in Hong Kong in 1999–2008 including in therapeutic areas such as oncology, endocrinology, gastroenterology and hepatology, cardiology and respiratory. Ibid., appendix 2.

[13] Hong Kong 1997 Patents Ordinance Cap 514 also provides the substantive rules for an invention to be patentable. See in particular Sections 93–97.

[14] See the World Justice Project, "Rule of Law Index 2016" (2016), http://worldjusticeproject .org/sites/default/files/media/wjp_rule_of_law_index_2016.pdf, accessed 6 March 2017.

the Protection of Industrial Property (Stockholm Act 1967) in 1985 and is bound to adhere to the Patent Cooperation Treaty (PCT). While the first two treaties are of marginal importance to the regulations on guaranteeing patent validity and the like, Hong Kong is a Member of the WTO in its own right and thus must comply with the TRIPS Agreement, which is an integral part of the WTO Agreement.

2.1.2   The Public Healthcare System

Hong Kong is in the luxurious position of being able to afford and prioritize its public healthcare system, with the government committed to "develop and maintain...a health care system which protects and promotes the health of the population, which provides lifelong holistic care to each citizen, and which is affordable and financially sustainable in the long term".[15] As a result, Hong Kong maintains a world-class system that rivals most in the world.

The Hong Kong healthcare system is more heavily dependent on government subvention than most other economically advanced jurisdictions, with 95 percent of the cost for across-the-board public hospital services and 97 percent for in-patient care subsidized by the government.[16] As a result, public funding largely supports primary and specialist care, and most medicines are fully or partially subsidized through a Drug Formulary, which aims to ensure equal access to affordable medicine of proven safety and quality through standardized drug procurement and utilization policies across all public hospitals and clinics. Moreover, the public healthcare system provides an additional safety net in the form of specially allocated funding that provides financial resources to patients needing medicines that are not procured under the subsidized Drug

---

[15] *Hong Kong SAR 2001 Policy Address, Health Services: Policy Objective and Key Result Areas,* the Government of the Hong Kong SAR 2 (2001), www.policyaddress.gov.hk/pa01/sim/pdf/healthe.pdf, accessed 6 March 2017. The Policy Address is the Chief Executive's annual strategy paper, which defines the policy agenda and initiatives.

[16] Hong Kong SAR Food and Health Bureau, "Your Health, Your Life: Healthcare Reform Consultation Document" (2008) Annex B, at B.22 at 125, www.fhb.gov.hk/beStrong/files/consultation/Condochealth_full_eng.pdf, accessed 6 March 2017. As an illustration, a visit to the accident and emergency department costs HK$100 (equivalent to US$12.50) regardless of the reason for the visit or necessary treatment. For this reason, Hong Kong's healthcare system is skewed and wastefully dependent on public hospitals, with over 90 percent of patient care received at public hospitals compared with 92 percent of patients in England receiving care from general practitioners at private clinics. Business Monitor International, "Hong Kong Pharmaceuticals & Healthcare Report Q4," 2015.

Formulary. At the same time, the government encourages the populace to make use of private healthcare, which offers additional medical treatment options for those willing to pay for them.

Public healthcare is delivered through the Department of Health and the Hospital Authority, the former being a government body charged with the implementation of the public health policy and the latter being a statutory body that manages all public hospitals (including resource allocation and drug procurement). In accordance with the Hospital Authority Ordinance (Cap 113), the Hospital Authority is directed to provide equitable and accessible quality public healthcare services to the population[17] and ensure that "no one [is] denied adequate healthcare through lack of means."[18]

Similar to many other jurisdictions, public spending on medical and health services has been rapidly rising over recent years due to increased demand for hospital services, the implementation of measures to improve clinical care and the introduction of newer and more costly drugs to the Drug Formulary.[19] For the reporting year of 2016–2017, the government allocated the Hospital Authority a budget of HK$57 billion (equivalent to US$7.3 billion), which is more than 90 percent higher than a decade ago and represents approximately 16.5 percent of the Hong Kong government's general expenditures – on top of a new HK$200 billion grant provided as part of a ten-year plan to upgrade hospital facilities.

The issue of "rising health expenditure, which [is growing] at a rate faster than that of the economy" is increasingly making it more difficult for Hong Kong to maintain a world-class healthcare system.[20] The government has long realized the growing problem, with the 2007–2008 Policy Address even stating that it would be "impossible for the Government to increase public health care expenditure indefinitely" and calling for the

---

[17] See 1990 Hospital Authority Ordinance (amended 2007) O.H.K., Cap 113, at 4(a)(i) (providing that the Hospital Authority is to "use hospital beds, staff, equipment and other resources efficiently to provide hospital services of the highest possible standard within the resources obtainable").

[18] P. Y. Leung et al., "Sustaining Quality, Performance and Cost-Effectiveness in a Public Hospital System," Hong Kong Hospital Authority 32 (2011), www.ha.org.hk/upload/presentation/347.pdf, accessed 21 February 2017.

[19] See "Hong Kong SAR 2016–17 Budget Speech," www.budget.gov.hk/2016/eng/speech.html, accessed 21 February 2017.

[20] Ko Wing-Man, "HK Healthcare Is a Dual-Track System," Hong Kong, 9 April 2013, www.news.gov.hk/en/record/html/2013/04/20130409_190409.shtml, accessed 21 February 2017.

introduction of "supplementary financing."[21] Following this Address, the government initiated public consultations on "comprehensive and fundamental" healthcare reform in order to address the challenges of rising costs and the substantial increase in the healthcare budget due to the rise in the demand for healthcare services.[22] And make no mistake, demand for healthcare services in Hong Kong will rise – the population is growing and life expectancy in Hong Kong (currently at eighty-four years) is already among the highest in the world.[23] At the same time, the incidence of chronic diseases is also on the rise,[24] and the labor force is expected to start to decline from 2018 onward due to the rapidly aging population.[25]

Unsurprisingly, the consultation focused on the implementation of supplementary and alternative financing options in order to combat the rising public health expenditure, with a key outcome being the adoption of the Health Protection Scheme, which shifts more of the cost burden to patients. More recently, the 2013 Policy Address stressed the further development of the private healthcare sector, finding that

> our rapidly ageing population has increased demand for healthcare services. The growing prevalence of certain diseases, advances in healthcare technology and public expectations for healthcare services to keep up with the latest medical practices have led to a rise in medical costs. We must tackle the root of the problem to ensure the sustainable development of our healthcare system.[26]

The conclusions of the consultation were given a further boost when then-Hong Kong Financial Secretary John C. Tsang stated:

---

[21] "Hong Kong SAR 2007–2008 Policy Address," Health Care Reform, the Government of the Hong Kong SAR at 98 (2007), www.legco.gov.hk/yr07–08/english/panels/0708speech_e.pdf, accessed 21 February 2017.

[22] See "Report of the Review Committee on Regulation of Pharmaceutical Products in Hong Kong," Hong Kong SAR Food and Health Bureau and Department of Health (December 2009), www.ppbhk.org.hk/eng/files/Report_of_Review_Committee_eng.pdf, accessed 21 February 2017. For consultation reports and related materials, see "Your Health, Your Life, Consultation Documents and Materials," www.fhb.gov.hk/beStrong/eng/consultation/consultation_cdhcr_shfs.html, accessed 21 February 2017.

[23] World Bank, "Life Expectancy at Birth," (2016), http://data.worldbank.org/indicator/SP.DYN.LE00.IN, accessed 21 February 2017. See also "Hong Kong Major Health Indicators in 2015 and 2016," the Department of Health, the Government of the Hong Kong SAR, www.chp.gov.hk/en/data/4/10/27/110.html, accessed 4 August 2017.

[24] See "Hong Kong SAR 2013 Policy Address," above n. 8 at 105 (2013) www.policyaddress.gov.hk/2013/eng/pdf/PA2013.pdf, accessed 21 February 2017.

[25] "Hong Kong SAR Budget Speech 2015–16," Hong Kong SAR Finance Bureau (2015) at 134, www.budget.gov.hk/2015/eng/speech.html, accessed 21 February 2017.

[26] See "Hong Kong SAR 2013 Policy Address," above n. 8, at 158.

[The population] aged 65 or above will increase from the current 0.9 million to 2.1 million in 2030. To cope with this long-term issue, both the community and the Government will have to make sustained efforts in various respects. Measures implemented in certain policy areas, such as the *healthcare financing reform*, will help us get ready for the future.

(emphasis added)[27]

In the 2015–2016 Budget Speech, the Chief Executive further announced plans to "alleviate pressure on the public healthcare system due to manpower shortages and surge in demand" through a Hospital Authority fund for public-private partnership initiatives.[28] Other initiatives, such as the expansion of the Elderly Health Care Voucher Scheme,[29] provide stop-gap measures but are not viewed as long-term solutions.

When attempting to limit healthcare budget increases, an obvious target is the high cost of pharmaceuticals. Public procurement of medicines forms a sizable chunk of the Hong Kong healthcare budget, although as with many pharmaceutical-related issues in Hong Kong, acquiring actual figures has proven difficult. That said, it is known that drug expenditures nearly doubled between 2005 and 2015, with expenditures recently rising approximately seven percent a per annum and reaching HK$6.156 billion (US$1.7 billion) in 2017.[30] This level of pharmaceutical expenditure accounts for nearly ten percent of Hong Kong's entire health budget.[31] While respect for patent rights and innovation is important, it must be understood that a central part of the balance between the maintenance

---

[27] "Hong Kong SAR Budget Speech 2012–13," Hong Kong SAR Finance Bureau (2012) at 176, 212, www.budget.gov.hk/2012/eng/pdf/e_budgetspeech2012–13.pdf, accessed 21 February 2017.

[28] "Hong Kong SAR Budget Speech 2015–16," above n. 25, at 142.

[29] Used by 640,000 people, the program provides elderly residents with a HK$2,000 voucher and has an annual expenditure of some HK$600 million. See "Hong Kong SAR Budget Speech 2014–15" (2014), at 153, www.budget.gov.hk/2014/eng/budget42.html, accessed 21 December 2017.

[30] "Drug Expenditure in Hong Kong Doubled to HK$4.3b," *Hong Kong Business*, 11 April 2016, http://hongkongbusiness.hk/healthcare/in-focus/drug-expenditure-in-hong-kong-doubled-hkd43b#sthash.YykHpHtx.dpuf; Hospital Authority, Annual Report 2016–17, at 70, available at http://www.ha.org.hk/ho/corpcomm/AR201617/PDF/HAAR_2016-17_PDF.pdf. accessed 21 December 2017. While statistics comparing the percentage of pharmaceuticals (by cost) purchased by the Hospital Authority versus privately are not readily available, by combining data garnered from government statistics and research consultants it is possible to conclude that the Hospital Authority accounts for roughly 54 percent of drug spending.

[31] Ibid., Hospital Authority.

of a world-class healthcare system with necessary cost containment measures occurs through the public procurement of medicines.

Unfortunately, and somewhat bizarrely, the Hong Kong government claims that it does not maintain statistics on the actual ratio between generic and branded drugs purchased by the Hospital Authority. That being the case, the Secretary for Food and Health is on the record as stating that "the annual percentage of expenditure on generic drugs procured through tenders by the [Hospital Authority] account[s] for more than 80% of the total expenditure on drugs."[32] Discussions with government officials confirm a policy favoring generic substitution as part of the cost-containment strategy. These figures, however, are somewhat at odds with those compiled by a leading healthcare consulting group, which found that generic pharmaceuticals currently account for 20.6 percent of the total market.[33]

The sale and supply of pharmaceutical products in Hong Kong are regulated through a system of registration and classification.[34] In order to market pharmaceutical products in Hong Kong the product must be registered with the Pharmacy and Poisons Board (PPB). The PPB is a statutory body that assesses applications for registration (marketing approval) on the basis of their safety, efficacy and quality through two Committees: the Registration Committee and the Poisons Committee. In order to approve any pharmaceutical product, applicants must submit to the PPB valid Certificates of Pharmaceutical Product (CPPs) issued by countries making up the International Conference on Harmonisation of Technical Requirements for Registration of Pharmaceuticals for Human Use (ICH);[35] that is, Hong Kong will not grant marketing approval to any product unless it has been approved in two ICH counties – namely, the United States,

---

[32] "Official Record of Proceedings" (May 11, 2011), Hong Kong SAR Legislative Council 10128–9 (2011), www.legco.gov.hk/yr10–11/english/counmtg/hansard/cm0511-translate-e.pdf, at 10130.

[33] Business Monitor International, Q4 2013, above n. 48 at 42 (projecting the share of generics to rise to 27 percent of the total market by 2017). The Report separates the total market into three categories: patented drugs, generic drugs and (curiously) over-the-counter medicines (which it would seem would either be patented or generic).

[34] See Pharmacy and Poisons Ordinance (PPO) (Cap. 138).

[35] The ICH is a grouping that "bring[s] together the regulatory authorities and pharmaceutical industry to discuss scientific and technical aspects of drug registration ... [and whose] mission is to achieve greater harmonisation worldwide to ensure that safe, effective, and high quality medicines are developed and registered in the most resource-efficient manner." The ICH produces a number of guidelines, including on pharmaceutical product registration. For more information, see the ICH website at www.ich.org/products/guidelines .html, accessed 14 August 2017.

EU, Japan, Australia or Canada.[36] The process for generic pharmaceutical products to enter the market is even more onerous and takes more time as the applicant must acquire and present a Free Sales Certificate from the country of origin, the manufacturer's license, a Good Manufacturing Practice certificate and other documents that adequately track the manufacturing and logistics chain. Hong Kong does not treat originator products made from chemical entities differently from biological materials (i.e., products derived from living organisms). Unlike generic versions of pharmaceutical products made from chemical entities, generic versions of biological drugs are not exact copies but rather similar as a result "of the inevitable differences in molecular structures and quality attributes arising from their different manufacturing processes."[37] For these reasons, such generic versions are referred to as "biosimilars." Hong Kong has a special process for the granting of marketing approval of biosimilars that is heavily based on guidelines developed by the World Health Organization (WHO) and practical experience of a number of jurisdictions, most notably the EU. In order to receive marketing approval in Hong Kong, biosimilar product applicants need to provide proof that the product has been approved in one other select market (the United States, Europe, Japan, Australia or Canada).[38] Moreover, marketing approval will not be granted to a biosimilar until the original biological drug (called the "reference product") has been on the Hong Kong market for a period of at least eight years.[39] Furthermore, the biosimilar cannot rely on another biosimilar for the purposes of gaining marketing approval but must instead demonstrate similarity with the originator reference product.[40]

Following endorsement by the PPB, the Drug Advisory Committee of the Hospital Authority will consider applications from newly registered

---

[36] The PPB not only requires proof of registration in the other jurisdictions but also seeks to understand why the drug was registered (or, if applicable, initially rejected). That is, the PPB does not simply approve and register all applications that produce CPPs but instead uses those prior registrations to assist in its own investigation. The need for two CPPs has been criticized for delaying the registration process and limiting the availability of products for treatment of rare diseases, but is consistently defended as necessary to guard against premature and potentially dangerous drugs that are approved in only one jurisdiction before being withdrawn. See, e.g., Business Facilitation Advisory Committee, "Second Meeting of the Business Facilitation Advisory Committee," BFAC Paper 3/06, paras. 18–19, available at www.gov.hk/en/theme/bf/pdf/2bfacpaper3–06.pdf, accessed 14 August 2017.

[37] Hong Kong Department of Health, Drug Office, Drug Registration and Import/Export Control Division, "Guidance Notes for Registration of Biosimilar Products" (with effect from 1 January 2016), para. 3, available at www.drugoffice.gov.hk/eps/do/en/pharmaceutical_trade/guidelines_forms/pr_guide_main.html, accessed 23 August 2017.

[38] Ibid., para. 10.   [39] Ibid., para. 14.   [40] Ibid.

pharmaceutical products (whether chemically or biologically derived) to be included on the Drug Formulary. If successful, the product would be government-funded to the public and available at public hospitals and clinics, whereas unlisted products are available only on a user-pays, self-funded basis for patients. Approximately 70 percent of drugs sold in Hong Kong are listed on the Drug Formulary, which is revised every twelve to eighteen months to take account of the decisions of the Drug Advisory Committee.[41]

At the same time, Hong Kong's Legislative Council must amend the Pharmacy and Poisons Regulations and the Poisons List Regulations before the product can be marketed in Hong Kong. The usual time for drug approval and registration in Hong Kong is on average between eight and twelve months, but can be as short as four months.[42] That being said, and as mentioned above, once approval has been granted by the PPB, the manufacturer must wait for legislative approval by the Legislative Council. This process regularly adds on average an additional three to nine months to the process, and with the current state of Hong Kong politics in a state of paralysis owing to domestic political factors, routine items such as pharmaceutical approvals often get sidelined and pushed back on the agenda. The result over the recent few years has been further delays to the registration process.

The registration of pharmaceutical products is a purely scientific decision based on the safety, efficacy and quality of the submission. The PPB is qualified to make such a decision, and there does not seem to be a need for Legislative Council approval prior to approving the drug for registration. In other jurisdictions, including Australia, the EU and the United States as well as Asian neighbors Korea, Singapore and Taiwan, the process is entirely delegated to the relevant health authority and completed without legislative intervention. The need for legislation approval in Hong Kong unnecessarily delays the registration of new pharmaceutical products, to the detriment of patients and community health.

---

[41] For the current list of listed pharmaceuticals, see HA Drug Formulary Management, available at www.ha.org.hk/hadf/en-us/Updated-HA-Drug-Formulary, accessed on 14 August 2017.

[42] While Hong Kong does have a fast track approval scheme when there are "unmet needs" in the community, there are high procedural hurdles to overcome to implement the scheme and the procurement of the drug will likely have to be self-funded by the patient. Moreover, even when unmet needs have been established, the government still requires prior approval in two other jurisdictions.

Thus, on average an applicant can expect to wait eighteen to twenty-four months to receive marketing approval. This is far longer than other regional jurisdictions, which either make their own determination on the safety and efficacy or rely on only one other jurisdiction (usually being the United States or EU) as a guide. For instance, Singapore targets an approval time of forty working days for certain submissions and less than one year for all submissions.[43] Moreover, while Singapore regularly approves between 100 and 200 new pharmaceutical products a year,[44] Hong Kong by comparison approves only twenty to fifty new products.[45]

While the delays ensure only high-quality pharmaceutical products are registered and that a healthcare system that is heavily reliant on public funding and subvention operates in a cost-effective manner, physicians and patients have complained that the length in processing time results in unnecessary suffering and even deaths as life-saving drugs readily available elsewhere cannot be marketed in Hong Kong. In so doing, however, quite a number of physicians conflate the marketing approval process with that of the government-funded Drug Formulary – to be clear, a drug can be approved for marketing in Hong Kong but not added to the government-funded procurement list, meaning that the patients must pay for it themselves. For instance, William Chui Chun-ming, president of the Society of Hospital Pharmacists, suggested that the long drug approval process may be due to the fact that the government subvention rate is exceedingly high in Hong Kong.[46] Likewise, Dr. Stephen Chan, assistant

---

[43] See Singaporean Health Sciences Authority, "Target Processing Times," available at www.hsa.gov.sg/content/hsa/en/Health_Products_Regulation/Western_Medicines/Application_Registration/Target_Processing_Timelines.html, accessed on 14 August 2017. See also Kitty Tsz Ki Chan, "Evaluation of the Drug Regulatory Systems in Hong Kong, Singapore, Taiwan, United States and European Union," submission for Master of Public Health, University of Hong Kong, February 2013, pp. 1, 6 (on file with author) (reporting the average approval time of sixty days).

[44] These figures are sourced from the annual reports of Singapore's Health Sciences Authority, with reports from 2001 to 2016 available at www.hsa.gov.sg/content/hsa/en/Publications/Annual_Reports/Annual_Report_FY2015_16.html, accessed 14 August 2017.

[45] This figure is sourced from the annual reports of the Pharmacy and Poisons Board of Hong Kong, with reports from 2001 to 2015 available at www.ppbhk.org.hk/eng/index.html, accessed 14 August 2017.

[46] Emily Tsang, "Patients Forced to Wait Up to 24 Months for New Drugs to Be Approved in Hong Kong, as Experts Call for Simpler System," *South China Morning Post* (31 August 2015), available at www.scmp.com/news/hong-kong/health-environment/article/1853881/experts-call-hong-kongs-drug-approval-system-be, accessed on 14 August 2017.

professor of oncology at the Chinese University of Hong Kong, stated: "It is the government's responsibility to consider the cost and benefits of certain new drugs, especially if they are very expensive, as they are managing taxpayers' money... In Singapore, there is less concern for the government as patients are usually covered by medical insurance."[47] These may be arguments for not listing the new pharmaceutical product on the Drug Formulary, but they are irrelevant to the length of time it takes for a drug to receive market approval, or even whether the product should receive marketing approval. The statements do, however, demonstrate how the issues of the pharmaceutical approval process and funding of pharmaceuticals are misunderstood, even by those close to the system.

In Hong Kong, as in many jurisdictions, patented products are usually purchased through a single tender, while off-patent/generic drugs are procured through open tender.[48] In some ways, this system serves to unwittingly delay the entry of generics into the market even further due to the tendering process, which grants access to successful tenders for a two- to three-year period. In so doing, depending on the timing of the tendering process, a monopoly on sales can be extended beyond the expiration of the patent period.

The healthcare situation in Hong Kong is thus somewhat complex and difficult to categorize. At the same time as the government attempts to reduce costs, it recently increased the cost burden of medicines on the budget in at least two ways. First, the government allocated additional funding to the Hospital Authority in order to expand the Drug Formulary so as to "introduce additional drugs of proven cost-effectiveness and efficacy as standard drugs."[49] The addition of new drugs on the Drug Formulary seems reasonable if not overdue, as medical practitioners have long complained about the restricted nature of the list and the corresponding inability to prescribe what some may deem to be more preferred medicines. Second, Hong Kong negotiated free trade agreements (FTAs) which bind the government to introduce measures that in all likelihood will increase the cost of the procurement of medicines. The most notable example of this is included in the Hong Kong–European Free Trade Association FTA (HK-EFTA FTA), which extends the period of test data

---

[47] Ibid.

[48] Business Monitor International, "Hong Kong Pharmaceuticals & Healthcare Report Q4 2013," 68 (2013). See also "Official Record of Proceedings" (May 11, 2011), Hong Kong SAR Legislative Council 10128–9 (2011).

[49] "Hong Kong SAR 2012–13 Budget," above n. 27, at 426.

exclusivity in Hong Kong to eight years.[50] More perplexing is that multiple sources have confirmed that it was Hong Kong that advocated and negotiated for the inclusion of this provision in the FTA.

The current state of public healthcare policy and pharmaceutical procurement is thus rather confusing – at the same time the government is publicly announcing its intent to contain the costs of healthcare and promoting a policy of generic substitution of medicines (presumably with cost-containment in mind), it is negotiating treaty text that delays the introduction of generic competition for medicines. The seemingly contradictory nature of the measures could be understandable if rationalized and based on solid evidence and reasoning. However, it appears that neither of the measures was accompanied by or based on any thorough study evaluating the actual role of generic and branded suppliers in drug procurement. For instance, and again rather bizarrely, the "comprehensive" consultations on public health reform completely neglected the area of pharmaceutical patent protection and did not even attempt to assess the impact of public procurement or drug pricing practices on the economics of the healthcare system. Likewise, the government did not commission or refer to any consultation or study to evaluate the effect of data exclusivity on the public healthcare system before negotiating for the extension in the HK-EFTA FTA. Thus, this author cannot avoid making the accusation that two important (and seemingly contradictory) policy developments were not taken as a result of integrated, informed and systematic decision-making but rather may be a case of one government department simply being uninformed about or ignoring what the other is doing, that is, government departments not acting in concert and in line with a clear policy directive.

2.1.3   The Pharmaceutical Industry

The importance of establishing and maintaining a domestic pharmaceutical industry is controversial. Many developing country governments believe that the sector is beneficial for economic development in that it provides foreign investment, infrastructure, technology transfer and employment opportunities as well as using it as a way to provide for "pharmaceutical security." For more advanced economies, the sector is a worthwhile driver of innovation, source of high-quality employment for the populace and a boost to export trade terms. Still yet other

---

[50] For more detail and discussion, see Chapter 6.

countries, both developing and advanced, do not attempt to establish or bolster a local pharmaceutical industry and are content with importing medicines.

The direction of domestic policy objectives, priorities and strategies should ideally directly shape patent laws. For instance, as the United States and Switzerland are advanced nations and home to several multinational branded pharmaceutical companies with large investments in both R&D and manufacturing and source of employment to many thousands of workers, it is not surprising that both are strong proponents of a maximalist IP regime. On the other end of the spectrum are Brazil and India, both large developing countries with large and highly advanced generic pharmaceutical industries, which seek to minimize IPRs and take advantage of all existing flexibilities built within the IP regime for both local consumption and export opportunities. Between these two extremes lie most nations, each with varying degrees of health priorities, pharmaceutical R&D, manufacturing capacity and the like.

Hong Kong is host to one of the smallest pharmaceutical markets in Asia, and given its already high level of wealth and limited capacity for population growth, it has few prospects for industry growth. Sales and profits, however, have been rising in recent years due to increased volume and price increases – which have been attributed to population increase, rising per capita pharmaceutical expenditures, geographical proximity to mainland China and other emerging markets in the region and the presence of international leading innovative pharmaceutical companies (as marketers and lobbyists).[51] However, the overall impact of the pharmaceutical industry remains modest: In 2014, pharmaceutical sales accounted for only 0.52 percent of GDP (US$1.57 billion) and are expected to reach only 0.56 percent of GDP (US$2.14 billion) in the coming years.[52] The sector is nevertheless a source of employment as it hosts approximately 240 importers/exporters, 720 wholesalers and 4,500 pharmaceutical retailers.[53]

Hong Kong possesses limited manufacturing capacity. More specifically, as of 2017 Hong Kong hosts twenty-two licensed pharmaceutical

---

[51] Business Monitor International, "Hong Kong Pharmaceuticals & Healthcare Report," above n. 31.

[52] Ibid.

[53] Legislative Council Panel on Health Services, "Legislative Proposals to Enhance the Regulation of Pharmaceutical Products in Hong Kong," LC Paper No. CB(2)254/13–14(03) (2013), www.legco.gov.hk/yr13–14/english/panels/hs/papers/hs1118cb2–254-3-e.pdf, p. 3 accessed 21 February 2017.

manufacturers (down from twenty-four in 2015 and thirty-five in 2013),[54] and it has been reported that domestic production of pharmaceuticals and medical products employs up to 6,324 people (although it should be noted that the employment figure is conflated with other chemical sectors and therefore rather inflated).[55] Pharmaceutical production is focused on basic generic products for domestic consumption,[56] but the jurisdiction also produces consumer health products and Chinese medicines.[57] Overall, Hong Kong is a net importer of pharmaceuticals: In 2016, Hong Kong imported HK$5.381 billion and exported HK$628 million of domestic pharmaceuticals and medicinal products (down from HK$860 million in 2015).[58]

---

[54] For the current list of licensed pharmaceutical manufacturers operating in compliance with Good Manufacturing Practices Guidelines for Pharmaceutical Products of the Pharmacy and Poisons Board of Hong Kong, see the Government of Hong Kong SAR, Department of Health, List of Licensed Pharmaceutical Manufacturers, www.drugoffice.gov.hk/eps/do/en/pharmaceutical_trade/news_informations/relicList.html?indextype=ML, accessed 4 August 2017.

[55] The figure is reported in the category "chemical products and pharmaceutical." See "Hong Kong Annual Digest of Statistics," Hong Kong Census and Statistics Department (2017), p. 150, http://www.statistics.gov.hk/pub/B10100032017AN17B0100.pdf . Branded pharmaceutical companies are represented by HKAPI; as of April 2017, thirty-eight international members of the association are claimed to account for the provision of over 70 percent of prescription medicines in Hong Kong; see Membership of HKAPI, www.hkapi.hk/membership.asp. Local pharmaceutical manufacturers are represented by the Chinese Manufacturers' Association, see the Chinese Manufacturer's Association of Hong Kong, www.cma.org.hk. Links accessed 21 December 2017.

[56] See Benjamin Tak-Yuen Chan, "Pharmaceutical Policy in Hong Kong: Defining an Evolving Area of Study," presented at the First Conference on Pharmaceutical Policy Analysis, Zeist, Netherlands (19–21 September 2007), at 10. The government reports that exports of pharmaceuticals and medicinal products amounted to 6.2 percent of the territory's exports in 2015, but seemingly fails to distinguish between products manufactured in Hong Kong and those imported into the jurisdiction (most often from China) before being reexported elsewhere. See Hong Kong Trade and Industry, "The Facts: Trade and Industry," available at www.gov.hk/en/about/abouthk/factsheets/docs/trade&industry.pdf, accessed on 4 August 2017.

[57] The notion of "proprietary Chinese medicine" essentially requires that the product is composed solely of the following as active ingredients: (i) any Chinese herbal medicines; or (ii) any materials of herbal, animal or mineral origin customarily used by the Chinese; or (iii) any medicines and materials referred to in subparagraphs (i) and (ii), respectively. See Chinese Medicine Ordinance (1999, last amended 2010) O.H.K., Cap 549, at 2. Since this research focuses on the regulation of pharmaceutical products, proprietary Chinese medicine is excluded from the scope of the research. It should be noted, however, that a method for preparation of a Chinese medicine composition, such as the method of extraction of a natural substance, can be patentable.

[58] Hong Kong Census and Statistics Department, above n. 55, at 299. Hong Kong also reexported HK$1.544 billion in pharmaceuticals and medicinal products. Ibid.

Faced with increasing competition from imports from China (or, more accurately, multinational companies manufacturing in China),[59] the outlook for Hong Kong's pharmaceutical industry is bleak and its capacity is "shrinking or at least consolidating."[60] This is unsurprising, as land, infrastructure, inputs and labor are all significantly cheaper in China and elsewhere in Asia than they are in Hong Kong. Without government intervention, the industry will continue to follow the textiles and electronics industries, which significantly contracted and virtually disappeared as lower cost producers from elsewhere claimed market share.

Somewhat surprisingly, Hong Kong does not host any significant R&D activity in the pharmaceutical sector, and none of the major multinationals in the industry conducts any R&D in the territory. In a comprehensive review of patent databases in Hong Kong and all major markets conducted for this project, Daria Kim found that pharmaceutical patenting activity among Hong Kong residents is "quite modest [and] slightly declining recently," that nearly half of all Hong Kong filings do not ultimately receive a patent and that the vast majority of patent applications and approved patents were filed by universities.[61] Even with the universities, Hong Kong pharmaceutical patent activity results only in approximately twenty patent filings per year.

Another point of consideration is that the vast majority of university patents are ultimately licensed to other entities to further develop and exploit. This further development and exploitation occurs outside Hong Kong. Thus, while the government presumes that there will be a positive impact of patenting on national innovation policy,[62] this is not the case. In order for industrial policy to benefit, Hong Kong needs to consider how it can further derive benefits from the patent system; that is, how the patent

---

[59] Business Monitor International Report Q2 2014, above n. 32, at 29.

[60] Ibid., at 43–44. However, see Business Monitor International Report Q4 2013, above n. 48, at 69 (recognizing that although Hong Kong currently has little pharmaceutical R&D activity, "given its relatively advanced regulatory regime ... [it has] considerable potential as a base for biotechnology activity").

[61] Daria Kim, "Patenting Activity in the Pharmaceutical Sector in Hong Kong: National Innovation Perspective" (unpublished, 2015) (on file with author). The sources of data for the study include Patentscope (WIPO); Espacenet, Inpadoc, Patstat (EPO); USPTO, SIPO and HK IPO.

[62] See, i.e., "Hong Kong SAR 2013 Policy Address," above n. 8, at 43. ("We attach great importance to the significant contribution of innovation and technology to the development of the economy and industries. There are a number of drivers for technological innovation in Hong Kong, including our rule of law, internationally acclaimed universities and sound intellectual property rights protection.")

system "interrelates and interacts with other elements of national innovation system."[63] More specifically, it must "consider how technologies developed by universities can be further absorbed by the domestic industrial sector and benefit the local consumer."[64] To date, this discussion has simply not occurred and the disconnect between the reality of patenting activity "sharply contrasts the policy aspirations"[65] of the government as "an innovation-led, technology-intensive economy in the 21st century."[66]

This is in stark contrast to friendly rival Singapore,[67] and even more curious given the level of R&D conducted in other regional markets such as Taiwan, China and Malaysia. Of course, Hong Kong has long championed laissez-faire-style economic liberalism, which means that the pharmaceutical industry does not benefit from large-scale grants/subsidies, tax breaks, preferences or other government largesse. While pharmaceutical companies – like any other technology or research-based company – can benefit by subsidized rent at the Hong Kong Science Park, this is the extent of governmental assistance. Thus, and despite being "a textbook case for an open FDI climate, with international investors treated the same as national counterparts, and with no limits on the extent or type of foreign investment,"[68] Hong Kong has failed to attract significant investment in the pharmaceutical sector. In fact, investment in pharmaceuticals does not rate among the top ten investment sectors – nor was it deemed important enough to merit even in a mention in the direct investment statistics reports published annually over the last five years.[69]

As mentioned above, the government has also recently attempted to establish the territory as a regional hub for clinical trials. These efforts have been hampered by high costs relative to competitors (such as those in China). The government does not offer much in the way of direct subsidies and offers no incentive for companies to conduct trials in Hong Kong. This is unlike several other jurisdictions, which offer a fast-track approval

---

[63] Kim, above n. 61.   [64] Ibid.   [65] Ibid.

[66] Ibid., citing the 1998 Report of the Hong Kong Commission on Innovation and Technology.

[67] See, i.e., Bryan Mercurio and Daria Kim, "Foreign Direct Investment in the Pharmaceutical Industry: Why Singapore and Not Hong Kong" (2016) 10 *Asian Journal of Comparative Law* 235.

[68] Ibid.

[69] See, for instance, "External Direct Investment Statistics of Hong Kong 2011," Hong Kong SAR Census and Statistics Department (2011), www.statistics.gov.hk/pub/B10400032011AN11B0100.pdf, and "External Direct Investment Statistics of Hong Kong 2015," Hong Kong SAR Census and Statistics Department, www.statistics.gov.hk/pub/B10400032015AN15B0100.pdf, accessed 4 August 2017.

process where the drugs have been trialed locally. In addition, clinical trial certificates in Hong Kong are valid for only two years (as opposed to five years in several other jurisdictions), and as trials regularly last ten to twelve years this can mean frequent interruptions and delays in the trials and increased costs and administrative burden to the clinicians.

To some extent, it is unsurprising that no branded multinational pharmaceutical company engages in any significant R&D, that local manufacturing is shrinking in the face of increased competition and that the policy push to become a regional hub for clinical trials has largely failed. The jurisdiction is renowned for its open economy, regulatory stability, low tax rates and educated workforce, but fails to offer any specific investment incentives. In itself, this indicates the extent to which other jurisdictions have actively sought to attract and retain the industry through inducements. The contrast is succinctly summarized in the following quotation: "[Hong Kong's] policy for strategic development of [the pharmaceutical] sector is lacking when compared to Singapore and Malaysia [both of which] have actively promoted biotechnology and pharmaceuticals as new growth areas of their national economy."[70]

2.2   Policy Planning on Pharmaceutical Innovation

Having described Hong Kong's general economic and legal climate, the state of the healthcare system and pharmaceutical landscape, it is time to now turn to consider the issue of policy planning in relation to innovation in pharmaceutical products, focusing on current policies and priorities.

Despite the fact that Hong Kong has little manufacturing capacity and no R&D activity, the government has at times discussed the possibility of the jurisdiction becoming a "pharmaceutical centre." For instance, in October 2012 the Hong Kong Legislative Council discussed a call from industry groups to "develop Hong Kong into a 'pharmaceutical centre'... [and] attract world-renowned pharmaceutical manufacturers" in order to export to China, as well as to promote Hong Kong as a destination for clinical testing and manufacturing.[71]

---

[70] Chan, above n. 56, at 10.

[71] See Hong Kong Legislative Council, "Official Record of Proceedings of Wednesday, 24 October 2012," at 587, www.legco.gov.hk/yr12–13/english/counmtg/hansard/cm1024-translate-e.pdf; see also Hong Kong SAR Legislative Council, Press Release: "LCQ6: Development of Pharmaceutical Industry in Hong Kong," www.info.gov.hk/gia/general/201210/24/P201210240450.htm. Links accessed 6 March 2017.

In the ensuing discussion, Dr. Ko Wing-Man, the Secretary for Food and Health, made two important statements. First, that the Hong Kong Census and Statistics Department "does not have figures on the gross domestic output of the industry of manufacture of western drugs"[72] and, second, that the Hospital Authority "does not have detailed statistics on the quantity of different types of generic drugs procured by various clusters [i.e., groups of hospitals] and their respective proportions to the total drugs procured."[73]

That the government would not collect statistics on the production and quantity of medicines is curious, if not somewhat revealing about the state of the local pharmaceutical industry. It is also revealing of the state of the government, which it would appear fails to understand the linkage between patent protection, public health and the pharmaceutical industry. These are startling admissions, which evidence the lack of an integrated approach to pharmaceutical policy.

The second statement of interest is that "specific policies [are] to be put in place in the future to facilitate the development of the pharmaceutical industry, so as to develop Hong Kong into the pharmaceutical centre of the Asia Pacific Region."[74] As well as admitting that as of that date Hong Kong had not put the necessary policies in place, it is worth noting that the government has still failed to take any steps to develop Hong Kong into a "pharmaceutical centre" nor has it outlined a policy focus or priorities for the development of the pharmaceutical sector or even whether such a center would focus on manufacturing or R&D. The likelihood of these discussions maturing into policy is indeed remote.

Innovation promotion is a key component of Hong Kong's policymaking for future development, but innovation in relation to pharmaceutical products has been left unconsidered in the most recent policy documents. As mentioned above, the 2013 Policy Address signaled the government's intention to enhance innovation capacity by attaching "great importance to the significant contribution of innovation and technology to the development of the economy and industries" and reinforced its commitment to "focus on the development of the highly competitive sectors of the innovation and technology industries in light of Hong Kong' strengths."[75]

---

[72] Ibid., at 588.
[73] Hong Kong Legislative Council, "Official Record of Proceedings," 10128–29 at 10130 (2011), www.legco.gov.hk/yr10–11/english/counmtg/hansard/cm0511-translate-e.pdf.
[74] See above n. 71.
[75] The Government of the Hong Kong SAR, "The 2013 Policy Address," above n. 8 at 43.

However, innovation here is mentioned only in vague terms and without a focus being placed on pharmaceuticals.

More recently, the government has virtually ignored the sector. For instance, the 2015 Policy Address[76] notes that Hong Kong is one of "the 10 most innovative places"[77] and emphasizes that the government is setting up "a strategic environment for innovation and technology development" based on five "core strategies," i.e., (1) providing world-class technology infrastructure for enterprises, research institutions and universities; (2) offering financial support to stakeholders in the industry, academia and research sector to commercialize their R&D deliverables; (3) nurturing talent; (4) strengthening collaboration with the Mainland (China) and other places in science and technology; and (5) fostering a vibrant culture of innovation.[78] The Policy Address also reiterates that in the near future the government will create an Innovation and Technology Bureau (ITB), that Hong Kong's R&D expenditure has already increased from $7.1 billion in 2001 to $15.6 billion in 2013, and the government's ITF has provided about $8.9 billion for more than 4,200 projects.[79] Virtually nothing, however, was mentioned regarding the pharmaceutical sector.[80]

More recently, the 2016 Policy Address confirmed the successful establishment of the ITB and clarified its proactive coordination role in supporting "the development of Hong Kong's innovation and technology industry" as well as the work of the various research actors (such as universities, the Hong Kong Science Park, industrial estates, Cyberport and the Productivity Council) and in "set[ting] up a robust system for scientific research, development and production."[81] Nonetheless, while Hong Kong's policy plans announced research collaboration with sixteen key laboratories,[82] enhanced protection of the elderly (as a key feature of

---

[76] The Government of the Hong Kong SAR, "The 2015 Policy Address, Uphold the Rule of Law, Seize the Opportunities, Make the Right Choices, Pursue Democracy, Boost the Economy, Improve People's Livelihood," www.policyaddress.gov.hk/2015/eng/pdf/PA2015.pdf, accessed 21 February 2017.

[77] Ibid., at 41.   [78] Ibid., at 42.   [79] Ibid., at 43–48.

[80] In fact, the only reference made to the subject matter consist of mentioning increased efforts to promote Chinese medicines and the development of "authoritative international benchmarks to pave the way for the internationalization of Hong Kong's Chinese medicine industry." Ibid., at 194.

[81] The Government of the Hong Kong SAR, "The 2016 Policy Address: Innovate for the Economy, Improve Livelihood, Foster Harmony, Share Prosperity," at 68 www.policyaddress.gov.hk/2016/eng/pdf/PA2016.pdf, accessed 21 February 2017.

[82] Ibid., at 71.

the health agenda) and increased spending to strengthen the ambulance service and provide some 5,000 public hospital beds and more than 90 operating theaters over a ten-year period,[83] pharmaceutical development is again not considered in its plans for innovation.

This lack of political intent can also be seen in terms of institutional support. For example, when the head of the Food and Health Bureau – a government authority in charge of pharmaceutical regulatory matters – was called to report on the pharmaceutical industry performance and development, it became patently clear that Hong Kong does not have a special body in charge of the strategic development of the pharmaceutical industry. More importantly, the discussion revealed that the government had not considered the pharmaceutical industry when it formulated its "key" and "emerging" industries list.[84] Even more stunning is that the Hong Kong Census and Statistics Department neither lists the pharmaceutical industry as a separate economic sector nor provides industry-specific statistics – "possibly because it is simply not important enough."[85] This omission is striking and, in combination with the sector being ignored in recent policy address, is at odds with the legislative session on the future development of the pharmaceutical sector in Hong Kong. It thus cannot be said that development of the pharmaceutical sector is a policy priority for the government.

This conclusion may come as a surprise, if only because the vision of transforming Hong Kong into an innovation center for Asia-Pacific has long been a recurring focal point of legislators, if not the government. The first report of the newly established Commission on Innovation and Technology in 1998 envisaged Hong Kong as an "innovation-led, technology-intensive economy in the 21st century, serving the region not only as a business and financial centre, but also a world centre for the development

---

[83] Ibid., at 220–40.

[84] See Hong Kong Census and Statistics Department, "Hong Kong Monthly Digest of Statistics" (April 2013) at FC1, www.statistics.gov.hk/pub/B10100022013MM04B0100 .pdf, accessed 21 February 2017. The four "key industries" considered by the Hong Kong government to drive Hong Kong's economic growth provide impetus to the development of other sectors and create employment, including financial services, trading and logistics, tourism and professional and producer services. The government has also identified "emerging industries" as "enjoying advantages for further development," namely, cultural and creative industries, medical services, education services, innovation and technology, testing and certification services and environmental industries.

[85] BMI Report Q2 2014, above n. 31, at 55.

of health food and pharmaceuticals" and a marketplace for technology transfer between the mainland and the rest of the world.[86]

Yet in 2016, the promise is unfulfilled and the reality is that Hong Kong's innovation focus has shifted to reindustrialization – described as "a potential new area of economic growth for Hong Kong"[87] – as well as to supporting technology start-ups so as to promote and commercialize Hong Kong's digital development.[88] The 2016 Policy Address mentions "three cross-disciplinary platforms, namely 'smart city,' 'robotics' and 'healthy ageing'" as a focus for the territory.[89]

Given the shifting nature of Hong Kong's "innovation," one may ask why, fifteen years later, this vision of Hong Kong as a pharmaceutical center reappeared on the policy agenda of legislators. One also wonders why the initial vision failed to materialize. While the former is difficult to assess at this point in time, the latter is clear: Hong Kong lacked an integrated and comprehensive pharmaceutical policy framework. Broad statements declaring the zest for technological innovation and a general recognition of the importance of strong intellectual rights protection are not sufficient; rather, forethought, planning and precision as to the particular policy objectives and targeted assistance for pharmaceutical R&D and innovations are necessary in order to turn this vision into reality[90] – only then can the role of pharmaceutical patent provisions and policy choices in promoting pharmaceutical innovation be considered and evaluated.

2.3   Constructing a Policy Objective in Hong Kong

Based on the above analysis, it is essential for Hong Kong to define its overall position and strategy in the pharmaceutical sector. The effort thus far has been half-hearted and without sustained progress. Even advocates and supporters of pharmaceutical innovation in Hong Kong have not been

---

[86] Hong Kong Legislative Council, "Official Record of Proceedings of Wednesday 20th March, 2013, at 7678–79, www.legco.gov.hk/yr12–13/english/counmtg/hansard/cm0320-translate-e.pdf, accessed 21 February 2017 (with Council Member Ng Leung-Sing quoting the report of the Hong Kong SAR Commission on Innovation and Technology as "set[ting] forth a vision of making Hong Kong an innovation centre for the Asia Pacific Region").

[87] Policy Address 2016, above n. 81 at 77.   [88] Ibid., at 75, 80–86.   [89] Ibid., at 76.

[90] See, e.g., Hong Kong SAR Legislative Council, Official Record of Proceedings of 30 January 2013, at 5610, www.legco.gov.hk/yr12–13/english/counmtg/hansard/cm0130-translate-e .pdf, accessed 21 February 2017 (citing Dr. Lo Wai-Kwok's observation that "in order to achieve the long-term and sustainable development of Hong Kong economy, the SAR Government should formulate a balanced and visionary industrial policy so as to establish a clear policy vision and targets").

clear in their ambitions and goals – do they want Hong Kong to develop innovative capabilities in certain pharmaceutical sectors or across a wide range of sectors? Are they seeking to develop local innovative capacity in order to supply the domestic and/or export market or to place Hong Kong as an R&D "hub" for multinational pharmaceutical companies specializing in research and clinical trials activities for discovery and product development? Should Hong Kong attempt to attract branded and/or generic manufacturers for employment purposes?

Pharmaceuticals "help patients live longer, healthier and more productive lives,"[91] but it is unnecessary for every jurisdiction to engage in pharmaceutical manufacturing innovation. Comparative advantage and economies of scale will naturally mean that certain jurisdictions will be able to produce pharmaceuticals cheaper than others, while government incentives are necessary to attract and maintain large-scale R&D.

Transforming Hong Kong into a pharmaceutical production hub may be too much of a challenge, even with concerted government effort. While Singapore has largely succeeded in becoming a regional pharmaceutical hub over the past two decades, it has done so through meticulous and long-term planning and government support. Hong Kong did not and has not formulated any sector-specific policy and (unsurprisingly) has attracted little to no investment in the sector. Both are comparable "small, high-income, free market economies with an attractive business and investment climate, close in geographic proximity, comparable in terms of population, and sharing a common colonial background"[92] – both enjoy similar market sizes, have adequate access to skilled workforce, provide similar levels of regulatory, legal (including IPR) protection and enforcement and political stability.[93] The stark difference in performance is owing to the vastly dissimilar policy framework.

As I have written elsewhere with Daria Kim, Singapore has taken great care in prioritizing the pharmaceutical sector (within the more comprehensive framework of the Biomedical Sciences Initiative) and skillfully created a regulatory framework conducive to foreign and domestic investment for high-value R&D and manufacturing. In contrast, Hong Kong continues to lack a clear pharmaceutical policy of any kind.[94] As a result, while Hong Kong's domestic pharmaceutical industry consists of around

---

[91] Pharmaceutical Research and Manufacturers of America (PhRMA), "PhRMA Statement on Partnership to Support Innovation," www.phrma.org/press-release/phrma-statement-on-partnership-to-support-innovation, accessed 28 March 2017.

[92] See Mercurio and Kim, above n. 67.   [93] Ibid., at 8–12.   [94] Ibid., at 13.

thirty companies producing primarily generic pharmaceuticals predominantly for the local market, Singapore's industry grew from S$6 billion to S$23.3 billion between 2000 and 2010, making pharmaceuticals the leading sector for manufacturing FDI in Singapore[95] and transforming the nation into a pharmaceutical "trading base for the South East Asian region."[96]

Statements indicating Hong Kong's desire to become a pharmaceutical hub appear to be little more than puffery without the necessary accompanying policy and regulatory action; such statements also do not appear to be feasible given Hong Kong's present capabilities and forecasted future. Several jurisdictions in the region, such as Singapore, China, Taiwan and Malaysia, among others, have established and well-developed pharmaceutical R&D and manufacturing sectors, making the possibility of transforming Hong Kong into a regional "hub" unlikely even if the government were to deem it a priority. For these reasons, and for the economic and healthcare factors explored in this chapter, Hong Kong would be better served developing a policy of cost containment that seeks to maintain high quality standards and availability of medicines at the cheapest possible prices.

Of course, designing a policy objective and implementing it through amendments to existing legislation is complicated and nuanced. Broadly, the objective of pharmaceutical policy should be both to provide as much access as possible to innovative drugs in order to meet challenges of complex diseases and to procure the drugs at an affordable rate so as to better serve the broader needs of the population.

At present, Hong Kong has no discernible objective for the patent system in relation to pharmaceuticals. Like many other nations, Hong Kong must use the patent system to balance the incentive to create (globally, as Hong Kong benefits from innovation elsewhere) with broader societal interests. In this regard, Hong Kong must seek to provide the populace with high-quality healthcare, including ample access to affordable and safe medicines, while at the same time restrain rising healthcare costs. Hong Kong is similar to many jurisdictions in that healthcare costs are rising both as a percentage of government spending and at a rate faster than the GDP, necessitating cost-cutting measures such as the reduction of pharmaceutical expenditures through greater use of generic pharmaceuticals.

---

[95] Ibid., at 5.
[96] Espicom Business Intelligence, *The Pharmaceutical Market: Singapore* (London: Business Monitor International, 2012).

Without industrial policy concerns, the only choice is to clearly identify access to medicines and cost containment as priorities and construct the pharmaceutical patent system accordingly.

Of course, such a policy cannot be implemented to the detriment of the IP system. Hong Kong has worked for many years solidifying its reputation as a safe and secure jurisdiction that seriously protects IPRs and should not seek to dismantle its standing. This book proposes, however, that Hong Kong devote time, energy and resources into crafting a suitable system for the jurisdiction based on the constructed objective that at the same time is fully compliant with its international commitments.

3

Standards of Patentability

3.1 Introduction

The positive effects of patents are well known – patents provide an incentive to invest in costly research and reward scientific progress. Patents can also have significant downsides such as distorting competition through the granting of monopoly power. In regard to pharmaceuticals, it is almost a truism to say that without the temporary monopoly rights granted by patent protection there would be little incentive for investment and pharmaceutical R&D and far fewer breakthrough and follow-on drugs. As a result, the populace would be unhealthier and less productive. Quite obviously, no individual or company would invest hundreds of millions of dollars in medical R&D without at least an opportunity for a return on investment.[1] At the same time, the granting of a patent inevitably raises the cost of the product to a level that greatly exceeds the marginal production cost for as long as the patent remains in force – medicines are expensive to invent and bring to market, but inexpensive to produce. Monopoly rights granted by the patent thus allow the inventor to price the product at a rate that far exceeds the cost of production, and in so doing makes it more difficult for people to access the medicines at reasonable costs. Moreover, patents (and in particular pharmaceutical patents) could also stifle

---

[1] Plausible estimates on the cost of inventing and bringing a drug to market vary widely, but range from USD$800 million to USD$2.6 billion. See Steve Morgan et al., "The Cost of Drug Development: A Systematic Review," (2011) 100 *Health Policy*, 4 (concluding after a review of original data published between 1980 and 2009 that "[e]stimates of the cost of drug development ranged more than 9-fold, from USD$92 million cash (USD$161 million capitalized) to USD$883.6 million cash (USD$1.8 billion capitalized)"); Tufts Center for the Study of Drug Development, "Cost to Develop and Win Marketing Approval for a New Drug Is $2.6 Billion" (18 November 2014), http://csdd.tufts.edu/news/complete_story/pr_tufts_csdd_2014_cost_study, accessed 21 February 2017 (estimating costs at $2.558 billion, which is comprised of average out-of-pocket cost of $1.395 billion and time costs (expected returns that investors forgo while a drug is in development) of $1.163 billion).

follow-on innovations, increase legal risk for competitors and decrease competition for periods far exceeding the original patent term.

With both industrial development and human health at stake, the patent system must act to effectively balance the objectives of securing timely access to competitively priced pharmaceuticals, fostering R&D and innovation, supporting employment and facilitating scientific and industrial progress. Of course, it must be remembered that a nation's patent system does not operate in a vacuum. International treaty obligations serve as an umbrella guiding both the substance and procedures of domestic law.

That being the case, scope exists for countries to tailor patent laws in a manner that is both compliant with the international standard and in harmony with broader governmental objectives. In this regard, countries such as India, Brazil and Argentina have prioritized the availability of cheap medicines to the populace. Accordingly, these countries narrowly define patentability provisions in domestic law, thereby restricting the number of patents granted. It is also no coincidence that these nations (and in particular India and Brazil) have thriving generic industries, which suggests that industrial policy sits beside health policy as a relevant governmental objective behind the policy. The recent Brazilian task force on patent reform admitted as much when it stated: "With the employment of higher standards for patentability requirements, one is encouraging the capacity building and technological development in Brazil."[2]

On the other hand, countries such as the United States and Switzerland are home to the world leaders of the innovative/branded pharmaceutical industry and thus provide for strong and broad patent protection. Still others are stuck in the middle, with undefined or conflicting objectives. China is a good example of such a nation, having prioritized and encouraged 'innovation' by rewarding patent filings. Unsurprisingly, this policy has resulted in a substantial increase in the number of patents filed and granted by Chinese nationals. But such inducements have done little to encourage scientific progress or real innovation. In this regard, the fundamental objective of the patent system has been lost. Still other jurisdictions do not shape patent policy through domestic objectives but merely

---

[2] See "Brazil's Patent Reform: Innovation Towards National Competitiveness," *Brazilian Chamber of Deputies, Center for Strategic Studies and Debates, Estudos Estratégicos* 1 (2013), p. 62, http://infojustice.org/wp-content/uploads/2013/09/Brazilian_Patent_Reform .pdf, accessed 6 March 2017.

follow the path taken by others. Hong Kong appears to be in this category, with its laws shaped not through governmental objectives, planning
or review but simply through a mixture of the law leftover from the former colonial government and heavy reliance on the laws of select other
jurisdictions.

Regardless of how a domestic law is formed or the policies behind
such formation, the shadow of the international standard as set out in
the TRIPS Agreement (to continue the umbrella metaphor) is large. More
specifically, Article 27.1 of the TRIPS Agreement, entitled "Patentable
Subject Matter," reads:

> patents shall be available for any inventions, whether products or processes,
> in all fields of technology, provided that they are new, involve an inventive
> step and are capable of industrial application. (5)
> (Footnote 5: For the purposes of this Article, the terms "inventive step"
> and "capable of industrial application" may be deemed by a Member to be
> synonymous with the terms "non-obvious" and "useful" respectively.)

Therefore, in order to comply with the international standard, patents
should be granted for "inventions" that are "new" and "inventive." This
is sensible, given the justification for providing patents as a limited term
monopoly is to reward and encourage further creation – granting patents
for inventions previously known or obvious would be inimical to the very
reason we provide the monopoly rights. The international standard also
provides that a patentable invention must be "capable of industrial application," that is, have utility or be useful.

Similar to most jurisdictions, Hong Kong virtually repeats the TRIPS
standard through Section 93(1) of the Patents Ordinance, entitled
"Patentable Inventions," which states:

> An invention is patentable if it is susceptible of industrial application, is
> new and involves an inventive step.

Of course, jurisdictions often require more in order for an "invention"
to gain patent protection. For instance, the invention defined in the
claims, and thereby the scope of rights obtained, must be commen-
surate with what is described in the specification.[3] Moreover, as the
granting of a patent is a matter of public interest, disclosure is a fundamental principle of the patent system. One US court succinctly stated
that "the whole purpose of a patent specification is to disclose one's

---

[3] Hong Kong Patents Ordinance, S 76.

invention to the public. It is the quid pro quo for the grant of the period of exclusivity."[4]

More specifically, applicants must provide in the patent specification sufficient information for the invention to be repeated. In this way the public has access to useful information regarding new technologies and both the jurisdiction and future inventors can use the invention after the patent term expires or is otherwise no longer in force.[5] At the same time, the sufficiency of the disclosure (or enablement) requirement demands that the product or process for which the patent is filed is clearly and sufficiently described so that a person skilled in the art can be fully capable of producing the patent.[6] Complete disclosure is important in order to set and adequately define the scope of the patent. Remembering that "[p]atents, unlike blocks of land, do not come with settled boundaries"[7] and that patent specifications "are drafted by patent attorneys in a species of legalese that mocks the values of open science and communication,"[8] governments must set clear standards and patent examiners must be equally vigilant in ensuring the standards have been met. A related requirement directly incorporated into some legislation (but not that of Hong Kong) is "best mode," which mandates that the applicant expressly detail "the best mode contemplated by the inventor" of execution of the invention in the filing.[9] The best mode requirement is essentially a public interest safeguard that provides transparency and legal certainty for downstream users by disciplining applicants that attempt to obtain patent protection without making a full disclosure (as is often required by the patent legislation).[10]

---

[4] See *LizardTech, Inc. v. Earth Res. Mapping, Inc.*, 433 F.3d 1373, 1375 (Fed. Cir. 2006).

[5] In this regard, Peter Drahos states that the purpose of disclosure is "to provide search systems that would allow members of the public a meaningful exercise of their rights to access invention information, and rights that they hold by virtue of the patent social contract." Peter Drahos, *The Global Governance of Knowledge: Patent Offices and Their Clients* (Cambridge University Press, 2010), at 300.

[6] Hong Kong Patents Ordinance, S 77.

[7] Peter Drahos, "Patent Reform for Innovation and Risk Management: A Separation of Powers Approach" (2007) 1 *KEStudies* 1, at 8. www.anu.edu.au/fellows/pdrahos/articles/pdfs/2007patentreformforinnovriskmgmt.pdf, accessed 6 March 2017.

[8] Ibid., at 5.

[9] See, e.g., Title 35 of the United States Code, 35 USC. 112(a).

[10] Owing to recent changes in the US Patent Act, there is some doubt as to whether best mode remains a requirement. See Eric Combs, "Uncertainty Surrounds the Best Mode Requirement in the Wake of the America Invents Act" (February 13, 2013), www.mondaq.com/unitedstates/x/222416/Patent/Uncertainty+Surrounds+The+Best+Mode+Requirement+In+The+Wake+Of+The+America+Invents+Act, accessed 21 February 2017.

In other words, the best mode requirement prohibits applicants from disclosing only what they know to be their second-best embodiment, while retaining the best mode for themselves.[11]

This chapter reviews the key features of patentability standards. Using the international standard and comparative experience of several jurisdictions as a guide, the chapter aims to make recommendations for possible amendments to the Hong Kong Patents Ordinance so as to take advantage of the available policy space to bring the Ordinance more in line with the constructed governmental objectives and priorities developed in Chapter 2. In the following sections, discussion and analysis is followed by targeted recommendations. Section 3.2 reviews the policy considerations relevant to patentability and the examination of desired standards. Section 3.3 analyzes the substantive conditions of patentability, including novelty, inventive step/obviousness and industrial application/utility. Section 3.4 briefly discusses the boundaries of patentable subject matter. Section 3.5 provides analysis on the controversial and topical issue of second use patents. Section 3.6 offers concluding comments.

3.2   Policy Considerations

The TRIPS Agreement sets minimum standards and criteria of patentability, but as noted above, Members have the discretion to craft the precise contours of each of the criteria for patentability. The first choice to be made in this regard is how the standards of patentability are to be judged. Many advanced economies utilize a "positive grant" system, where the substance of applications is scrutinized and only applications that fully meet the patentability standards are granted. There is, however, no international requirement to conduct a substantial examination of a patent application. Like Hong Kong,[12] Thailand and several other countries register patents without a substantive examination and on the basis of examination and registration elsewhere. Still others, such as South Africa[13] and until recently Singapore, simply grant a patent for any subject matter that is not explicitly excluded from patentability under the Patents Act (intrinsic

---

[11] For a more detailed explanation, see *In re Nelson*, 280 F.2d 172, 126 USPQ 242 (CCPA 1960).

[12] Legislative Council Panel on Commerce and Industry, "Review of the Patent System in Hong Kong," LC Paper No. CB(1)534/12–13(05), 19 February 2013, at P2–6, www.legco.gov.hk/yr12–13/english/panels/ci/papers/ci0219cb1–534–5-e.pdf, accessed 6 March 2017.

[13] South African Patents Act, Section 25.

patentability) and that is in compliance with the requirements of the standards of patentability (extrinsic patentability) as per the criteria modeled after Article 27(1) of the TRIPS Agreement. Following a "self-assessment" by the applicant, the patent is granted not after an examination of intrinsic or extrinsic patentability but only following a cursory examination as to whether the applicant has complied with the formal requirements of the Patents Act within the time periods set by the Act. Under such a system, the patent specification is accepted as the subject matter is described, and, within a certain time period (e.g., three months in South Africa), the patent is granted. Other forms of limited substantive examination or supplementary substantive examination in support of a positive grant system are used by various other counties. Of course, in any system the grant of the patent is a mere presumption and opposition proceedings can subsequently be launched to invalidate the patent.

The main justification for a substantive examination system and stricter patentability standards is to improve patent quality, eliminate frivolous patents and allow for localized and tailored policy. Domestic patent law should, on the one hand, be compliant with the TRIPS Agreement and, on the other, reflect local socioeconomic factors, national objectives and priorities and arguably differences in technologies.[14] As Burkt and Lemley correctly point out, in implementing TRIPS standards in relation to pharmaceutical patents Members can select from policy levers in varying combinations in order to "modulate the scope and frequency of patents" and encourage innovation beyond the mere chance of registering a patent – by increasing the value of the patent once it is granted.[15]

A joint publication of the World Trade Organization (WTO), the World Intellectual Property Organization (WIPO) and the World Health Organization (WHO) substantiates this claim in relation to the promotion of

---

[14] See, e.g., Max Planck Institute for Innovation and Competition, "Declaration on Patent Protection. Regulatory Sovereignty under TRIPS" (2014), Max Planck Institute for Innovation and Competition Research Paper No. 14 19 at para. 14 ("The non-discrimination principle in Article 27(1) of the TRIPS Agreement does not prevent states from adapting the subject matter and requirements of patentability to the characteristics inherent in the technology at issue. They may, for example, apply a different demarcation line between inventions and discoveries in different fields of technology; different standards of novelty, non-obviousness and disclosure depending on the technology's maturity and dissemination").

[15] Dan L. Burkt and Mark A. Lemley, "Policy Levers in Patent Law" (2003) 89 *Virginia Law Review* 1575, 1684–87. See also Geertrui van Overwalle, "Policy Levers Tailoring Patent Law to Biotechnology: Comparing US and European Approaches" (2011) 1 *UC Irvine Law Review* 435.

access to medical technologies and innovation: "Patent application, examination and grant procedures, as well as opposition, appeal, and other review procedures allow courts and other review bodies to correct erroneous decisions and give relief where necessary, in order to ensure that the patent system as a whole functions as a public interest policy tool."[16] One of the main concerns in this respect is to counter "evergreening" – which has been defined as "the practice of making incremental, patentable innovations for medicines without corresponding benefit, particularly if patients are aggressively or forcibly transitioned to the new product."[17] Most onlookers, including three prominent NGOs engaged in the access to medicines movement, conclude that countries with registration systems are "more likely to grant multiple patents on a single medicine, and to allow evergreening to occur."[18] In this regard, Vawda states that a "major complication is that the South African patents office does not conduct substantive examinations as to the merits of each patent application, nor is there any opportunity for an interested party to oppose such applications."[19]

Of course, it is not enough to merely have an examination system. The legislation must be conducive to national priorities, and, as important, the patent examiners must be properly trained to implement the legal standards. In regard to the former, it is generally accepted that "developing countries need to have lower and more flexible IPRs standards than do their developed counterparts"[20] – and of course, the only way for

[16] WTO, WIPO and WHO, "Promoting Access to Medical Technologies and Innovation Intersections between Public Health, Intellectual Property and Trade" (2012) at 56, www.wto.org/english/res_e/booksp_e/pamtiwhowipowtoweb13_e.pdf, accessed 3 March 2017.

[17] Reed F. Beall, Jason W. Nickerson, Warren A. Kaplan and Amir Attaran, "Is Patent 'Evergreening' Restricting Access to Medicine/Device Combination Products?" (2016) 11(2) PLoS One, www.ncbi.nlm.nih.gov/pmc/articles/PMC4766186/.

[18] Treatment Action Campaign (TAC), Médecins Sans Frontières (MSF) and Research and Information System for Developing Countries (RIS), "Why South Africa Should Examine Pharmaceutical Patents" (2013), at 3, www.msfaccess.org/content/why-south-africa-should-examine-pharmaceutical-patents, accessed 21 February 2017. As an example, the briefing uses the case of Darunavir, an antiretroviral medicine used to treat HIV/AIDS: "Although the patent on the base compound (1993) was never filed in South Africa, a number of patents have been granted on different versions of this drug that do not expire till 2028."

[19] Yousef A. Vawda, "'Patent Law in Emerging Economies: South Africa," in Frederick M. Abbott, Carlos M. Correa and Peter Drahos (eds.), Emerging Markets and the World Patent Order (Edward Elgar, 2013), at 290.

[20] World Bank, Global Economic Prospects and the Developing Countries 2002 (2001) 147, http://documents.worldbank.org/curated/en/285571468337817024/310436360_20050012014722/additional/multi0page.pdf, accessed 3 March 2017.

developing countries to do this is to apply strict criteria for the granting of patents. Leading IP and access to medicines scholar Carlos Correa expands on this idea by stating that "low standards of patentability may lead to unnecessary limitations on competition without any significant trade-off in terms of more innovation to address society's needs."[21] He concludes that "[t]he best policy from the perspective of public health would seem to be the application of a strict standard of inventiveness so as to promote genuine innovations and prevent unwarranted limitations to competition and access to existing drugs."[22] With public health at the core of his argument, Correa proposes national guidelines for the evaluation and assessment of pharmaceutical patent applications in a manner that is conducive to public health policy goals.

Public health is not the only argument for strict patentability standards and an examination system. The joint NGO report mentioned above recommends that South Africa adopt a strict examination system, not only for public health reasons, but also in order to aid the development of local production of pharmaceuticals in the (often dubious and unfulfilled) hopes that a domestic industry can supply drugs more cheaply than imported drugs.[23]

It is also important to highlight that while an examination system could be superior to a registration system in controlling and managing standards, it cannot and should not be adopted by every country. Designing, implementing and maintaining a well-functioning patent examination system is costly in terms of both monetary and human capital. Finding, hiring, training and retaining enough qualified patent examiners capable

---

[21] Carlos Correa, "WHO, ICTSD, UNCTAD, Guidelines for the Examination of Pharmaceutical Patents: Developing a Public Health Perspective" (2007) at 3, www.ufrgs.br/antropi/lib/exe/fetch.php?media=correa_pharmaceutical-patents-guidelines.pdf, accessed 3 March 2017.

[22] Ibid., at 4.

[23] See above n. 18, at 3. This claim is dubious, as ensuring a steady stream of high-quality pharmaceuticals at a reasonable price is difficult to achieve in much of the developing world. See Warren Kaplan and Richard Laing, "Local Production of Pharmaceuticals: Industrial Policy and Access to Medicines," HNP Discussion Policy (June 2005), http://medeor.de/images/themen/konferenz/KaplanLocalProductionFinal5b15d.pdf, accessed 21 February 2017; Roger Bate, "Local Pharmaceutical Production in Developing' Countries Campaign for Fighting Diseases," Discussion Paper no. 1, www.unido.org/fileadmin/user_media/Services/PSD/BEP/Local%20Pharmaceutical%20Production%20web.pdf, accessed 21 February 2017; United Nations, "Local Production of Pharmaceuticals and Related Technology Transfer in Developing Countries: A Series of Case Studies by the UNCTAD Secretariat" (2011), http://unctad.org/en/PublicationsLibrary/diaepcb2011d7_en.pdf, accessed 3 March 2017.

of examining innovations in all fields of technology would also be difficult for many countries. This cost would be borne by the host state, but also by patent applicants in the form of higher application fees. Other, non-monetary costs include a more complicated process and increased time to grant the patent. Simply stated, an examination system is not suitable for all countries. Cost and resource issues may dictate that a country maintain a registration or self-assessment system. For these reasons, a World Bank report in 2002 recommended a registration system for low-income countries, registration or limited substantive examination system for middle-income countries and a substantive examination system for high-income countries.[24]

Hong Kong has decided to transition from a registration to an examination system. Even though costs will rise and the move may not be entirely necessary given that currently Hong Kong registers patents from only a few select jurisdictions, from a policy perspective the arguments for a positive grant system based on a substantive examination and for the adoption of stricter/higher patentability standards are compelling. As detailed in Chapter 2, Hong Kong is a relatively wealthy jurisdiction with an aging population, rising health costs and very little innovation or manufacturing capabilities. These factors should be borne in mind with regard to both Hong Kong's legal framework and the regulations used to guide future patent examiners.

The next section focuses on the substantive criteria used to evaluate a patent application, with particular attention paid to the international standard and comparative practice to be used as guidance in developing an examination system in Hong Kong.

3.3   Substantive Conditions

As mentioned above, the TRIPS Agreement does not define the criteria of novelty, inventive step and industrial applicability. Instead, the Agreement leaves Members with a certain degree of flexibility to fashion their own interpretations. While the WTO has not even attempted to harmonize standards, the WIPO's Standing Committee of the Law of Patents (SCP) – as part of its Patent Law Treaty harmonizing regulations on patent formalities and procedures, adopted in 2000[25] – unsuccessfully attempted

---

[24] See World Bank, above n. 20, at 141.
[25] Diplomatic Conference for the Adoption of the Patent Law Treaty on 1 June 2000, www .wipo.int/meetings/en/details.jsp?meeting_id=4057, accessed 3 March 2017.

to draft a Substantive Patent Law Treaty. The negotiations commenced in 2001 but were put on hold in 2006 following a breakdown due to the absence of consensus on the issues.[26]

Given that Hong Kong will soon transition to an examination system, the time is ripe for the jurisdiction to tailor its patent provisions to best suit its own needs and priorities instead of following the idiosyncratic provisions of other jurisdictions. Following the conclusions reached in Chapter 2, Hong Kong should prioritize access to cost-efficient medicines while maintaining respect for international standards and its well-earned reputation for rule of law and friendliness toward business interests. In this regard, Hong Kong should follow the advice of Correa when he stated that "[l]ess technologically advanced countries may prefer to set higher standards of novelty and inventive step in order to preserve and enhance competition without violating minimum international standards."[27] Although Correa was writing in the context of developing countries, the scenario of Hong Kong necessitates equivalent advice. With scant manufacturing abilities and limited research capacities, Hong Kong should maintain strict patentability standards that, while serving to encourage and reward innovation, do not unnecessarily overprotect inventions in a manner that would curtail access to affordable medicines or the ability of the government to provide world-class healthcare to the populace. The remainder of this section will further explain the advice and make recommendations in regard to novelty standards (Section 3.3.1), inventive step/non-obviousness (Section 3.3.2) and utility (Section 3.3.3).

3.3.1 Novelty Standards

Article 27(1) of the TRIPS Agreement requires WTO Members to protect inventions that are, among other things, "new." There is consensus among Members that the subject matter of a patent application is "new" if it does not form part of the prior (or existing) art. However, there have been some historical differences in interpretation as to what constitutes the boundaries of prior art, and the TRIPS Agreement allows for each Member to decide the scope for themselves.

---

[26] For more information and a critical review of the drafting process, see Jerome H. Reichman and Rochelle Cooper Dreyfuss, "Harmonization Without Consensus: Critical Reflections on Drafting a Substantive Patent Law Treaty" (2007) 85 *Duke Law Journal* 85.

[27] Carlos M. Correa, "Public Health and Patent Legislation in Developing Countries" (2001) 3 *Tulane Journal of Technology and Intellectual Property* 1, 49.

The Patent Cooperation Treaty (PCT) is equally unhelpful as a guide. While Article 33(2) of the PCT defines novelty for the purposes of the international preliminary examination – "a claimed invention shall be considered novel if it is not anticipated by the prior art" – Article 33(5) makes clear that each Member may apply additional or different criteria, and, in regard to what the standard of novelty should be applied, the PCT remains silent. Each jurisdiction can decide this important question for itself through a factual assessment.

In regard to pharmaceuticals, a novelty threshold that is too lax could grant patent protection for medicines for which the active ingredient (or otherwise) is already known, and therefore provide monopoly rights over a product that could otherwise be manufactured and sold to the populace as a generic far more cheaply.

Most jurisdictions (including Australia, the EU, India, Japan, Russia, Singapore and Taiwan) attempt to draw clear boundaries of what is referred to as "absolute" novelty – that is, an "invention [that] is not publicly known anywhere in the world" prior to the filing of the patent application or priority filing date.[28] An invention is therefore novel if it does not form part of the state of the art, or prior art, anywhere in the world immediately before the priority date of that invention, which includes any disclosure of the invention made available to the public, such as written publications, sales, public oral disclosures and public demonstrations or use.[29] Such is the case in Hong Kong, with Section 94 of the Patents Ordinance providing the elements that make up the state of the art, and thereby destroy novelty: "The state of the art shall be held to comprise everything made available to the public (whether in Hong Kong or elsewhere) by means of a written or oral description, by use or in any other way," before the date of filing of an application or, if priority was claimed, before the date of priority.[30] Thus, if the invention already exists in the state of the art anywhere in the world, it is not "new" or novel and would not receive a patent.

---

[28] Review of the Patent System in Hong Kong, above n. 12, at 193.

[29] See, e.g., Indian Patents Act, No. 39 of 1970, §2(1)(l) (Universal 2005) (amended 2005) ("any invention or technology which has not been anticipated by publication in any document or used in the country or elsewhere in the world before the date of filing of patent application with complete specification, i.e. the subject matter has not fallen in public domain or that it does not form part of the state of the art").

[30] See also Article 54(2) of the European Patent Convention: "The state of the art shall be held to comprise everything made available to the public by means of a written or oral description, by use, or in any other way, before the date of filing of the European patent application."

In certain other jurisdictions a "relative" standard of novelty is used, and only the use of the invention or public knowledge of the invention in the jurisdiction itself constitutes prior art. For example, until 2012, US Patent Code defined novelty as "[t]he invention was known or used by others *in this country*, or patented or described in a printed publication in this or a foreign country, before the invention thereof by the applicant for patent."[31]

The difference in standards between countries has revealed itself in a number of instances, with perhaps the most notable being the status of neem oil. The European Patent Office (EPO) revoked a patent for lack of novelty (under Article 54(1)(2)) when evidence showed that extracts of neem oil were mixed, diluted and used to treat crops, fruits and vegetables against pests and diseases in western India prior to the filing of the patent application. In the United States, which at the time maintained a relative standard of novelty, the patent was granted.

Other interpretive issues that legislation commonly fails to address but need resolution often revolve around the concepts of absolute or relative novelty. This dichotomy is somewhat unhelpful as even the definition of "absolute" differs between and among jurisdictions. Instead of using the absolute/relative terms, it is more useful to deconstruct novelty into its constituting elements in order to understand what advantages and disadvantages each element provides.

Perhaps the most important part of novelty is the scope of the terms "use" or "public knowledge" of the invention. This is especially the case in regard to pharmaceuticals, with novelty and prior art sometimes difficult to determine when distinguishing between different types of "uses" for an invention – for example, first medical use, second and subsequent medical use and second nonmedical use. Resolution is dependent on the policy choices made within the jurisdiction, and the outcome is of great importance. If a second or further medical (or nonmedical) use is deemed to be new, such further uses will be eligible for patent protection, and thus the system is designed to stimulate follow-on innovation. On the other hand, a regime could prohibit the patenting of such further uses because it deems these practices to be a form of "evergreening," which serves mainly if not exclusively to maintain monopoly pricing and delay competitive

---

[31] S 102(a)(1). Amended as a result of the Leahy–Smith America Invents Act, the current S 102(a)(1) reads: "(1) the claimed invention was patented, described in a printed publication, or in public use, on sale, or otherwise available to the public before the effective filing date of the claimed invention."

conditions. In this case, the regime is favoring cheaper access to the product over longer-term innovative potential of follow-on drugs.

Given the importance of this issue, second and further use patents are the focus of Section 3.5 of this chapter, but brief discussion is warranted at this point. Suffice to say, opinion is divided on this issue of whether to issue second and further use patents. For instance, the UK Commission on Intellectual Property Rights (CIPR) in 2002 cautioned against regarding a product to be new, even if a new use is identified, as a safeguard against the rising costs of medicines: "[W]e caution against developing countries simply taking over from the comparatively recent European jurisprudence the counter-intuitive notion that a product may be regarded as new, if a new use is identified for it. Such an approach is not required by TRIPS."[32]

However, one can also make the opposite argument that humanity (and thus individual countries) should encourage the exploitation of proven drugs – a single active ingredient or medicine can yield multiple and diverse benefits. In the words of Jacob J (as he was known then), "patents are provided to encourage research. If new and non-obvious improved methods of administration of known drugs for known diseases are not patentable in principle ... then there will be less of a research incentive to find such methods."[33]

Another important issue is whether the jurisdiction should provide a grace period for nonprejudicial disclosure to protect an inventor or their successor in title from authorized and/or unauthorized disclosure of the invention prior to the filing date. The rationale for a grace period exception is that it promotes access to knowledge and innovation while still maintaining the inventor's right to patent the invention within the grace period. Under such an exception, inventors have the opportunity to publish their research in scientific journals, which is an important incentive for scientists, or demonstrate the marketability of the invention to potential investors in order to acquire funding for, among other things, the costly process of obtaining a patent. In some jurisdictions, the grace period applies to any disclosure, while in others the exception is limited to disclosure in certain forms. The US pre-filing grace period exception is an example of the former: "These exceptions limit the use of an inventor's own work as prior art, when the inventor's own work has been

---

[32] Commission on Intellectual Property Rights (CIPR), "Integrating Intellectual Property Rights and Development Policy" (2002), at 116, www.iprcommission.org/papers/pdfs/final_report/ciprfullfinal.pdf, accessed 3 March 2017.

[33] *Merck & Co Inc's Patents* [2003] FSR 298.

publicly disclosed by the inventor, a joint inventor, or another who obtained the subject matter directly or indirectly from the inventor or joint inventor not more than one year before the effective filing date of the claimed invention."[34] The length and language of the US provision has been accepted and essentially adopted into numerous recently negotiated FTAs, including the ill-fated Trans-Pacific Partnership (TPP).[35] India provides an example of a more limited exception, as it only provides a twelve-month pre-filing grace period for disclosures made with the inventor's consent in government-designated exhibitions or before learned societies.[36]

The grace period exception seems to be a matter of common sense – the objective of the patent system is to encourage and reward innovation; the normal course of business dictates that one should acquire as much information as possible before investing and the standard in academia is to publish findings as quickly as possible for personal satisfaction, promotion and most importantly lest another scientist subsequently reach the same conclusion and get the credit because they first published the findings. Thus, while the UK CIPR stated that "[f]or those developing countries having few prospective patentees, there may therefore be little to gain from providing a grace period,"[37] this author would caution that while such advice may be temporarily utilized by LDCs, it would not be in the long-term interests of most developing and developed economies to adopt such an approach.

As the statistics presented in Chapter 2 reveal, Hong Kong is not a highly innovative jurisdiction and may under some definitions even have "few prospective patentees." But it does value IPRs and its place as a good international citizen.[38] Moreover, the vast majority of local inventors in the fields of pharmaceutical and biotech are universities – exactly the type of inventor that will be looking to publish findings in journals, present at conferences and seek licensing opportunities to enable further development and bring the invention to market. For these reasons, Hong Kong should

---

[34] America Invents Act 35 USC 102(b)(1)(A).
[35] See, e.g., Australia–United States FTA, Article 17.9(9); TPP, Article 18.38.
[36] India Patents Act, Sections 29–34.   [37] CIPR, above n. 32, at 116.
[38] For this reason, Hong Kong should not adopt a strategy like that of South Africa, where its Review recommended setting strict levels of patent criteria in order to incentivize only genuine innovation, and as an "additional motivation . . . to set strict patentability criteria arises where the vast majority of patent applicants are from abroad." South African Department of Trade and Industry, "National Policy on Intellectual Property (IP) of South Africa: A Framework," *Government Gazette*, 4 September 2013 (No. 36816), at 26 (2013).

not only maintain but expand its grace period exception. Modeled on Article 55 of the European Patent Convention (EPC), Hong Kong provides that a disclosure of the invention shall not be taken into consideration if it occurred no earlier than six months before the filing of the application, if (a) the disclosure resulted from an evident abuse (i.e., nonauthorized disclosure by a third party) or (b) the applicant or any proprietor of the invention displayed the invention at a prescribed exhibition or meeting.[39] It would seem sensible to expand the term to a twelve-month window and, at the very least, as a regional convention and exhibition center hub, to consider expanding on its limited grace period exception of "prescribed" exhibitions and meetings beyond the officially recognized exhibitions[40] in order to become even more attractive to innovation conferences, conventions and meetings. In fact, taking into account the heavy reliance in Hong Kong on university research in the pharmaceutical and biotech sector for local patenting activity, there does not seem to be any substantive reason to argue against broadening the standard to include *any* public disclosure by the inventor.

Hong Kong should also maintain its version of absolute novelty (subject to an expanded grace period exception) and, for reasons explained below, recognize and grant further second use patents.

3.3.2   Inventive Step/Non-Obviousness

The second criteria set out in Article 27(1) of the TRIPS Agreement is that an invention "involve an inventive step" or, as footnote 5 makes clear, is "non-obvious." Article 27 does not define the terms "inventive step" or "non-obviousness."

The rationale of the inventiveness or non-obviousness requirement is to encourage sequential innovation (follow-on innovation). Setting non-obviousness standards too low could allow companies to accumulate patents on incremental improvements, maintain patent pools and block local improvers and ultimately stymie innovation.[41] This could in turn

---

[39] Hong Kong Patents Ordinance 1997, S 95 and 109. If making use of the convention or exhibition exception, an applicant must disclose that the invention has been displayed at the time of filing.

[40] Convention on International Exhibitions, signed in Paris, 22 November 1928, www.bie-paris.org/site/images/stories/files/BIE_Convention_eng.pdf, accessed 4 March 2017.

[41] See Jerome Reichman, "Intellectual Property in the Twenty-First Century: Will the Developing Countries Lead or Follow?" (2009) 46 *Houston Law Review* 1115, 1134.

create formidable barriers to entry and impact on the competitive conditions within the jurisdiction. On the other hand, setting the standard too high is also dangerous, as it will not incentivize or reward R&D and could threaten the availability of advanced technology in the jurisdiction.[42] Striking a delicate balance is therefore crucial.

As with novelty, whether a claimed invention involves an inventive step/non-obviousness is evaluated by the state of the art, excluding prior art and grace periods for nonprejudicial disclosures. Most jurisdictions set out only the general principle, which is applied to each specific case, as opposed to attempting to precisely define what is an "inventive step" or "non-obvious."[43] Thus, as opposed to attempting a factual comparison between a claimed invention and prior art (as is the case in determining the novelty), the assessment of an inventive step relies on a more vague, qualitative approach.[44] The Standing Commission of the Law of Patents endorsed such an approach, considering it "suitable for the application of the patentability criteria to each invention on its merit, bearing in mind that inventions may relate to a different field of technology. It also accommodates future technological development that cannot be foreseen."[45]

The vast majority of advanced jurisdictions find that the threshold of an inventive step/non-obviousness has been met when the invention is not obvious to a hypothetical person having ordinary skill in the art,[46] having regard to the prior art (the so-called person having ordinary skill in the art (PHOSITA) in the United States[47] and also adopted in this

---

[42] Michael J. Meurer and Katherine J. Strandburg, "Patent Carrots and Sticks: A Model of Non-Obviousness" (2008) 12 *Lewis & Clark Law Review* 547, 563.

[43] See, e.g., Article 13 of Law No. 9.279 (14 May 1996) (Brazil Industrial Property Law).

[44] See, e.g., W. R. Cornish, David Llewelyn and Tania Aplin, *Intellectual Property: Patents, Copyright, Trademarks and Allied Rights*, 8th edition (Sweet & Maxwell, 2013), at 205.

[45] Standing Committee on the Law of Patents, Twenty-Second Session, Geneva, 27–31 July 2015, SCP/22/3, at para. 11.

[46] See *Lubrizol v. Esso* [1998] RPC 727, 738 ("Patent specifications are intended to be read by persons skilled in the relevant art, but their construction is for the court. Thus the court must adopt the mantle of notional skilled addressee, and determine . . . what the notional skilled addressee would understand to be the ambit of the claim"). See also Pfizer's Patent [2001] FSR 201; and *Nichia Corporation v. Argos Limited* [2007] EWCA Civ 741.

[47] See 35 USC §103(A). The term "Phosita" appears to have first appeared in Cyril A. Soans, "Some Absurd Presumptions in Patent Cases" (1966) 10 *IDEA* 433, 438–39 (passionately arguing against the court's creation of a "superhuman Frankenstein monster Mr. Phosita," whose powers extended far beyond those of the ordinarily skilled mechanic). In time, "Mr. Phosita" became "PHOSITA" in the literature.

publication) that exists before the filing date or priority date.[48] What constitutes an inventive step is therefore foremost a qualitative question that occurs *ex post* and is often done by a fact finder that lacks the skills of the art (although it should be noted that patent examiners are often specialized and grouped accordingly by the patent office).[49]

Hong Kong, in Section 96 of the Patents Ordinance, utilizes such an approach:

(1) An invention shall be considered as involving an inventive step if, having regard to the state of the art, it is not obvious to a person skilled in the art.
(2) For the purpose of subsection (1), if the state of the art also includes documents within the meaning of section 94(3), these documents are not to be considered in deciding whether there has been an inventive step.[50]

The remainder of this subsection evaluates the fictitious PHOSITA standard (3.2.1) and concludes with a review of different tests relevant for inventive step (3.2.2).

PHOSITA

As stated above, many jurisdictions explicitly state that the inventive step is determined by the PHOSITA standard.[51] Other jurisdictions do not explicitly refer to a PHOSITA but rather an "average" person,[52] which in practice requires a similar level of required skill. Regardless, the obvious question is who exactly is this PHOSITA, average person, or in the words of one UK judge, this "nerd"?[53] What knowledge and ability does he or she possess?

---

[48] On the relevant date to be used, see *Sara Lee Household & Body Care v. Johnson Wax* [2001] EWCA Civ 1609.
[49] Nathalie A. Thomas, "Secondary Considerations in Nonobviousness Analysis: The Use of Objective Indicia Following KSR v. Teleflex" (2011) 86 *New York University Law Review* 2070, 2072.
[50] See also EPC, Article 56.
[51] These include Japan, Malaysia, the Republic of Korea, China, Sri Lanka, Thailand and the United States.
[52] These include Argentina, Chile, Colombia, Costa Rica, Ecuador, Israel, Panama, Peru and Vietnam.
[53] See Jacob LJ in *Rockwater Ltd v. Technip France SA & Anor* [2004] EWCA Civ 381 (01 April 2004) at 7. ("It is settled that this man, if real, would be very boring – a nerd.")

Paragraph 13.11 of the PCT International Search and Preliminary Examination Guidelines describes some of the commonalities in PHOSITA's interpretation across many jurisdictions:

> The person skilled in the art should be presumed to be a hypothetical person having ordinary skill in the art and being aware of what was common general knowledge in the art at the relevant date. He should also be presumed to have had access to everything in the "prior art," in particular, the documents cited in the international search report, and to have had at his disposal the normal means and capacity for routine experimentation. If the problem on which the invention is based and which arises from the closest prior art prompts the person skilled in the art to seek its solution in another technical field, the person skilled in the art in that field is the person qualified to solve the problem. The assessment of whether the solution involves an inventive step must therefore be based on that specialist's knowledge and ability. There may be instances where it is more appropriate to think in terms of a group of persons, for example, a research or production team, than a single person. This may apply, for example, in certain advanced technologies such as computers or telephone systems and in highly specialized processes such as the commercial production of integrated circuits or of complex chemical substances.

Even this definition raises several questions and leaves sufficient scope for differentiation. For instance, what forms part of "common general knowledge"? In this regard, public knowledge can be distinguished from common general knowledge. Information in the public domain does not automatically become part of the common general knowledge. That said, publications such as a description in a standard textbook will provide a strong indication of common general knowledge. Singapore's approach to this issue seems sensible – the PHOSITA is not expected to know of all the information, but rather he or she would know where to find all the relevant information.[54]

Moreover, and perhaps most importantly, the definition of PHOSITA is left for jurisdictional interpretation. In the United Kingdom, courts have defined the person "skilled in the art" as someone who is familiar with the background literature but is "incapable of a scintilla of invention." For instance, the court in *Technograph Printed Circuits Limited v. Mills and Rockley (Electronics) Limited* stated:

---

[54] *Nokia v. IPCom* [2009] EWHC 3482 (Pat), at 38. Likewise, in the United States the PHOSITA is expected to understand what he or she finds. See, e.g., *Ex parte Hiyamizu*, 10 USPQ2d 1393, 1394 (Bd. Pat. App. & Inter. 1988) (The "hypothetical [PHOSITA] to which the claimed subject matter pertains would, of necessity have the capability of understanding the scientific and engineering principles applicable to the pertinent art").

To whom must the invention be obvious? It is not disputed that the hypothetical addressee is a skilled technician who is well acquainted with workshop technique and who has carefully read the relevant literature. He is supposed to have an unlimited capacity to assimilate the contents of, it may be, scores of specifications but to be incapable of a scintilla of invention. When dealing with obviousness, unlike novelty, it is permissible to make a "mosaic" out of the relevant documents, but it must be a mosaic which can be put together by an unimaginative man with no inventive capacity.[55]

The South African Patent Review interprets this to mean in practice that unless the prior literature contains what often amounts to an explicit instruction or suggestion to make the invention, especially when two or more pieces of prior art need to be combined or mosaicked, the invention will be deemed sufficiently non-obvious to meet the inventive step requirement.[56] The Indian Intellectual Property Appellate Board describes the PHOSITA in slightly broader terms:

We must remember that this ordinary man has skill in this art. He is not ignorant of its basics, nor is he ignorant of the activities in the particular field. He is also not ignorant of the demand on this art. "He is just an average man . . . Well . . . just an ordinary man." But he is no dullard. He has read the prior art and knows how to proceed in the normal course of research with what he knows of the state of the art. He does not need to be guided along step by step. He can work his way through. He reads the prior arts as a whole and allows himself to be taught by what is contained therein.[57]

Correa also attributes some specialized knowledge to the PHOSITA as opposed to viewing that person as simply someone with very general or ordinary knowledge in the relevant technical field: "A person skilled in the art is not just an expert in his technical field but a person who should have some degree of imagination and intuition."[58] Regardless of definition, the

---

[55] *Technograph Printed Circuits Limited v. Mills and Rockley (Electronics) Limited* (1972) RPC, 346 at 355. See also *General Tire v. Firestone Tire & Rubber* [1972] RPC 457, at 506 ("In our judgment the evidence in the instant case shows that there is far more than a 'scintilla of invention' in the process for which protection is claimed in the patent-in-suit"). For a similar finding in the United States, see *Standard Oil Co. v. Am. Cyanamid Co.*, 774 F.2d 448, 454 (Fed. Cir. 1985).

[56] South African IP Review, above n. 38, at 32.

[57] *Sankalp Rehabilitation Trust v. F. Hoffmann-La Roche AG and the Asst. Controller of Patents & Designs, Intellectual Property Appellate Board*, Order No. 250/2012, 2 November 2012 (India) at 42. See also *KSR Int'l Co. v. Teleflex Inc.*, 550 US 398 (2007), at 421 ("A person of ordinary skill is also a person of ordinary creativity, not an automaton").

[58] Correa, above n. 21, at 4. Exceptions include Australia and Papua New Guinea, which state that common general knowledge is taken into account for the assessment of inventive step.

US Supreme Court in *KSR Int'l v. Teleflex, Inc.* warned that "[r]igid preventative rules that deny factfinders recourse to common sense, however, are neither necessary under our case law nor consistent with it."[59]

Jurisdictions have developed various tests in order to assist in identifying the PHOSITA for the purposes of determining novelty. One of the lead cases in this regard is the UK case of *Windsurfing International v. Tabur Marine*, which developed a four-step test:

1. identify the inventive concept of the claim in question or, if that cannot readily be done, construe it;
2. identify the notional "person skilled in the art" and the relevant common general knowledge of that person;
3. identify what, if any, differences exist between the matter cited as forming part of the "state of the art" and the inventive concept of the claim or the claim as constructed; and
4. determine whether, viewed without any knowledge of the alleged invention as claimed, if those differences constitute steps which would have been obvious to the person skilled in the art or do they require any degree of invention.[60]

While this test has slightly shifted over time,[61] it nevertheless remains a useful and illustrative guide to our discussion.

---

[59] *KSR Int'l v. Teleflex, Inc.*, above n. 57, at 421.

[60] *Windsurfing International Inc. v. Tabur Marine (Great Britain) Ltd.*, [1985] RPC 59 (CA) at 73–74. ("There are, we think, four steps which require to be taken in answering the jury question. The first is to identify the inventive concept embodied in the patent in suit. Thereafter, the court has to assume the mantle of the normally skilled but unimaginative addressee in the art at the priority date and to impute to him what was, at that date, common general knowledge in the art in question. The third step is to identify what, if any, differences exist between the matter cited as being 'known or used' and the alleged invention. Finally, the court has to ask itself whether, viewed without any knowledge of the alleged invention, those differences constitute steps which would have been obvious to the skilled man or whether they require any degree of invention.") This test proved influential in other jurisdictions. See, e.g., *Apotex Inc. v. Sanofi-Synthelabo Canada Inc.*, [2008] 3 R.C.S. 265, 2008 CSC 61, at 268 ("An obviousness inquiry should follow a four-step approach"). For the Court's reasoning, see para. 67.

[61] See *Pozzoli Spa v. BDMO SA & Anor* [2007] EWCA Civ 588 (22 June 2007). See also *Actavis v. Novartis* [2010] EWCA Civ 82. It should be noted that the UK's concept of "common general knowledge" differs slightly from the traditional US test as set out in *Graham* and that of the EPC's "problem-solution approach." The risk of the UK approach is that too much knowledge is imparted on the skilled person and fewer inventions are deemed to be inventive. For illustration, see the decision in *Teva UK Limited & Another v. AstraZeneca AB* [2014] EWHC 2873 (Pat).

Inventive Step Tests

If the objective of the inventiveness/obvious requirement is to craft a rigorous system that rewards true innovation (such as higher-level incremental improvements but excluding small or minor improvements), a jurisdiction should use the inventive step/non-obvious standard to eradicate poor quality patents. This is easier to do in theory rather than in practice. In practice, jurisdictions have struggled to design a standard that is fair and applicable in many circumstances. For example, in *Graham v. John Deere Co.* the US Supreme Court developed a four-step test on an obviousness inquiry. First, courts must determine the scope and content of the prior art; second, courts must identify the differences between the prior art and the claims at issue; third, courts must ascertain the level of ordinary skill in the art; and fourth, courts must make use of secondary considerations as an aid.[62]

US courts have subsequently refined the test in numerous ways. For instance, in an effort to avoid hindsight bias the Federal Circuit developed the teaching, suggestion or motivation test.[63] Simply, if a teaching, suggestion or motivation in the prior art pointed to the invention, then it was obvious. Other supplementary, secondary consideration tests (also known as an "objective indicia of non-obviousness"[64]) have been used in the United States since *Graham* and elsewhere in recent years. One such test is the economic significance test (also used in other jurisdictions, most notably India) and the commercial success test in South Africa.[65] The most influential recent case is *KSR v. Teleflex World*,[66] which criticized the teaching, suggestion and motivation test and "identified a number of rationales to support a conclusion of obviousness which are consistent with the proper 'functional approach' to the determination of obviousness as laid down in *Graham*."[67] This case, along with several subsequent

---

[62] *Graham v. John Deere Co.*, 383 US 1 (1966), at 17.

[63] *Ruiz v. A.B. Chance*, 234 F.3d 654, 665–66 (Fed. Cir. 2000). A study conducted by the Federal Trade Commission found that there was much uncertainty about the test, which, according to the National Research Council, led to some dilution of the non-obviousness standard. See Amanda Wieker, "Secondary Considerations Should Be Given Increased Weight in Obviousness Inquiries under 35 U.S.C. §103 in the Post-KSR v. Teleflex World" (2008) 17 *Federal Circuit Bar Journal* 665, 671.

[64] See generally Thomas, above n. 49.

[65] *Schlumberger Logelco Inc. v. Coflexip*, 2003 (1) SA 16 (SCA).

[66] *KSR Int'l Co. v. Teleflex Inc.*, above n. 57, 415–21.

[67] See the updated US Patent and Trademark Office, "Examples of Basic Requirements of a Prima Facie Case of Obviousness [R-08.2012]," www.uspto.gov/web/offices/pac/mpep/s2143.html, accessed 3 March 2017.

cases, led to the US Patent and Trademarks Office (USPTO) providing a nonexhaustive list of exemplary rationales that may support a conclusion of obviousness:

(A) Combining prior art elements according to known methods to yield predictable results;
(B) Substituting one known element for another to obtain predictable results;
(C) Using known technique to improve similar devices (methods, or products) in the same way;
(D) Applying a known technique to a known device (method, or product) ready for improvement to yield predictable results;
(E) Choosing from a finite number of identified, predictable solutions, with a reasonable expectation of success (so-called "obvious to try");
(F) Known work in one field of endeavor may prompt variations of it for use in either the same field or a different one based on design incentives or other market forces if the variations are predictable to one of ordinary skill in the art;
(G) Some teaching, suggestion, or motivation in the prior art that would have led one of ordinary skill to modify the prior art reference or to combine prior art reference teachings to arrive at the claimed invention.[68]

These tests are not without controversy or problems, as they tend to favor the patent holder and could be construed to work against the interest of the public health policy goals. Then again, the advantage of the secondary consideration tests is that they are more objective than the non-obviousness test. Regardless of the chosen manner, jurisdictions would be wise to heed the caution of the US Supreme Court in *KSR Int'l v, Teleflex, Inc.* that rejecting or invalidating patents claiming obvious subject matter "must not be confined within a test or formulation too constrained to serve its purpose."[69]

The issue is even more complicated in regard to pharmaceuticals. There is a growing body of evidence that questions the inventiveness of the majority of patented drugs. While the literature is too complex and extensive to discuss at length here, the crux is that the incentive structure of the patent system at present encourages minor incremental changes to existing drugs so as to extend the term of monopoly protection in what

[68] Ibid.   [69] *KSR Int'l v. Teleflex, Inc.*, above n. 57, at 423.

is called "evergreening."[70] In a majority of these cases, there is little if any therapeutic benefit to such changes.[71] The result is that startling few new medicines on the market can be labeled highly innovative or breakthrough drugs, defined as the first pharmaceutical product that effectively treats a given disease or promotes considerable treatment gains in comparison with existing drugs.[72]

India has adopted a clear and proactive stance against evergreening through the adoption of its inventiveness standard with the specific goal of narrowing the patentability threshold. With a higher standard than most countries, which has been referred to as a "non-obviousness-plus" standard,[73] India defines an inventive step not only to mean non-obvious to a person skilled in the art, but also to "involve technical advance as compared to the existing knowledge or have economic significance or both." The burden of proof is on the applicant to show a technical advance.[74]

Under such a standard, the subject matter of an extended Swiss-type or second use claim may be deemed to be a mere discovery that does not fulfill the "inventive step" requirement of patentability. Australia too has discussed setting a threshold to "inhibit the patenting of follow-on pharmaceuticals which promote evergreening with no material therapeutic benefit."[75] The difficulty in establishing such a standard is establishing the proper "size of the step" required for patentability – setting the bar too

---

[70] At the same time, it is widely known that the industry abandons R&D into promising new drugs due to questions regarding the patentability of the resulting medicine.

[71] For instance, only 25 percent of medicines patented in the period 1989–2000 showed any therapeutic benefit. James Love, "Evidence Regarding Research and Development Investments in Innovative and Non-Innovative Medicines" (September 2003), www.cptech.org/ip/health/rnd/evidenceregardingrnd.pdf, accessed 4 March 2017.

[72] See, e.g., CDER NDAs Approved in Calendar Years 1990–2004 by Therapeutic Potential and Chemical Type, www.fda.gov/cder/rdmt/pstable.htm, accessed 21 February 2017 (finding that only 11 percent of new drugs patented between 2000 and 2004 were considered highly innovative). See also Morris L. Barer, Patricia A. Caetano, Charlyn D. Black, Steven G. Morgan, Kenneth L. Bassett, James M. Wright and Robert G. Evans, "'Breakthrough' Drugs and Growth in Expenditure on Prescription Drugs in Canada" (2005) 331 *British Medical Journal* 815 (finding only 5.9 percent of newly patented drugs in Canada between 1990 and 2003 were labeled "breakthrough drugs").

[73] Janice M. Mueller, "The Tiger Awakens: The Tumultuous Transformation of India's Patent System and the Rise of Indian Pharmaceutical Innovation" (2007) 68 *University of Pittsburgh Law Review* 491, 564.

[74] Indian Patents Act, Section 2(1)(j)(a).

[75] Commonwealth of Australia, "Pharmaceutical Patents Review Report 2013," conducted by Dr. Nicholas Gruen, Professor Dianne Nicol and Tony Harris at the request of the Parliamentary Secretary for Innovation, at xi.

high will discourage continual but incremental improvement from follow-on inventors, whereas setting the bar too low may tilt the balance too much toward such smaller increments and discourage R&D into what could be ambitious breakthroughs.[76]

There is emerging consensus in a number of jurisdictions that a higher threshold for inventiveness will improve the quality of the system and lead to fewer patented pharmaceuticals, more generic competition/lower prices and perhaps a more sustainable supply of high-quality drugs given the potential for multiple manufacturers. It is also plausible that higher patentability criteria will lead to greater innovation as inventors have increased incentives to spend valuable resources on R&D, which could lead to real breakthroughs and decreased incentives to allocate R&D to incremental improvements that may not lead to patent protection. Like-wise, as found in the EU Commission Pharmaceutical Sector Inquiry Report, a higher standard of inventiveness could avoid (1) the filing of numerous patents for the same medicine, leading to patent thickets or clusters; (2) excessive patent litigation, which normally revolves around "secondary" patents in order to prevent entry to the market by generic competition; and (3) life-cycle management strategies used by companies to slightly amend a formulation or dosage and orchestrate a switch away from the soon-to-be-off-patent medicines to the second-generation phar-maceutical covered by subsequent patents.[77]

The recommendations of the Brazilian patent review on inventive step could be a useful model for Hong Kong to adopt:

> The invention carries inventive activity when, for a person skilled in the art, it does not derive in an obvious or evident manner from the state of the art, and provided it represents a significant technical advance in regards to the state of the art.[78]

It makes sense for Hong Kong to follow the burgeoning intellectual trend and define the standards for non-obviousness at a relatively high level in order both to eliminate frivolous and/or the evergreening of patents in

---

[76] See Federal Trade Commission, The Evolving IP Market Place – Aligning Patent Notice and Remedies with Competition, (2011), chapter 4, pp. 4–6, as cited in the Patent report of the Brazilian Chamber of Deputies, above n. 2, at 64.

[77] European Commission, "Pharmaceutical Sector Inquiry Final Report," adopted 8 July 2009, at 10–15, http://ec.europa.eu/competition/sectors/pharmaceuticals/inquiry/staff_working_paper_part1.pdf, accessed 3 March 2017.

[78] Patent report of the Brazilian Chamber of Deputies, above n. 2, at 67.

order to reduce pharmaceutical spending and to encourage local development of incremental innovations in the sector, which may be within reach of the jurisdiction's innovative capabilities. In this regard, the adoption of the Brazilian model could limit the granting of poor-quality patents, safeguard the public health system and at the same time perhaps even assist local inventors in the market.

3.3.3   Industrial Applicability/Utility

In most jurisdictions, the PCT and of course in Article 27(1) of the TRIPS Agreement, industrial applicability/utility is another of the requirements for patentability. While the TRIPS Agreement does not attempt to define industrial application/utility, Article 33(4) of the PCT states:

> For the purposes of the international preliminary examination, a claimed invention shall be considered industrially applicable if, according to its nature, it can be made or used (in the technological sense) in any kind of industry. "Industry" shall be understood in its broadest sense, as in the Paris Convention for the Protection of Industrial Property.

In most jurisdictions there is almost an assumption that any invention is capable of industrial application. This is the case in the EU and the United States, where an applicant needs only one credible assertion of utility to satisfy the standard.[79] Referred to as "uncontroversial" and "easily met," the utility standard in the United States can, according to a 1998 US Patent Examination Manuel, be defeated only with "proof of total incapacity."[80] Mexico's Law of Industrial Property (Ley de la Propiedad Industrial) is even more lenient, with Article 12 defining "industrial application" as "the *possibility* that an invention may have a practical utility or can be produced or used in any branch of economic activity, for the purposes described in the patent application."[81] Section 96 of Hong Kong's Patents Ordinance is likewise broad in scope, providing that "[a]n invention shall be considered as susceptible of industrial application if it can be made or used in any kind of industry, including agriculture." One has to imagine that the interpretive threshold for industrial application/utility under Section 96 would likewise be exceptionally low.

---

[79]   EPC 2000, Article 57; 35 USC 101.

[80]   1998 US Patent Examination Manual, as cited by Eli Lilly in *Eli Lilly v. Government of Canada*, in the Arbitration under the Arbitration Rules of the UNCITRAL and NAFTA, Notice of Arbitration, 12 September 2013, para. 32.

[81]   Cited in ibid., para. 33.

In regard to pharmaceuticals, examiners and courts sometimes actively inquire into what constitutes credible utility. In the United States, any substantial, nonfrivolous use has traditionally qualified as credible activity. As such, proof of in vitro pharmacological activity has been deemed to qualify as credible utility.[82] Likewise, the Boards of Appeal of the EPO attempted to place some threshold for the requirement when it held that there must be some "profitable use for which the substance can be employed" in order to be deemed capable of industrial application.[83]

In recent years, additional and (slightly) more stringent standards in recent years is in large part due to the "difficulty of determining whether certain biotechnology-related inventions, such as those covering genes or proteins, really have any industrial application."[84] In an attempt to forestall speculative patents, the United States established guidelines requiring applicants to disclose a "specific, substantial and credible utility" for the invention.[85] The European Patent Office (EPO) and others have followed suit with a similar requirement.[86]

The United States has also taken the lead in setting a standard for the threshold required for pharmaceutical inventions. Recognizing the nature and realities of pharmaceutical R&D, the US Court of Appeals for the Federal Circuit stated in *In re Brana*:

> Usefulness in patent law, and in particular in the context of pharmaceutical inventions, necessarily includes the expectation of further research and development. The stage at which an invention in this field becomes useful is well before it is ready to be administered to humans. Were we to require Phase II testing in order to prove utility, the associated costs would prevent many companies from obtaining patent protection on promising new inventions, thereby eliminating an incentive to pursue, through research and development, potential cures in many crucial areas such as the treatment of cancer.[87]

---

[82] Ibid., para. 30.

[83] Board of Appeal of the European Patent Office, Decision of 11 May 2005, p. 4, www.epo.org/law-practice/case-law-appeals/pdf/t040870eu1.pdf, accessed 22 February 2017 (2005).

[84] CIPR, above n. 32, 116.

[85] See Utility Examination Guidelines, Federal Register 66(4), January 5, 2001, Notices, 1092, www.uspto.gov/sites/default/files/web/offices/com/sol/notices/utilexmguide.pdf, accessed 22 February 2017, as cited in CIPR, above n. 32, 117.

[86] CIPR, above n. 32, 117.

[87] *In re Brana*, 51 F.3d 1560, 1568 (Fed. Cir. 1995). Cited in *Eli Lilly v. Canada*, above n. 81, at para. 31.

The outlying country in terms of the industrial application/utility standard is Canada. Since 2005, the Canadian courts have diverted from the "mere scintilla of utility" doctrine[88] and applied a so-called promise doctrine whereby a patented invention must actually do what the inventor claimed, or implied, it would do when at the time of making the patent application, backed by evidence, to satisfy the utility requirement.[89] This is referred to in the courts as the "doctrine of sound prediction." In *Apotex Inc. v. Wellcome Foundation Ltd.* the Supreme Court of Canada set out the three conditions of the doctrine of sound prediction as (a) a "factual basis" for the prediction, (b) an "articulable and sound line of reasoning from which the desired result can be inferred from the factual basis," and (c) "proper disclosure."[90]

The promise doctrine most often affects the pharmaceutical industry (and medical inventions), as the specification in further and second use patents – that is, where the patent is for a new use of a known compound – must assert that the compound is useful for the claimed purpose.[91] The promise doctrine has proven particularly difficult for the pharmaceutical industry, where patent applications are generally made at an early stage of pharmaceutical development and long before any stage 2 and 3 clinical trials (and often before stage 1 trials). It is therefore difficult for an applicant to precisely identify with any accuracy the effect of the drug at issue. This difficulty has proved fatal to numerous pharmaceutical applicants. For instance, between 2009 and 2011 the Federal Court in Canada invalidated patents that had been granted prior to 2005 – Zyprexa (olanzapine)

---

[88] Eli Lilly quotes a 1990 Canadian Patent Office Manual, which states: "Utility [is] an essential feature of invention. If an invention is totally useless, the purposes and objects of the [patent] grant would fail and such [patent] grant would consequently be void . . . Utility, as related to inventions, means industrial value." From this Eli Lilly concludes that "as long as an invention had some industrial purpose and was not inoperable, the invention satisfied the utility requirement." *Eli Lilly v. Canada*, above n. 81, para. 29 (citing MOPOP §§12.02.01 and 12.03 (January 1990)).

[89] Information obtained after the date of filing is irrelevant to satisfy the criteria. *Apotex Inc. v. Wellcome Foundation Ltd.* 2002 SCC 77 (AZT) at para. 84. Pre-filing data must be sufficiently disclosed (as opposed to merely referenced) in the patent application in order to meet the requirement. *Teva Canada Ltd. v. Pfizer Canada Inc.* 2012 SCC 60 (sildenafil) at para. 42.

[90] *Apotex Inc. v. Wellcome Foundation Ltd.* 2002 SCC 77 (AZT) at para. 70.

[91] Other situations requiring a promise include a selection patent claiming compounds that fall within a previously disclosed genus and where an advantage is necessary to establish inventiveness. See further *Eli Lily Canada Inc. et al. v. Novopharm Limited* 2010 FCA 197 (olanzapine) at para. 78; *Hoffmann-La Roche Limited v. Apotex Inc.* 2011 FC 875 (mycophenolate mofetil) at para. 22.

and Strattera (atomoxetine) – for failing to meet the utility threshold.[92] In the case of Zyprexa, the Federal Court found that the drug did not meet the implied promise that the drug is "markedly superior" to other drugs for the same disease; in the case of Strattera, the Court determined that a seven-week double-blind placebo-controlled study of twenty-two patients was too small and too short in duration to provide anything more than interesting but inconclusive data.[93]

As a result of the invalidation, pharmaceutical giant Eli Lilly brought a claim against Canada under Chapter 11 of the North American Free Trade Agreement (NAFTA) when it filed a Notice of Arbitration on 12 September 2013 claiming violations of several provisions.[94] In its statement of defense, Canada argued that "allowing patent protection in these circumstances would permit applicants to obtain and uphold patents based on speculation, and in the absence of any adequate disclosure to the public. It would also have the effect of dissuading innovation by pre-emptively fencing off areas of research in the absence of a realized invention, undermining a primary policy goal of the Patent Act."[95] More directly, Canada argued that the core patent criteria must be fulfilled no later than at the time of filing: "[W]hether or not the applicant ultimately demonstrates its alleged invention to be 'useful in fact' (years after the filing of the invention, on the basis of wholly different research) is not the relevant inquiry."[96] Thus, the fact that both drugs were marketed and sold in Canada – and therefore were proven to be medically useful – is irrelevant under the Canadian doctrine.

Canada also disputed that the promise doctrine only became "good law" in 2005, instead asserting that since 1959 Canadian courts have endorsed the doctrine that inventions must be useful as specified.[97] As evidence, Canada pointed to a 1981 case in the Supreme Court of Canada that quotes the Halsbury Laws of England as stating that an invention lacks utility

---

[92] Under Canada's Patent Law, "the initial administrative grant was only presumptively valid. It remained subject to challenge, review and potential invalidation by Canada's Federal Court through private-party litigation." Patent Act, RSC 1985, c. P-4. *Eli Lilly and Company v. Government of Canada*, Statement of Defence of the Government of Canada, 30 June 2014, at 1. See also *Eli Lilly & Co. v. Teva Canada Limited* 2011 FCA 220 (atomoxetine) at paras. 31–43.

[93] *Eli Lilly v. Canada*, above n. 81. [94] *Eli Lilly v. Canada*, above n. 81.

[95] *Eli Lilly v. Canada*, Statement of Defence of the Government of Canada, above n. 92, at 2.

[96] Ibid., at 8.

[97] *Rodi & Wienenberger Aktiengeschaft v. Metalliflex Ltd.* (1959), 32 CPR 102 (Que CA), paras. 15–17. Affirmed in *Metalliflex Ltd. v. Rodi & Wienenberger Aktiengesellschaft* [1961] SCR 117.

when the invention will not work, either in the sense that it will not operate at all or, "more broadly, that it will not do what the specification promises that it will do."[98] Thus, Canada asserted that although the default rule is that there is no general obligation to promise a specific utility of the invention, other than a mere scintilla of utility, this does not apply in cases where the applicant promises a particular degree of utility or selection patents – in such cases the utility must be demonstrated or "soundly predicted" as of the date of the patent application filing date.[99] Canada therefore admitted that its "promise doctrine" deviates from the accepted "mere scintilla of utility" doctrine.

Canada's view that a promise somehow raises the threshold is unorthodox. It could also be viewed as distortion and an abuse of the phrase "capable of industrial application" – whether a drug is "markedly superior" to any other drug on the market seems irrelevant to whether it is capable of industrial application or has any utility. Further, invalidating a drug that has been approved by the health authorities as being safe and effective in the treatment of a certain disease or ailment (and is currently marketed and sold in Canada) for not having utility twists the obvious meaning of the word and pushes the envelope of compliance with Article 27(1) of the TRIPS Agreement.

The novelty and inventiveness standards would seem to be better equipped to factor in the degree of inventiveness of an invention. While not a perfect substitute for the promise doctrine, these factors are far more appropriate to determine how and what a process/product does than the standard of whether the invention is capable of industrial application.

Interestingly, Canada successfully defended its approach in the investor-state dispute settlement (ISDS) decision in March 2017, but just a few months later the Supreme Court of Canada declared the promise doctrine to no longer be good law. In the ISDS dispute, the Final Award emphasized the high bar to success first in noting that the tribunal "is not

---

[98] *Consolboar Inc. v. MacMillan Bloedel (Saskatchewan) Ltd.* [1981] SCR 504, 1981 CArswell-Nat 582, para. 36.

[99] *Eli Lilly v. Canada*, Statement of Defence of the Government of Canada, above n. 92, at 11, 24–26. See also *Sanofi-Aventis v. Apotex Inc.* 2013 FCA 186 (clopidogrel), at para. 46; *Apotex Inc. v. Wellcome Foundation Ltd.* 2002 SCC 77 (AZT) at para. 70. See also *Eli Lilly Canada Inc. v. Apotex Inc.* 2009 FCA 97 (raloxifine) at para. 15; *Eli Lilly and Company v. Teva Canada Limited* 2011 FCA 220 (atomoxetine) at para. 57; *Bell Helicopter Textron Canada Limitée v. Eurocopter* 2013 FCA 219 at para. 155.

an appellate tier in respect of the decisions of national judiciaries"[100] and second in setting out the customary international law minimum standard of treatment as per NAFTA Article 1105(1) as follows:

> [A] violation of the customary international law minimum standard of treatment... requires an act that is sufficiently egregious and shocking – a gross denial of justice, manifest arbitrariness, blatant unfairness, a complete lack of due process, evident discrimination, or a manifest lack of reasons – so as to fall below accepted international standards and constitute a breach of Article 1105. Such a breach may be exhibited by a "gross denial of justice or manifest arbitrariness falling below acceptable international standards"; or the creation by the State of objective expectations in order to induce investment and the subsequent repudiation of those expectations... although bad faith may often be present in such a determination and its presence certainly will be determinative of a violation, a finding of bad faith is not a requirement for a breach of Article 1105(1).[101]

Moreover, the tribunal made it clear that "there are distinctions to be made between conduct that may amount to a denial (or gross denial) of justice and other conduct that may also be sufficiently egregious and shocking, such as manifest arbitrariness or blatant unfairness."[102] In light of the fact that the tribunal's task is not to act as a review mechanism over national courts, the Award stated that "considerable deference is to be accorded to the conduct and decisions of such courts [and] it will accordingly only be in very exceptional circumstances, in which there is clear evidence of egregious and shocking conduct, that it will be appropriate for a NAFTA Chapter Eleven tribunal to assess such conduct against the obligations of the respondent State under NAFTA Article 1105(1)."[103]

After setting out the interpretive framework, the tribunal moved to the substance of the claim and found that Eli Lilly "has not demonstrated a fundamental or dramatic change in Canadian patent law... [T]he Tribunal finds that Claimant has not demonstrated, as a factual matter, that its legitimate expectations were violated by the application of Canadian patent law to the Zyprexa and Strattera Patents."[104] This despite the fact that the tribunal accepted the point that prior to the products at issue "no commercially successful products were found to lack utility, whereas now

---

[100] Eli Lilly and Company v. Government of Canada, International Centre For Settlement of Investment Disputes in an Arbitration under Chapter Eleven of the NAFTA and the UNCITRAL Arbitration Rules, 1976, Case No. UNCT/14/2, Final Award, 16 March 2017, paras. 221 and 224.

[101] Ibid., para. 222.   [102] Ibid., para. 223.   [103] Ibid., para. 224.   [104] Ibid., para. 387.

this is not uncommon. This is a notable fact, but Claimant has not established this to be the result of changed law."[105] In sum:

> [T]he Tribunal recognizes that the outcome in AZT was unexpected for some practitioners and even judges who had understood the language of [a previous decision of the Court of Appeal] to mean that utility could be demonstrated through post-filing evidence (most notably commercial success). Still, having considered all of the evidence, the Tribunal cannot conclude that the Supreme Court effected a dramatic change from previously well-established law when it clarified this rule in AZT.[106]

For these, and other, reasons the Tribunal dismissed the claim.

In regard to the Supreme Court of Canada overturning the promise doctrine on 30 June 2017,[107] the case stems from a trial judge in the Federal Court of Canada finding AstraZeneca's patent for its blockbuster Nexium drug (a proton pump inhibitor that decreases the amount of acid produced in the stomach) invalid for lack of utility under Section 2 of the Patent Act. While the trial judge found the patent novel and non-obvious, the patent was invalidated for lacking utility under the promise doctrine, with the judge stating that "the promise of the patent is the yardstick against which utility is measured."[108] In essence, while the patentee fulfilled one promise (use as a proton pump inhibitor to reduce acid in the stomach), it did not fulfil a second promise (improved metabolic properties). More specifically, the patent read:

> It is desirable to obtain compounds with improved pharmacokinetic and metabolic properties which *will give an improved therapeutic profile* such as a lower degree of individual variation. The present invention provides such compounds, which are novel salts of single enantiomers of omeprazole.[109]

Having determined that the promise of a "lower degree of individual variation" was not achieved by the drug, the judge concluded:

> Had the patent stated that such compounds "may" or "could" give an improved therapeutic profile, then the argument that such statements referred merely to a goal would be more compelling. The same cannot be said of "will." Will does not convey a low threshold of potential outcomes, but to the contrary, a high threshold of probable or certain outcomes that

---

[105] Ibid., para. 336, citations omitted.   [106] Ibid., para. 337.
[107] *AstraZeneca Canada Inc. v. Apotex Inc.*, 2017 SCC 36 (30 June 2017).
[108] Trial judgment, para. 86, cited in SC para. 28.
[109] *AstraZeneca v. Apotex*, 2014 FC 638 (esomeprazole) (F.C. per Rennie J.) at para. 113.

will occur, which in turn, suggests that such outcomes are promised by the patent.[110]

The decision, upheld by the Federal Court of Appeal,[111] thus turns on the phrasing used in the patent application rather than the actual utility of the product.

The Supreme Court's recent ruling in *AstraZeneca* removes the promise doctrine as a basis for declaring a Canadian patent invalid, and it did so in blunt terms: "The Promise Doctrine is not the correct method of determining whether the utility requirement under [Section 2] of the Patent Act is met."[112]

The Court then attacked both the sensibility and textual support for the doctrine:

> [The promise] doctrine holds that if a patentee's patent application promises a specific utility, only if that promise is fulfilled, can the invention have the requisite utility, but where no specific utility is promised, a mere scintilla of utility will suffice. Generally, an analysis regarding issues of validity will focus on the claims alone, and only considers the disclosure where there is ambiguity in the claims. This is in accordance with the Court's direction that claims construction precedes all considerations of validity. The Promise Doctrine, by contrast, directs courts to make determinations regarding utility by reading both the claims and the disclosure to identify potential promises, even in an absence of ambiguity in the claims. The Promise Doctrine then provides that if any one of the promises is not fulfilled, the utility requirement in [Section 2] is not met and the patent, in its entirety, is invalid.
>
> The Promise Doctrine is incongruent with both the words and the scheme of the Patent Act. First, it conflates [Sections 2 and 22(3)] by requiring that . . . to satisfy the utility requirement in [Section 2], any use disclosed in accordance with [Section 27(3)] must be demonstrated or soundly predicted at the time of filing. If that is not done successfully, the entire patent is invalid, as the pre-condition for patentability – an invention under the [Section 2] of the Act – has not been fulfilled. Second, to require all multiple uses be met for the patent's validity to be upheld, runs counter to the words of the Act and has the potential for unfair consequences. The Promise Doctrine risks, as was the case here, for an otherwise useful invention to be deprived of patent protection because not every promised use was sufficiently demonstrated or soundly predicted by the filing date.[113]

---

[110] Ibid., at para. 120.
[111] *AstraZeneca Canada Inc. v. Apotex Inc.*, 2017 SCC 36 (30 June 2017), para. 24. See also para. 2.
[112] Ibid.   [113] Ibid., at paras. 1–2.

The Court continued the attack on the doctrine by stating:

> The effect of the Promise Doctrine to deprive such an invention of patent pro-
> tection if even one "promised" use is not soundly predicted or demonstrated
> is punitive and has no basis in the Act. Furthermore, such a consequence
> is antagonistic to the bargain on which patent law is based wherein we ask
> inventors to give fulsome disclosure in exchange for a limited monopoly. To
> invalidate a patent solely on the basis of an unintentional overstatement of
> even a single use will discourage a patentee from disclosing fully, whereas
> such disclosure is to the advantage of the public. The Promise Doctrine in
> its operation is inconsistent with the purpose of s. 27(3) of the Act which
> calls on an inventor to "fully describe the invention and its operation or
> use." Thus, the Promise Doctrine undermines a key part of the scheme of the
> Act; it is not good law.[114]

The Supreme Court then set out the correct two-step approach that Courts
should take in assessing utility – that is, to first identify the subject matter
of the invention as claimed in the patent and, second, to ask whether that
subject matter is useful – "is it capable of a practical purpose (i.e. an actual
result)?"[115]

As to the "degree or quantum of usefulness" required, the Supreme
Court reverted to the traditional requirement that "a scintilla of utility will
do," stating:

> The Act does not prescribe the degree or quantum of usefulness required,
> or that every potential use be realized – a scintilla of utility will do. A single
> use related to the nature of the subject-matter is sufficient, and the utility
> must be established by either demonstration or sound prediction as of the
> filing date.[116]

This decision represents a rather significant reversal of the requirement
for utility, and one that brings Canada back in line with international standards (and significantly lowers the threshold for defending against a challenge on the grounds of utility). While Canada successfully defended the
promise doctrine against a challenge in ISDS, it is less certain whether the
doctrine is compliant with the TRIPS Agreement. Canada may have been
able to successfully argue that given the territorial nature of IPRs it has
wide leeway in setting out the standards and perimeters for what qualifies
as an "invention" and that its requirement in regard to utility was both fair
and sensible; it is just as likely that a court would have seen the doctrine
as counter to Article 27(1) of the TRIPS Agreement.

---

[114] Ibid., at paras. 50–51, emphasis added, citations omitted.
[115] Ibid., at para. 54.   [116] Ibid., at para. 55.

Given the state of the marketplace in Hong Kong, and the legal uncertainty associated with the recent (but no longer relied on) Canadian approach, it would not seem in the interest of the territory to adopt the promise doctrine. Instead, Hong Kong should simply follow the path of the United States and EU in ensuring through interpretive guidelines that speculative inventions in the biotechnology field (or other fields) meet the traditional minimum standard of utility.

3.4 Subject Matter

This section briefly discusses the general legislation on patentable subject matter. In most jurisdictions there are a number of things that simply are not patentable or inventions "as such," namely, discoveries, scientific theories and mathematical methods. For instance, finding a naturally occurring compound in the human body is a nonpatentable discovery. On the other hand, developing processes used to isolate or purify such a compound or producing a synthetic version of the naturally occurring compound would be a patentable invention. In many jurisdictions, aesthetic creations such as literary, dramatic, musical and artistic works are not inventions "as such."[117] Jurisdictions are more divided on the granting of patents for computer programs and software-related patents as well as for business method patents.

Jurisdictions also deem some inventions to simply be not patentable. These include inventions contrary to *ordre public* or morality, "diagnostic, therapeutic and surgical methods for the treatment of humans and animals" and "plants and animals other than micro-organisms, and essentially biological processes for the production of plants or animals other than non-biological and microbiological processes."[118] These exclusions are allowable under Articles 27(2)–(3) of the TRIPS Agreement. While the exclusion for public order and morality and plants or animals needs no further explanation, the exclusion for medical techniques warrants further discussion. The rationale behind the exclusion for medical techniques is that medical practitioners should be free to use any medical method they deem necessary to treat patients. More than eighty countries currently prohibit medical method patents, including countries in the EU,

---

[117] Patent Act 1977 s.1(2)(b).
[118] The exception being that Members must provide protection, whether by patents or a sui generis right, to plant varieties.

Asia, Africa, North America and South America.[119] This exclusion of patentability is reached in different ways, even in Europe. For instance, some countries (including the United Kingdom, Germany and France) have incorporated provisions affirming such methods are not capable of industrial application, whereas Sweden, Italy and Denmark have declared such methods to be noninventions. For its part, Switzerland characterizes medical techniques as legal exceptions to patentability.[120]

In contrast, methods of medical treatment are patentable in the United States and Australia.[121] In the United States, however, medical practitioners benefit from immunity from liability. In Australia, there is no such immunity. In Section 93(4) of the Patents Ordinance, Hong Kong follows the major European countries in using industrial application to exclude patentability:

> A method for treatment of the human or animal body or surgery or therapy and a diagnostic method practiced on the human or animal body shall not be regarded as an invention which is susceptible of industrial application ... but this subsection shall not apply to a product, and in particular a substance or composition, for use in any such method.

Section 93(5) of the Hong Kong Patents Ordinance also deems that "the publication or working of which would be contrary to public order ('ordre public') or morality shall not be a patentable invention"; however, "the working of an invention shall not be deemed to be so contrary merely because it is prohibited by any law in force in Hong Kong" and the patenting of "plant or animal variety or an essentially biological process for the production of plants or animals, other than a microbiological process or the products of such a process." Hong Kong drew heavily on European, UK and Irish law in formulating Section 93(5),[122] and it does not appear that any modifications relating to pharmaceutical patents are required.

3.5 Second Use

This section revisits in greater detail second or subsequent medical use (second use) patents. Originators have long argued for the adoption of

---

[119] Oksana Mitnovetski and Dianne Nicol, "Are Patents for Methods of Medical Treatment Contrary to the Ordre Public and Morality or 'Generally Inconvenient'?" (2004) 30 *Journal of Medical Ethics* 470.

[120] Ibid., at 471.

[121] *Anaesthetic Supplies Pty Ltd v. Rescare Ltd.* (1994) 28 IPR 383; confirmed by *Bristol Myers Squibb Co v. F H Faulding & Co Ltd.* (1998) 41 IPR 467.

[122] See EPC Arts. 52 and 53; 1977 c. 37 ss. 1 and 4 U.K.; 1992 No. 1 ss. 9 and 10 Eire.

second use patents in order to provide for a soft landing from the patent cliff.[123] Such an argument is weak, as originator companies should have taken the entirely foreseeable eventual expiration of patent protection into account and in their business models. To the contrary, some would argue that excluding second use patents will help originator companies divert attention away from less demanding research and focus on inventing new compounds.[124]

That said, more compelling arguments for second use patents exist. For instance, as science progresses it becomes harder to invent completely new compounds and substances (since the lower hanging fruits of the compounds have already been harvested). Moreover, during the life-cycle of the first medical use patent, (1) beneficial effects on another disease or part of the body can sometimes be observed in a patient group suffering from more than one disease, or (2) targeted research to a second use of the drug demonstrates beneficial effects in a patient group that suffers from another disease. In addition, it has been argued that patentability of second and subsequent medical use of known compounds is crucial[125] in order to reduce the cost of pharmacogenomics.[126]

The development of additional medicines based on existing drugs should be encouraged, as it represents a cheaper way to expand the medicinal toolkit and benefits human health. The legal issue is how the system can encourage such innovation while at the same time discouraging second use patents that confer additional monopolies on a product that is obvious to the PHOSITA or on an old/existing product (even if it has been unexploited).[127]

---

[123] "Patent cliff" is a phenomenon caused by the expiration of a patent whereby marketing exclusivity and monopoly pricing is lost, thereby resulting in a reduction in sales and profits for the originator company.

[124] Daniel Armstrong, "The Arguments of Law, Policy and Practice against Swiss-Type Patent Claims" (2001) 32 *Victoria University of Wellington Law Review* 201, 237 ("Even if conscious effort is required in the development of new uses, this is likely to be much less onerous than the research required in developing new compounds").

[125] The Boston Consulting Group, "A Revolution in R&D: How Genomics and Genetics Are Transforming the Biopharmaceutical Industry" (November 2001), www.bcg.com/documents/file13745.pdf, accessed 4 March 2017.

[126] Defined as "the study of how genes affect a person's response to drugs." See "What Is Pharmacogenomics?," US National Library of Medicine, http://ghr.nlm.nih.gov/handbook/genomicresearch/pharmacogenomics, accessed 22 February 2017.

[127] See *Teva Pharmaceutical Industries Ltd. v. Merck & Co Inc.*, [2003] EWHC 5 (Patent). There are many recent examples of novel and inventive second medical use of drugs that might be patentable and beneficial to human health. James Gallagher, "HIV Flushed Out by Cancer Drug," *BBC News Health* (31 July 2015), www.bbc.com/news/health-

3.5.1   The Basics of Second and Subsequent Medical Use

In principle, second use patents encourage further research and stimulate additional innovation, both of which can lead to more competition and access to more reasonably priced medicines. For this reason, advocates argue that without second use patents there is no incentive for continued R&D, and public health would suffer. Critics, on the other hand, contend that second use patents simply delay the availability of generic competition and artificially inflate prices.[128]

There may well be truth in both positions, and it is also important to understand the different context among jurisdictions. A jurisdiction such as the United States, EU or Switzerland will have different considerations, and different impact on the pharmaceutical industry, from those of a lower middle income country or LDC. For Hong Kong, several considerations come into play. Hong Kong is a small pharmaceutical market, and whether Hong Kong adopts second use patents is not going to be a deciding factor in a company's decision to conduct research into second medical uses. Moreover, given Hong Kong's current pharmaceutical capabilities, the adoption of second use will not result in more R&D being conducted in Hong Kong. On the contrary, the adoption of second or further use patents will lead to a transfer of funds out of Hong Kong. However, this is not to say that Hong Kong should not adopt second or further use patents – it is simply to understand that this transfer of funds out of the territory is the price Hong Kong has to pay for being an internationally responsible world-class city that respects IPRs.

This context also suggests two opposing objectives that should be at the core of Hong Kong's decision to legislate for a balanced regulation on second or further use patent protection:

(1) Second or further use patents should not restrict "first use" patents. To the contrary, first use should be in the public domain allowing generic manufacturers to use and sell the resulting product – Hong Kong can then benefit from the cost savings. Care must also be taken

---

33720325, accessed 22 February 2017; Smitha Mundasad, "Parkinson's: Diabetes Drug May Offer Clue to Treatment," *BBC News Health* (22 July 2015), www.bbc.com/news/health-33608725, accessed 22 February 2017.

[128] See, e.g., Patent Report of the Brazilian Chamber of Deputies, above n. 2, at 36 ("Most 'new' products placed in the pharmaceutical market would, in reality, be imitation products (me toos), meaning equivalent molecules to the ones already in the market that do not represent real innovation").

in this regard to ensure that practitioners can legally prescribe both the first and second use patented products. Legislation should therefore be mindful of and take into account potential adverse effects of second use patents on off-label use of medicines.

(2) The level of protection granted to second use patents should correspond to the level of their inventiveness: Therefore, crudely stated, more protection should be granted for pure second medical use patents, while less protection should be granted for second use claims that reside in a factor related to its efficacy, and an even lower level of protection should be granted for second use patents such as selection patents and polyphormism.

3.5.2   Hierarchy of Inventiveness

On an arguably lower level in the hierarchy of inventiveness – but of crucial importance for patients, the pharmaceutical industry and governments – are second use patents that combat the same disease or illness as the first use but demonstrate a greater efficacy by way of timing, frequency, dosage or sequence of the administration of the drug or in combination with a new compound. A growing variation of this is where the efficacy of a medicine is limited to a subset of the patients based on specific genome traits. Without such pharmacogenomic second use patents, there is simply no incentive for pharmaceutical companies to indicate the ineffectiveness of their drugs based on some genotypes or to indicate the effectiveness of a failed or expired drug for some subset of patients. Second use claims can remedy this and give pharmaceutical companies incentives to develop genetic tests and inform them about any potential adverse drug responses. This way the patent can be extended, although only for a fraction of the market, based on genotype. Pharmaceutical companies are also incentivized to improve efficacy or decrease side-effect profiles in particular patient subpopulations.

Granting such second or further use patents incentivizes pharmaceutical companies to improve efficacy or decrease side-effect profiles in particular patient subpopulations – again, this is to the benefit of human health. The proposal to use Swiss-type claims as a form of protection for pharmacogenomics inventions does not appear to have been widely considered. That being the case, the Examination Guidelines for Patent and Utility Model in Japan includes a provision that expressly approves of the application of second use claims, where novelty resides in the new patient group, in order to provide patent protection to pharmacogenomic inventions.[129]

On the same or arguably lower level of inventiveness are second use patents based on selection,[130] polymorphism,[131] optimal isomers,[132] analogy processes,[133] combinations,[134] active metabolites[135] and

---

[129] Part VII: Examination Guidelines for Inventions in Specific Fields, Chapter 2.2.1.1 Method of Judging Novelty (3–3)(a): "When it becomes clear that the claimed medicinal invention intended to specify by such mode of medical treatment is effective to a patient having, for example, a particular gene, and it becomes clear that it becomes possible for those skilled in the art to clearly distinguish the target patient groups of the both, which is specified hereunder, by a fact that the target patient group of the claimed medicinal invention is different from the target patient group which is not specifically specified in the cited invention." Medicinal Invention (Draft), Japan Patent Office Examination Guidelines for Patent and Utility Model in Japan (2005), p. 8, www.jpo.go.jp/iken_e/pdf/iken_e20050224_2/01.pdf, accessed 22 February 2017.

[130] The UK Court of Appeal rejected the contention that a specific compound lacks novelty as a matter of a priori reasoning (a generalized prior description does not disclose a specific matter within it). See *Dr Reddy's Laboratories (UK) Limited v. Eli Lilly and Company Limited*, Court of Appeal (Civil Division), UK, 18 December 2009, Docket No: Case No. A3/2008/2966.

[131] Crystal forms of the same compound. The search for the most adequate polymorph to improve stability, solubility, bioavailability and processability of the solid form of a certain substance may already be described in the state of the art and, therefore, if this is the case will not be characterized as novel and non-obvious – one of the essential patentability requirements. See *Janssen-Ortho Inc. et al. v. Novopharm et al.*, 2006 FC 1234. See further Joel Bernstein, *Polymorphism in Molecular Crystals* (Oxford University Press, 2010).

[132] Optical isomers are two compounds that contain the same number and kinds of atoms and bonds and different spatial arrangements of the atoms but that have nonsuperimposable mirror images.

[133] Analogy processes are noninventive processes but with a non-obvious product as a result, where the features can be derived only from an unknown and unsuspected effect (problem invention). For the EPC, see 9.17 Analogy process – envisageable product, Case Law of the Boards of Appeal (EPO), https://goo.gl/rGRBjx, accessed 4 March 2017. For the United States, see the Biotechnology Process Patents Act 1995.

[134] Since 2007 the US Supreme Court held that when elements, techniques, items or devices are combined, united or arranged, and when, in combination, each item performs the function it was designed to perform, the resulting combination – "ordinary innovation" – is not patentable. This can be true even if there is no teaching, suggestion or motivation to make the combination. See *KSR Int'l Co. v. Teleflex Inc.*, above n. 57.

[135] In most countries, active metabolites that are purified or synthesized in vitro are protected, contrary to those by metabolism. Section 3(d) of India's 2005 Patents (Amendment) Act recognizes metabolites as "new types of known substances," in principle considered identical to known substances and thus unpatentable. Only those metabolites that differ significantly in their characteristics regarding efficacy are deemed patentable. See further Richard Li-dar Wang and Pei-Chen Huang, "Patent Protection of Pharmacologically Active Metabolites: Theoretical and Technological Analysis on the Jurisprudence of Four Regions" (2013) 29 *Santa Clara Computer & High Technology Law Journal* 489.

prodrugs.[136] Thus, one can argue that the level of protection granted to such types of inventions depends on the level of inventiveness required in the jurisdiction, as well as the basic objectives of the domestic patent system.

3.5.3   Balance of Opposing Policy Objectives

Since Hong Kong's standard of inventiveness is not bound by any international obligation other than the requirement to protect novel, inventive and useful inventions for products or processes under Article 27(1) of the TRIPS Agreement – and provides flexibility in how Members meet this standard – it will be able to carefully craft the regulations in such a way as to optimally balance the two objectives that should drive Hong Kong's patent policy.

On the one hand, Hong Kong's internal objective must be to provide access to medicines at reasonable costs to its population. Industrial policy considerations should be an afterthought, as there is little local manufacturing (of which nearly all are low-tech generics) and almost a complete absence of serious originator R&D. It is thus in Hong Kong's interest to increase the standard of patentability such that more medicines become generic and the costs of medicines decrease. On the other hand, Hong Kong's external objective is to uphold its reputation as a world-class, business-friendly city that respects the rule of law and property rights. Maintaining strong levels of IPRs is thus also in Hong Kong's interest.

3.5.4   Methods Excluded as Subject Matter

As mentioned in Section 3.4 above, in most jurisdictions medical methods are excluded as patentable subject matter. Thus, medical practitioners are allowed to prescribe any method as they see fit. Instead, Swiss-type claims and more direct claims that reside in the use of the patented invention impose liability for infringement only on manufacturers. Moreover, the main characteristic of these second use claims is that novelty is not destroyed even though the same compound or substance is already known because of the first use of the patent. Swiss-type claims – that is, where "the

---

[136] Prodrugs are bioreversible, inactive derivatives of drug molecules that must undergo an enzymatic/chemical reaction in the body (in vivo) to release the active metabolite. See further Ralph Minderop, Arwed Burrichter and Nathalie Kirchhofer, "Prodrugs and Metabolites – In the Twilight of Patentability" (2013), *IP in the Life Sciences Industries 2013*, 8.

use of the known compound X in the manufacture of the medicament for the new therapeutic application Y" – are devised to avoid two obstacles to patentability: the novelty requirement and methods of medical treatment exclusion.

3.5.5   Novelty in Use

When the use in treating a medical condition might be new, novelty resides not in the subject matter of the claim but in some related use. In other words, the new use in treating a disease is included in the claim. The advantage of Swiss-type claims is that pharmaceutical companies are incentivized to continue research into new uses of known compounds and that medical practitioners' discretion to use the method of medical treatment of their choice is guaranteed. The EPO accepted the patentability of "the (second or subsequent) use of a substance or composition for the manufacture of a medicament for a specified new and inventive therapeutic application," because although the exclusion of therapeutic methods from patentability provided in Article 52(4) EPC 2000 on the ground that then these are not susceptible to industrial application has the effect of excluding from patentability a claim directed to the use of a substance for therapy, this type of claim would clearly be allowable (as susceptible to industrial application) for a nonmedical use: "the use of X for treating disease A in mammals" (not allowed), with "the use of X for treating disease B in cereal crops" (allowed).[137]

Since the decision in *Kos Life Sciences* (G02/08)[138] the EPO and the UKIPO no longer grant Swiss-type claims for patents covering second medical uses. Instead, patents will be granted with a more direct wording: for a pharmaceutical product with a specified (second or subsequent) medical use.

3.5.6   Options for Hong Kong

Section 94(2) of Hong Kong Patents Ordinance 1997 ("state of the art") does not provide any room for the patentability of new uses of existing compounds since novelty would be destroyed. Likewise, Section 93(4) of Patents Ordinance 1997 excludes methods of medical treatment to be

---

[137]   G 2/88, Decision of the Enlarged Board of Appeal dated 11 December 1989, at 106.
[138]   *Kos Life Sciences/Abbott Respiratory LLC* (G 0002/08), Enlarged Board of Appeal, EPO, 19 October 2010.

patented. Therefore, should Hong Kong decide to enable second or further medical use for existing compounds, it could craft a provision that resembles Section 4A(4) of the UK Patents Act 1977, as suggested by both the HKAPI and the American Chamber of Commerce in Hong Kong (AmCham).[139] Even though the new direct claims provided for under Section 54(5) EPC 2000 and Section 4A(4) of the UK Patents Act 1977 are directed to impose liability on manufacturers, there would also be a need to provide immunity against infringement liability for practitioners in order to avoid unnecessary interpretive problems. Whether the claim is phrased as a Swiss-type or more direct claim, it does not say much about novelty or obviousness. Therefore, Hong Kong can be flexible and cater to both sorts of claims, especially since Swiss-type claims are allowed in China.

Another option for Hong Kong would be to remove the method of treatment exception (Section 93(4) Patents Ordinance 1997) from the excluded subject matter for patentability. Such a model is adopted in the United States, which does not accept claims to use but instead accepts claims of method and process.[140] This is also possible in Singapore, with Section 14(7) of the Patents Act providing: "In the case of an invention consisting of a substance or composition for use in a method of treatment of the human or animal body by surgery or therapy or of diagnosis practised on the human or animal body, the fact that the substance or composition forms part of the state of the art shall not prevent the invention from being taken to be new if the use of the substance or composition in any such method does not form part of the state of the art."[141]

In addition, practitioners can be immunized against patent infringement for using the methods of medical (pharmaceutical), surgical and therapeutical treatment of their choice. If adopted, neither Swiss-type claims nor direct secondary use claims would be necessary. Next to novelty, inventiveness would be the only invalidating factor.

A survey of other jurisdictions indicates a mix of approaches and absence of international consensus. For instance, South Korea provides for wide-ranging legal protection of second medical use as long as it meets the patentability requirements normally provided by law, while Australia

---

[139] See "Review of the Patent System in Hong Kong," above n. 12, 174. It is worth noting that the Law Society of Hong Kong also recommended updating the substantive law with regard to second medical use and Swiss-type claims. Ibid., at 176.

[140] 35 USC Section 100(b).

[141] Singapore Patent Acts 1994 (revised edn. 2005), chapter 221.

provides a narrower version, with patent extensions of up to five years for claims to active ingredients or new formulations of a known active ingredient.[142] In regard to the lack of novelty, "patent extension" is the correct phrase. However, Australia also uses this patent extension for new and inventive substances,[143] which seems not in accord with the expression. Australia does not allow for patent extensions for new uses and methods.[144] On the other end of the spectrum, several countries including the Andean Community (Peru, Bolivia, Columbia and Ecuador) exclude new use patents.[145] Brazil and South Africa, meanwhile, are reportedly considering laws to remove the exception to novelty so as to prohibit second use patents in order to facilitate the entry of generic medicines in the market.[146]

Another issue that would need to be addressed relates to off-label prescriptions of medicines protected by second use patents. Without special attention, the prescription of such drugs could lead to primary liability of infringement by doctors, pharmacists and patients. In addition, the generic manufacturer will need certainty that it will not be exposed to the risk of secondary liability of infringement – such a risk would be a major disincentive to manufacture the product that was subject to the first use patent, even though manufacturing, marketing and selling the medicines with the appropriate label, package and patient information leaflet is legal because the first use patent has expired.

The analysis of second use patents is not complete without mention of the 2013 decision of the Supreme Court of India in *Novartis AG v. Union of India* (Glivec).[147] In this decision, the Supreme Court upheld the rejection of the patent application filed by Novartis AG for Glivec in 1998 (a so-called mailbox application) with the Indian Patent Office. In so doing, the Court held that Glivec (imatinib mesylate, a beta crystalline form of

---

[142] Australia Patents Review Report, above n. 75, at 93.   [143] Ibid.   [144] Ibid.
[145] Patent report of the Brazilian Chamber of Deputies, above n. 2, at 121–22.
[146] South African IP Review, above n. 38, at 29. Now Section 25(9) Patents Act 1978 (amended 2002) allows it: "In the case of an invention consisting of a substance or composition for use in a method of treatment of the human or animal body by surgery or therapy or of diagnosis practised on the human or animal body, the fact that the substance or composition forms part of the state of the art immediately before the priority date of the invention shall not prevent a patent being granted for the invention if the use of the substance or composition in any such method does not form part of the state of the art at that date." Patent Report of the Brazilian Chamber of Deputies, above n. 2, at 36 and 125.
[147] *Novartis AG v. Union of India, (UOI) and Ors.; Natco Pharma Ltd. v. UoI & Ors.; M/S Cancer Patients Aid Association v. UoI & Ors.*, Civil Appeal Nos. 2706–2716 of 2013, decided 1 April 2013.

the free base imatinib) did not meet the novelty and inventiveness requirements, since the beta crystalline form of imatinib mesylate was already included in Novartis's US patent on the free base imatinib, thereby becoming part of the prior art. Section 3(d) of India's Patent Act allows the mere discovery of a new use for a known substance to be patented only if the discovery can significantly improve the therapeutic efficacy of its properties.[148] This section is highly controversial and is responsible for two-thirds of all rejected pharmaceutical patents.[149]

The Supreme Court of India observed that the legislature enacted the provision "to prevent evergreening; to provide easy access to the citizens of this country to life saving drugs and to discharge their Constitutional obligation of providing good health care to its citizens."[150] While India no doubt had industrial as well as health objectives in mind when drafting such legislation (and leaving aside the merits of the application of facts to the law in the case), the provision and case presents a useful illustration of a jurisdiction that allows only conditional second use in order to avoid clear cases of evergreening of the patent, that is, the originator making only minor changes to the patent in order to register a new one and thereby extend protection. It would be in Hong Kong's interest to craft a second use provision based on India's Section 3(d) Patent Act 2005 where evergreening is discouraged but where the harnessing of true follow-on innovations that lead to net benefits are allowed and encouraged. However, it is perhaps in Hong Kong's interest to not be as strict with the "therapeutic efficacy" component of the standard, as a switch in dosage, form and the like could bring immense health benefits in patients.

---

[148] Section 3 of the Patents Act 1970 (Amendment 2005) reads: "The following are not inventions within the meaning of this Act, – (d) the mere discovery of a new form of a known substance which does not result in the enhancement of the known efficacy of that substance or the mere discovery of any new property or new use for a known substance or of the mere use of a known process, machine or apparatus unless such known process results in a new product or employs at least one new reactant." Explanation: For the purposes of this clause, salts, esters, ethers, polymorphs, metabolites, pure form, particle size, isomers, mixtures of isomers, complexes, combinations and other derivatives of known substance shall be considered to be the same substance, unless they differ significantly in properties with regard to efficacy. India reconfirmed the necessity for "therapeutic efficacy" as part of the inventive step criteria in relation to pharmaceuticals in response to questioning from, among others, the EU, United States, Japan, Australia and Switzerland. See Trade Policy Review India, Minutes of the Meeting, WT/TPR/M/313/Add.1, 31 July 2015, at 102–3.

[149] Peter Leung, "Most India Pharma Patent Denials Due to Single Provision," *BNA International Trade Daily* (28 July 2016).

[150] *Novartis AG v. Union of India*, paras. 12 and 19.

It is also in Hong Kong's overall interest as a strong proponent of IPRs and good international citizen to promote and encourage the pharmaceutical industry to invest R&D into existing drugs leading to the creation of new and useful products that benefit human health. It would seem to be a great pity if the potential of such research remains dormant due to lack of incentives and potential financial reward. That said, second and further use patents will not directly benefit the industry in Hong Kong, nor will they lead to any strengthening of the industry. Instead, the result will be that monopolies will be extended and thus Hong Kong will pay more for pharmaceuticals. For these reasons, it is strongly recommended that in adopting second and further use patents the government think carefully about how and to what extent it provides the additional protection, and then to pay attention to the drafting of the relevant legislation. The above analysis presents several models and argues for the adoption of a model that ensures manufacturing, use and prescription of the first use is legitimate and lawful and that also sets some standards for the grant of a second or further use patents and discourages evergreening so as to reward only true innovations that benefit human health.

3.6   Concluding Remarks

In moving from a registration to examination patent system, Hong Kong will need to better consider how the Patents Ordinance and its interpretation can reflect the territory's needs and developmental objectives in relation to patentability standards. Hong Kong is not an innovative pharmaceutical center, and without systemic and coordinated government efforts it will never be so. Neither is Hong Kong seeking to conflate industrial and health policy as a driver of pharmaceutical patents. Instead, Hong Kong should be concerned about its aging population and the steady rise in the costs of medicines. For this reason, Hong Kong should ensure that its transition to an examination system is accompanied by strict patentability standards that fully respect prevailing international standards while at the same time guard against overprotection and interests that run counter to those of the territory. This chapter provided comprehensive analysis of the most pressing patentability issues and made several recommendations that will assist Hong Kong in establishing a fair, predictable and efficient system based on a holistic view of health and other local priorities.

Extension of Patent Term for Pharmaceutical Products

4.1 Introduction

The availability of patent protection is essential to the innovative pharmaceutical industry as it provides incentives to engage in the R&D of new products. In order to encourage and reward innovation and the advancement of science, patents provide the inventor with the exclusive right to prevent third parties from making, using, offering for sale, selling or importing for these purposes the patented product or process. Such rights are fundamental to the proper functioning of a patent regime and are entrenched in Article 28 of the TRIPS Agreement. To safeguard these rights, Article 33 of the TRIPS Agreement requires that Members grant patent protection for a period of at least twenty years from the date of the patent application, this being generally in line with the term of protection granted by large industrialized countries prior to the advent of the Agreement.[1] The idea behind the set period of market exclusivity is obviously to allow inventors to recoup R&D costs and profit from the invention – thereby giving the incentive for continued creation and scientific advancement. While the patent term is ordinarily twenty years from the date of filing a patent application, in regard to pharmaceuticals the effective patent term[2] is significantly shorter due to delay resulting in the granting of the patent and/or from the health authorities in granting marketing approval for the pharmaceutical product. In fact, it takes on average between eight and twelve years to fulfill the requirements

---

[1] The TRIPS Agreement uses wording similar to that of Article 63.1 of the EPC. Other countries, including the United States and Canada, previously had provided protection for a period of seventeen years from the date of the grant.

[2] "Effective patent term" means the period from the date of approval of the product until the original expiration date of the patent.

necessary to gain marketing approval, meaning the effective patent term is on average eight to twelve years.[3]

The system of patent term extension (PTE) serves to compensate pharmaceutical companies/inventors for the loss during the period of regulatory delay. The PTE system is not explicitly recognized in the multilateral treaties such as the TRIPS Agreement or the Paris Convention;[4] instead, countries have introduced PTE on their own accord, and, more recently, PTEs have been included as part of IP obligations in FTAs. The most notable proponents of PTEs are the United States and the EU, both of which were earlier adopters of the system (United States in 1984 and the EU in 1992) and now export it to other counties via trade agreements.[5] Regionally, most of the more advanced economies have introduced PTE, including Australia,[6] Japan,[7] Singapore,[8] South Korea[9] and Taiwan.[10] The

---

[3] This often-cited figure can be found in, among other publications, European Commission, "Pharmaceuticals Sector Fiche" (16 December 2011), http://trade.ec.europa.eu/doclib/docs/2012/january/tradoc_148988.pdf, accessed 4 March 2017.

[4] It should be noted that Article 5 *bis* of Paris Convention contains a provision on patent restoration; however, it merely addresses the failure of the timely payment of fees for the maintenance of patent rights. Likewise, Article 11 of the WIPO Patent Law Treaty of 2000 provides relief in respect of time limits regarding an application for a patent. See WIPO, Patent Law Treaty, www.wipo.int/treaties/en/ip/plt/.

[5] For a fascinating historical record of the debate over term extension, see US Office of Technology Assessment, "Patent Term Extension and the Pharmaceutical Industry," NTIS order #PB82-100918 (August 1981), http://ota.fas.org/reports/8119.pdf, accessed 22 February 2017 (offering analysis of declining effective patent terms, effect of generic competition to innovation and benefits/costs of term extension).

[6] Australia attempts to provide pharmaceutical patents with an effective term of fifteen years. More specifically, Section 70 of Patent Act allows for applications for one PTE (to be made within six months of the date of the patent or marketing approval, whichever is later) where at least five years has elapsed between the period beginning on the date the patent was granted and ending on the first regulatory approval date for the substance and for those products where the term of patent has not been previously extended. The term of extension is equal to the period beginning on the date of the patent and ending on the first regulatory approval date of said pharmaceutical, reduced by five years, and not exceeding five years. See Articles 70, 71 and 77 of the Patent Act 1990 No. 83, 1990 (amended as of 2017), available from the Australian Government's Federal Register of legislation, www.legislation.gov.au/Details/C2017C00045, accessed 8 March 2017.

[7] Japan introduced PTE for a period not exceeding five years in 1987 to compensate for delays associated with marketing approval. See Patent Act, Article 67(2); Japan Patent Office, Revised Examination Guidelines for "Patent Term Extension," 1 (25 November 2014), www.jpo.go.jp/iken_e/pdf/pharmaceutical_141008_result/revised.pdf, accessed 22 February 2017. For further information, see Nari Lee, "Patent Term Extension in Japan in Light of the Pacific Capsule Decision' (2011) 42(4) *International Review of Intellectual Property and Competition Law* 442; William T. Christiansen II, "Patent Term Extension of Pharmaceuticals in Japan: So You Say You Want to Rush That Generic Drug to Market in Japan ... Good Luck!" (1997) 6 *Pacific Rim Law & Policy Journal* 613, 618.

structure of PTE differs among its adherents, but the intention behind PTE is shared – to counteract patent term erosion owing to regulatory delays as well as the expensive, complicated and lengthy premarketing approval testing necessary in order to bring a new pharmaceutical product to market.

On the one hand, this makes sense as the precious twenty-year patent clock begins not with the grant of the patent or of marketing approval but on the filing of the patent. Delays in the granting of a patent or marketing approval can significantly undercut the profits of a pharmaceutical product and reduce the incentive of the industry to invest in new medicines. On the other hand, issues involving affordability and accessibility to medicines mean that granting a PTE raises public health concerns. This tension between industry and wider community health concerns leads to the inevitable problem regarding how to reconcile the private or commercial interests of pharmaceutical industry with the public interests of consumers and patients. For this reason, the PTE system is not without criticism.

Hong Kong does not currently provide for PTE. This chapter seeks to ascertain whether Hong Kong should adopt PTE as it moves to a patent examination system. The chapter first briefly reviews the patent term restoration system in the United States and the supplementary protection certificate (SPC) in the EU and the incorporation of PTE into FTAs. The

---

[8] In line with the US-Singapore FTA, Singapore introduced PTE in June 2004, with Article 36A of the Singapore Patent Act granting a PTE for not more than five years where (a) there was an unreasonable delay in granting the patent; (b) where the patent was granted on the basis of prescribed information relating to a corresponding application, there was an unreasonable delay in the issuance/grant of the corresponding application, and the term of the corresponding application has been extended as a result of the delay; and (c) for a pharmaceutical product, there was an unreasonable curtailment of the opportunity to exploit the patent due to the process of obtaining marketing approval for a pioneering pharmaceutical product, and the term of the patent has not previously been extended because of the aforementioned delays. See Patent Act (Chapter 221) (Original Enactment: Act 21 of 1994), revised edition of 2005, https://goo.gl/FEj45a, accessed 8 March 2017.

[9] South Korea allows for a PTE for up to five years for delays in marketing approval as well as an extension for delays in the patent registration of over four years from the date of filing or three years from the examination request. See Patent Act, Act No. 950, 31 December 1961, Art. 89(1), amended by Act No. 11117, Dec. 2, 2011; Patent Act, Art. 92–2, added by Act No. 11117, 2 December 2011, respectively.

[10] Article 53 of Taiwan's Patent Act provides for a one-time PTE not exceeding five years for pharmaceuticals and agrichemicals (but not veterinary drugs), or the manufacturing process thereof, when the regulatory approval is obtained after the publication of the patent. See Intellectual Property Office of the Ministry of Economic Affairs, Patent Act (as amended in 2014) www.tipo.gov.tw/public/Data/691415513771.pdf, accessed 8 March 2017.

US and EU systems have been selected for review as both reflect typical systems of PTE for pharmaceutical products currently in operation and have served as a model in FTAs. Next, the chapter will review how the United States and EU have incorporated PTE provisions into FTAs. Having surveyed the current framework, Section 4.3 then discusses whether Hong Kong should adopt PTE and, if so, recommends some general principles for the jurisdiction to follow when crafting its PTE regime. Section 4.4 concludes.

4.2   Patent Term Extensions for Pharmaceutical Products: The United States and the EU

This section will briefly describe the rules and mechanism established in the United States and EU for the extension of patent term beyond the normal twenty-year period. The United States and EU are used as examples here as they represent the most widely disseminated models of PTEs for pharmaceutical products and have been replicated by numerous other countries.

4.2.1   The US Regime for Patent Term Extensions

The US patent system has several mechanisms available for adjusting the patent term. Most prominent among them are an adjustment due to delays in the review process by the Patent and Trademark Office (PTO) and for delays in the regulatory review process for marketing approval by the Food and Drug Administration (FDA). The United States provides for different and separate provisions regulating these two types of PTE.

Patent Term Extension for Delays at the Patent Office

Prior to the TRIPS Agreement, the United States granted a term of patent protection for a period of seventeen years from the date of the issuance of the patent. With the enactment of the Uruguay Round Agreement Act, the United States amended the patent term to twenty years from the date of filing in order to comply with obligations under the TRIPS Agreement.[11] As the exact period of patent protection is not preset, but rather depends on the length of time taken by the PTO in examining the patent, patent

---

[11] See 35 USC 154 Contents and term of patent; provisional rights, www.gpo.gov/fdsys/granule/USCODE-2011-title35/USCODE-2011-title35-partII-chap14-sec154, accessed 8 March 2017, particularly para. (a)(2).

owners are uncertain about the exact periods of effective patent term. This concern is exacerbated in relation to pharmaceuticals, where a patent must be applied for early in the R&D process, and often before stage 2 and stage 3 clinical trials.

In response to industry concern regarding the unpredictability of effective patent term, the Patent Term Guarantee Act (1999) provides for an adjustment of patent term in order to compensate the rights holder for delays caused by the PTO's review of patent application. More specifically, Section 154(b) provides for three types of delays that could trigger an adjustment of patent term.[12] The first delay is the failure of the PTO to take certain actions by specified deadlines, such as failure to notify or respond to a reply within specific periods of time.[13] When such delay occurs, Section 154(b) provides that the term of the patent shall be extended one day for each day after the end of specified period until the action prescribed is taken. Second, if the PTO fails to issue a patent within three years of the actual filing date of the application, the term of the patent shall be extended one day for each day after the end of that three-year period until the patent is issued.[14] Third, a one-day adjustment is added to the patent term for each day that the patent application is delayed due to the pendency of derivation proceedings, secrecy orders and successful appeals.[15]

The adjustment periods are cumulative, and the law does not provide a ceiling on the maximum amount of time that can be added to the patent term.[16] Moreover, the periods of adjustment are automatically determined by the PTO – meaning the patent owner need not request an extension,[17] but the applicant does have the opportunity to request reconsideration of

---

[12] For more detailed information, see Stephanie Plamondon Bair, "Adjustments, Extensions, Disclaimers, and Continuations: When Do Patent Term Adjustments Make Sense?" (2013) 41 *Capital University Law Review*, 445, 450.

[13] 35 USC 154 (b)(1)(A), above n. 11.   [14] 35 USC 154 (b)(1)(B), above n. 11.

[15] 35 USC 154 (b)(1)(C), above n. 11.

[16] However, the periods of adjustment shall be reduced by a period equal to the time during which the applicant failed to engage in reasonable efforts to conclude the prosecution of the application. See 35 USC 154(2)(C)(i). With respect to the three-year pendency delay (second type), an applicant shall be deemed to have failed to engage in reasonable efforts to conclude procession or examination of an application for the cumulative total of any periods of time in excess of three months that are taken to respond to a notice from the Office making any rejection, objection, argument, or other request, measuring such three-month period from the date the notice was given or mailed to the applicant. See 35 USC 154(2)(C)(ii), above n. 11.

[17] See 35 USC 154(3)(B)(i), above n. 11.

the adjusted patent term and even to appeal the PTO's adjustment determination to the federal court.[18]

Patent Term Extensions for Delays in Marketing Approval

The United States provides an alternative avenue for PTE available only to pharmaceutical products, medical devices and other products subject to regulatory review by the FDA under the Drug Price Competition and Patent Term Restoration Act of 1984 (also called the "Hatch-Waxman Act"). The Hatch-Waxman Act aims to balance the incentive for pharmaceutical innovations with access to new drugs. In essence, the Hatch-Waxman Act resulted from a "grand bargain" that facilitated the early introduction of generic pharmaceuticals into the marketplace in exchange for providing, inter alia, inventor pharmaceutical companies with the possibility of a PTE to compensate for the time taken by clinical trials and the regulatory review process necessary in order to obtain marketing approval.

Patents eligible for PTE include patents for products as well as methods for using or manufacturing products.[19] The PTO has set out clear regulations regarding an extension for a pharmaceutical patent, which include:

(a) the patent must be eligible to extension, namely, the patent claims a product or a method of using or manufacturing a product;

---

[18] See 35 USC 154(3)(B)(ii) and 35 USC 154(4), above n. 11.

[19] The term "product" includes a drug product, any medical device, food additive or color additive subject to regulation under the Federal Food, Drug, and Cosmetic Act. See 35 USC 156 – Extension of Patent Term, www.gpo.gov/fdsys/granule/USCODE-2011-title35/USCODE-2011-title35-partII-chap14-sec156, accessed 8 March 2017, at (f)(1). The term "drug product" means the active ingredient of a new human drug, antibiotic drug, or human biological product including any salt or ester of the active ingredient, as a single entity or in combination with another active ingredient, or the active ingredient of a new animal drug or veterinary biological product that is not primarily manufactured using recombinant DNA, recombinant RNA, hybridoma technology, or other processes including site-specific genetic manipulation techniques, including any salt or ester of the active ingredient, as a single entity or in combination with another active ingredient. See 37 CFR 1.710 – Patents subject to extension of the patent term, www.gpo.gov/fdsys/pkg/CFR-2016-title37-vol1/pdf/CFR-2016-title37-vol1-sec1-710.pdf, accessed 8 March 2017. See also 35 USC 156 (f)(1)–(2). The interpretation of "product" has led to inconsistent decisions at the Federal Court, although recent decisions attempt to provide clarity. See, e.g., *Ortho–McNeil Pharm., Inc. v. Lupin Pharm., Inc.*, 603 F.3d 1377, 1380–81 (Fed. Cir. 2010); *PhotoCure ASA v. Kappos*, 603 F.3d 1372, 1374–76 (Fed. Cir. 2010). These decisions adopt a narrow interpretation of "product" and in doing so arguably expand the range of pharmaceuticals that can benefit from the PTE. For critical analysis of the decisions, see Ann Kotze, "Reining in Patent Term Extensions for Related Pharmaceutical Products Post-Photocure and Ortho-McNeil" (2012) 106 *Northwestern University Law Review* 1419.

(b) the term of the patent has not been previously extended except for interim extensions or extensions due to the delay of the PTO's review process;

(c) an application for extension is submitted by the patent owner of agent;

(d) the product has been subject to a regulatory review period before its commercial marketing or use;

(e) the product has received permission for commercial marketing or use and such permission is the first received permission for commercial marketing or use;

(f) the application is submitted within sixty-day period beginning on the date the product first received permission for commercial marketing or use;

(g) the term of the patent has not expired before the submission of an application; and

(h) no other patent term has been extended for the same regulatory review period for the product.[20]

For a patented pharmaceutical eligible for extension, the patent term can be extended on application by the patent holder by the time equal to the regulatory review period for the approved product.[21] However, the duration of an extended patent is subject to limitations, which include:

(1) the duration of the extension can be reduced if it is determined that the applicant did not act with due diligence during regulatory review period;

(2) after any reduction due to the failure of the applicant to act with due diligence, the period of extension shall include only one-half of the time remaining in the periods of regulatory review;

(3) subject to the above time-period limitations, if the patent term remaining after the date of the FDA approval exceeds fourteen years, the extension shall be reduced so that the total of effective patent term, including original and extended periods, does not exceed fourteen years;[22] and

(4) in no event shall more than one patent be for the same regulatory review period for any product.[23]

---

[20] See 37 CFR 1.720 and 35 USC 156(a), above n. 19.
[21] The "regulatory review period" for a new drug, antibiotic or human biological product refers to the duration of the Investigational New Drug regulatory review period and the New Drug Application regulatory review period. See 35 USC 156(g)(1)(B), above n. 19.
[22] See 35 USC 156(c)(3), above n. 19.   [23] 35 US Code 156(c)(1)–(4), above n. 19.

For patents issued after the enactment of the Hatch-Waxman Act on 24 September 1984 (and those issued before this date but where clinical trials had not commenced), the maximum period of extension is available for five years.[24] If a patent was issued and clinical trials of such drug began prior to 24 September 1984, the maximum extension available is two years.[25]

Thus, the US system offers a maximum of a five-year extension as a result of delays in the marketing approval process, with the effective patent term capped at fourteen years. In practice, marketing approval times in the United States are now relatively quick and the extension provisions are accordingly rarely applied.

4.2.2 Supplementary Protection Certificate System in the EU

Unlike the United States, the EU has adopted a sui generis system of term extension, called a supplementary protection certificate (SPC), which blends IP protection with drug regulation. SPC protection is available to any patented product that must undergo an administrative authorization procedure prior to marketing as a "medical product" for human or veterinary use and operates by combining the two types of PTEs detailed above into a unified system. The system therefore addresses both regulatory delays due to review of the patent application and those relating to the marketing approval process for medical products.[26] The "certificate" takes effect at the end of the regular patent term and extends the same rights to the approved new medical product as conferred by the "basic patent" (and is subject to the same limitations and obligations).[27]

As with the US system, the purpose of an SPC is to compensate the patent owner for the time elapsed after the date of the patent application until the date the product is authorized for sale in the EU market. By granting an SPC, patents for medical products can effectively be extended

---

[24] See 35 USC 156(g)(6)(A)–(B), above n. 19.

[25] See 35 USC 156(g)(6)(C), above n. 19.

[26] See Regulation (EC) No. 469/2009 (formerly EU Regulation 1768/92) of the European Parliament and of the Council of 6 May 2009 concerning the supplementary protection certificate for medicinal products. See also Regulation (EC) No. 1610/96 of the European Parliament and of the Council of 23 July 1996 concerning the creation of a supplementary protection certificate for plant protection products.

[27] "Basic patent" is defined as "a patent which protects a product as such, a process to obtain a product or an application of a product, and which is designated by its holder for the purpose of the procedure for grant of a certificate."

beyond the statutory twenty-year term by up to five years.[28] Again, and unlike the PTE system in the United States, the EU's SPC legislation extends not the patent term but the period of market exclusivity of the medical products. Thus, the SPC offers similar protection for the patent owner through the denial of marketing approval to generic competitors while the SPC is in force.

Under the regulations, an applicant that applies within six months from the date the product received marketing authorization (or the patent was granted, if later in time) shall be granted a certificate if the medical product for which it was requested meets the following conditions at the time when the application was filed in a Member State where the basic patent has been issued and where the authorization to place the medical product on the market was obtained:

(a) the product is protected by a "basic patent" in force;
(b) the product, as a medicinal product, has been granted a valid marketing authorization;
(c) the product has not already been the subject of a certificate; and
(d) the marketing authorization is the first authorization to place the product on the market as a medicinal product.[29]

Unlike the US system, the duration of certificate is determined by combining regulatory delays due to the patent review process *and* the marketing approval for medical products. In essence, the duration of certificate – and thus the PTE – is equal to the period elapsed between the date of the patent application and the date of the first authorization to place the

---

[28] If the medical product has been tested for suitability for children, the SPC can be extended by an additional six months. See Regulation (EC) No. 1901/2006 of the European Parliament and of the Council of 12 December 2006 on medicinal products for pediatric use and amending Regulation (EEC) No. 1768/92; see also Directive 2001/20/EC of 4 April 2001 on the approximation of the laws, regulations and administrative provisions of the Member States relating to the implementation of good clinical practice in the conduct of clinical trials on medicinal products for human use; Directive 2001/83/EC of 6 November 2001 on the Community code relating to medicinal products for human use and Regulation (EC) No. 726/2004 of 31 March 2004 laying down Community procedures for the authorization and supervision of medicinal products for human and veterinary use and establishing a European Medicines Agency.

[29] Regulation (EC) 469/2009, above n. 26, Article 3. Applications to extend the duration of the SPC must be filed no later than two years before the expiration of the certificate. See also Article 7(4).

product on the market, reduced by a period of five years.[30] Importantly, as a safeguard against overprotection, the duration of the certificate may not exceed five years from the date on which it takes effect.[31] This means that the holder of the patent and SPC will benefit from an overall maximum of period of fifteen years' protection from the date at which the pharmaceutical first gains the authorization to be placed on the EU market.

4.2.3   Patent Term Extension in Free Trade Agreements

Despite not being required under the TRIPS Agreement, FTAs have for some time addressed PTE for pharmaceuticals. As highlighted above, both the United States and the EU attempt to export their respective models of PTE via trade agreements. Despite some differences among these FTAs, some trends regarding PTE can be noted and warrant further discussion.

From a Hortatory Norm to Mandatory Obligation

Until its incorporation into the NAFTA in 1993, PTEs had never been included as a mandatory obligation in an international agreement. Even in the NAFTA, Article 1709(12) simply provides a hortatory norm regarding the implementation of PTE as the parties find appropriate: "[The parties] may extend the term of patent protection, in appropriate cases, to compensate for delays caused by regulatory approval processes." The parties to the NAFTA therefore retain the discretion to decide whether or how to implement the PTE system in their respective jurisdictions.

The United States only maintained this approach in the early years of its FTA strategy,[32] with subsequent FTAs almost always imposing a mandatory obligation on partner countries to implement PTE with little room for policy space. With the Trade Promotion Agreements (TPAs) negotiated

---

[30]   Ibid., Article 13(1). The certificate can expire early if the certificate holder surrenders it; the annual fee is not paid on time; or the product covered by the certificate is no longer to be placed on the market. See ibid., at Article 14.

[31]   Ibid., Article 13(2). In cases where the medical products meet the requirements of pediatric use, an extra six months can be added to original certificate, but the duration of the period may be extended only once. See also Article 13(3), referencing Article 36 of Regulation (EC) No. 1901/2006, above n. 28.

[32]   See the list of the US FTAs on the website of the Office of the United States Trade Representative, https://ustr.gov/trade-agreements/free-trade-agreements. For instance, the US FTA with Jordan, Article 4.23.

in the late 2000s with Panama, Peru and Colombia as the exceptions,[33] mandatory PTE provisions have become a fixture in US trade agreements (whether concluded with developed or developing partners) and in relation to delays in the marketing approval process are also included in the ill-fated mega-regional TPP.[34] Likewise, while the EU has in the past negotiated FTAs with developing countries that make PTE optional, its normal practice is to include a system based on the SPC to be in its FTAs with partner countries.

The Template Approach to PTE for Delays Relating to the Granting of a Patent or Marketing Approval

The US FTA model requires PTEs to compensate the patent holder in the case of an "unreasonable delay" in the issuance of a patent, at the request of the patent owner.[35] The phrase "unreasonable delay" is often accompanied with a definition of what would constitute an unreasonable as opposed to reasonable delay. The exact periods of delay vary among different agreements. Most often, an unreasonable delay is defined as the lapse of four years from the date of filing of the patent application or two years after a request for examination of the application, whichever is later.[36] In other agreements, the periods of unreasonable delay are five years from the date of filing or three years after the request, whichever is later.[37] The Korea-United States Free Trade Agreement (KORUS), however, contains a different definition where a delay is considered as unreasonable if there is a

---

[33] In US TPAs with Peru, Panama and Colombia, PTE is optional for unreasonable curtailment of patent term caused by delays in the marketing approval process. However, PTE remains mandatory for unreasonable delays in the issuance of the patent.

[34] See the Trans-Pacific Partnership, Article 18.48, available from the New Zealand Foreign Affairs and Trade website, www.mfat.govt.nz/en/about-us/who-we-are/treaties/trans-pacific-partnership-agreement-tpp/text-of-the-trans-pacific-partnership, accessed 8 March 2017.

[35] The standardized wording is as follows: "Each Party, at the request of the patent owner, shall adjust the term of a patent to compensate for unreasonable delays that occur in granting the patent." See, e.g., KORUS, Article 18.8.8(a); US-Bahrain FTA, Article 14.8.6(a); US-Oman FTA, Article 15.8.6(a). Article 17.9.8(a) of the AUSFTA contains a slight variation: "If there are unreasonable delays in a Party's issuance of patents, that Party shall provide the means to, and at the request of a patent owner, shall, adjust the term of the patent to compensate for such delays."

[36] See AUSFTA, Article 17.9.8(a); US-Bahrain FTA, Article 14.8.6(a); US-Oman FTA, Article 15.8.6(a); US-Morocco FTA, Article 15.9.7; and US-Singapore FTA, Article 16.7.7.

[37] See Article 15.9.6(a) of the US-CAFTA-DR FTA; Article 17.9.6 of the US-Chile FTA; Article 16.9.6(a) of the US-Peru TPA; and Article 15.9.6(a) of the US-Panama TPA.

lapse of four years from the date of filing the application or three years after a request for examination, whichever is later.[38] Another provision frequently incorporated into US FTAs requires a country that relies on the examination and prior grant of patent in another jurisdiction to extend the patent term by a period equal to the period of extension granted by the authority in the original granting jurisdiction.[39]

In addition, US FTAs provide that where a pharmaceutical product is covered by a patent,[40] each party shall make available an adjustment/extension/restoration[41] of the patent term to compensate for the patent owner for "*unreasonable* curtailment" of the effective patent term as a result of the marketing approval process.[42] Unlike the first ground of extension, most FTAs do not provide clear guidance on the definition of "unreasonable curtailment" of the patent term. Such lack of clarity could lead to interpretive difficulties. For instance, is any delay automatically considered as unreasonable curtailment, or are delays resulting from clinical trials or where the regulator requests additional information an unreasonable curtailment of the "effective patent term"? Or is the definition of what constitutes an unreasonable curtailment decided by each party at its own discretion? These questions, and many others, are simply left unaddressed.

Yet another area of slight concern is that most US FTAs do not address whether the adjustment/extension/restoration applies to delays in the country where the marketing approval is sought or whether delays in the

---

[38] Time may be subtracted from the calculation of delay if the delay is attributable to actions of the patent applicant. In other words, if the delay of the issuance of patent was caused by the applicant, it will not be counted in determining the unreasonableness of such delay.

[39] See, e.g., US-Bahrain FTA, Article 14.8.7; US-Oman FTA, Article 15.8.7. See, contra, the US-Singapore FTA, which states that an extension of up to five years due to unreasonable delay for prior grant in another jurisdiction "may" be granted; there is thus no legally binding obligation to extend the patent term due to the unreasonable delay for prior grant of patent in another jurisdiction. US-Singapore FTA, Article 16.7.8.

[40] Unlike the first ground of extension, which applies to patents in all kinds of fields and any products or process, this extension applies only to pharmaceutical products subject to patent protection.

[41] The terms "adjustment," "extension" and "restoration" have all been used in US FTAs.

[42] For example, Article 17.9.8(b) of the AUSFTA provides: "With respect to a pharmaceutical product that is subject to a patent, each Party shall make available an adjustment of the patent term to compensate the patent owner for unreasonable curtailment of the effective patent term as a result of the marketing approval process." See, e.g., US-Bahrain FTA, Article 14.8.6(b)(i) (which substitutes the word "extension" for "adjustment" but is otherwise a replica of the other texts), and TPP, Article 18.48(2) (repeating the wording of the AUSFTA).

country where the first approval was obtained should also be taken into account. While the former interpretation would seem to be the most reasonable, the US FTA with Bahrain obliges the parties to take into account delays in the foreign country.[43] Curiously, US FTAs do not set out the maximum time period for the adjustment/extension/restoration. This is in contradistinction to US law, which sets out a time limit of not more than five years, with the additional safeguard of a maximum exclusivity period of fourteen years from the date of FDA approval.[44] Finally, while US law limits this extension to one patent per product, its FTAs provide no such limitation. While US partner countries can of course legislate for a similar restriction, the point here is simply that while US law provides safeguards, these provisions are lacking in the text of FTAs.

Using its own system as a template, the EU has been not only later to negotiate for PTE in its FTAs but also not as consistent. That being said, it is clear that the EU provisions are closely modeled on the concept of the SPC and in general seek an additional protection for a period of five years. For instance, Article 10–35.2 of the EU-Korea FTA provides an example of typical EU drafting:

> The Parties *shall provide*, at the request of the patent owner, for the extension of the duration of the rights conferred by the patent protection to compensate the patent owner for the reduction in the effective patent life as a result of the first authorization to place the product on their respective markets. The extension of the duration of the rights conferred by the patent protection may not exceed *five years*. [emphasis added]

The approach negotiated with Canada in the Canada-European Union Comprehensive Economic and Trade Agreement (CETA) is more nuanced and calls for sui generis protection equal to the period that elapsed between the date on which the application for a patent was filed and the date of the first authorization to place the product on the market of that party as a pharmaceutical product, reduced by a period of five years.[45]

---

[43] More specifically, where a party approves the marketing of a new pharmaceutical product on the basis of information concerning the safety or efficacy of a same or a similar product in another territory, such as evidence of prior marketing approval, the party shall make available a PTE to compensate the patent owner for unreasonable curtailment of the effective patent term in the party as a result of the marketing approval process in the other territory and in the party. See, e.g., US-Bahrain FTA, Art. 14.8.6(b)(ii).

[44] See 35 USC 156, above n. 19.

[45] Canada-European Union Comprehensive Economic and Trade Agreement (CETA) Article 9.2(4). The consolidated version of CETA as of 14 September 2016 is available from the European Council of the European Union, http://data.consilium.europa.eu/doc/document/ST-10973-2a016-INIT/en/pdf, accessed 8 March 2017.

Moreover, and despite the aforementioned requirement, "the duration of the sui generis protection may not exceed a period of two to five years, to be established by each Party."[46] While the EU will undoubtedly opt for five years' protection in line with domestic law, it has been reported that Canada will limit the extension to a period of two years.[47] Having never before legislated domestically for or negotiated PTE into FTAs, Canada is obviously attempting to limit the effects of the extension. The CETA is also more comprehensive than other EU FTAs, with Article 9.2(2) providing safeguards such as explicitly limiting the PTE provision to the first application for authorization to place the product on their market and to one extension per product. Moreover, and quite exceptionally, Article 9.2(5) contains an exception for generic drugs that are produced for export.

With certain developing countries, the EU has made PTE optional. This is the case in Article 223.4 of the EU-Columbia-Peru FTA:

> With respect to any pharmaceutical product that is covered by a patent, each Party *may*, in accordance with its domestic legislation, make available a mechanism to compensate the patent owner for unreasonable curtailment of the effective patent term resulting from the first marketing approval of that product in that Party. Such mechanism under this subparagraph shall confer all of the exclusive rights of a patent subject to the same limitations and exceptions applicable to the original patent. [emphasis added]

Here again, the EU practice is not standardized. For example, Article 17 of the proposed (and long delayed) EU-India FTA requires a PTE to be granted for a period equaling the time "between the filing of the application for a patent and the first authorization to place the product on their respective markets . . . reduced by a period of five years." While this is similar to the wording used in the CETA, it does not provide for the possibility of limiting protection to between two and five years.

4.3 Patent Term Extension in Hong Kong

Hong Kong does not grant PTEs for delays in either granting a patent or in the marketing approval process. With the coming shift to an examination patent system, the time is ripe for the territory to reconsider the

---

[46] Ibid.

[47] See Noel Courage, "Canadian Patent Term Extension – The Treaty Text is Released," Bereskin & Parr, 2 December 2014, www.bereskinparr.com/index.cfm?cm=Doc&ce=downloadPDF&primaryKey=481, accessed 22 February 2017.

issue. The issue has in fact been raised in Hong Kong, with both the American Chamber of Commerce and the Hong Kong Association of the Pharmaceutical Association calling for the government to introduce PTE for pharmaceuticals, substantiating their calls with the familiar reasoning of compensation to inventors, promotion of innovation and as a way to encourage investment and R&D in the jurisdiction.[48] On the other hand, critics would argue that PTE would bring few if any benefits to Hong Kong while costing the government (via the Hospital Authority) millions of dollars per year.[49]

The actual impact of PTE will largely depend on the content of specific rules and is difficult to evaluate without a holistic overview of the system. Nonetheless, it is obvious that the adoption of PTE could affect the various stakeholders – including patent holders, innovative pharmaceutical companies, generic pharmaceutical companies and patients – differently. While it is clear that innovative pharmaceutical companies and their licensees will benefit from any extension of the patent or monopoly selling period, conversely, generic pharmaceutical companies will suffer as they are delayed entry into the market. As the Hospital Authority purchases the vast majority of pharmaceuticals for the Hong Kong market, PTE will at first instance increase its costs as competition will be delayed. How much this will cost is debatable, as at present generic pharmaceutical companies do not usually apply for marketing authority until after the expiration of the patent, despite there being no barrier to submitting an application and gaining marketing approval during the life of the patent. The practical effect of this is that the introduction of generics into the market is delayed for a period regardless of any patent or associated legislation or regulations.

Another relevant point to consider is that at present both the registration of a patent and the granting of marketing approval are fairly quick in Hong Kong. Neither the granting of a pharmaceutical patent nor

---

[48] See AmCham, "Submission on the Consultation Paper on the Review of the Patent System in Hong Kong," American Chamber of Commerce in Hong Kong, available at www.cedb.gov.hk/citb/doc/en/submissions_list/070.pdf, accessed 22 February 2017; see also the Hong Kong Association of the Pharmaceutical Industry, "Position Paper of the Hong Kong Association of the Pharmaceutical Industry on the Review of the Patent System in Hong Kong," www.hkapi.hk/images/newsletter/Patent%20System%20in%20Hong%20Kong_30012012_161233.pdf, accessed 22 February 2017.

[49] According to one researcher, PTE lengthens protection for an average of 3.6 years and could account for up to 20 percent of annual pharmaceutical sales in the United States. See Charles Clift, "The Value of Patent Term Extensions to the Pharmaceutical Industry in the USA" (2008) 5 *Journal of Generic Medicines* 201.

the marketing approval process takes anywhere near as long a time period to trigger an "unreasonable delay" of the granting of the patent or "unreasonable curtailment" of the effective patent term due to the marketing approval process. The move to an examination system in Hong Kong will undoubtedly add time to the process, and it remains to be seen whether the Intellectual Property Department (IPD) will suffer from "unreasonable delays" in the future that reduce the effective patent term beyond a period of five years so as to trigger the PTE. Regardless, the self-examination process should not impact the time it takes for the Department of Health to grant marketing approval; thus, it is not anticipated that legislation providing for PTE in this regard would have any practical effect.

In essence, there is no easy way to determine the costs and benefits of PTE for Hong Kong. This will be the case for several years, until the amount of time it takes the IPD to examine pharmaceutical patents becomes clear. As with many issues, the reality is that Hong Kong's adoption or otherwise of PTE will have no impact on the innovative capacities and productivity of the pharmaceutical industry. Simply stated, the market is far too small and capacity for growth too limited to be of any consequence. Thus, while the US and EU adoption of PTE has arguably improved (or could improve) innovation in the industry and led to the development and marketing of drugs that would otherwise have been dormant, smaller jurisdictions are in a very different position. Even if one takes the position that in the longer term all stakeholders – including generic firms, the government and patients – benefit from a healthy and innovative pharmaceutical industry that produces a steady stream of new drugs and that if PTE leads to more innovative drugs being produced and marketed, the cost of the extra period of monopoly sales could be defrayed and significantly outweighed, no one can argue that Hon Kong's adoption of PTE will have any meaningful effect on this outcome.

Other governments have recently struggled with this issue. For example, a report commissioned by the former Australian government (and ignored by the current government) attempted to value PTE by linking it with pharmaceutical R&D expenditures in Australia, finding that while Australia contributes around 2 percent of global revenues for pharmaceutical companies, Australia received only approximately 0.3 percent (or AU$1 billion) of global pharmaceutical R&D expenditures. Thus, while Australia is paying for pharmaceuticals – in part through extended patent terms – it is not benefiting through investment in Australian R&D. This reasoning seems wholly flawed. Australian expenditures on pharmaceuticals are far higher than the corresponding level of pharmaceutical R&D

investment in Australia, but this does not mean that Australia does not benefit from a wider array of innovative and life-saving pharmaceutical products. Nor could every single country expect to host high levels of pharmaceutical R&D. The level of R&D is tied to other factors, such as investment incentives, skilled workforce and costs. There is no evidence that supports the claim that PTE leads to greater R&D expenditures in the host country, nor quite frankly could one expect there to be a causal link.

The question then becomes one of cost and potential savings. The Australian report then finds net savings of approximately AU\$50 million per year for each year of reduction in the term extension. More specifically, the report finds savings of AU\$45 million from a reduction in extension from five to four years, savings of AU\$95 million with a reduction to three years, up to \$244 million through the elimination of PTE. With an annual expenditure of more than AU\$9.25 billion for pharmaceuticals in 2012, the savings from a one-year reduction in term would represent 0.005 percent of the budget, while the complete elimination of PTE would represent only 2.6 percent of the budget. While not insignificant, the numbers demonstrate that PTE is not a significant burden nor would its reduction or elimination change the outlook of a health budget.

The percentages in Hong Kong would likely not substantially differ and could be far less depending on the rapidity with which the IPD examines the patent applications. Thus, even if Hong Kong would have some increased outlay for PTE, the cost would be minimal when put into the context of overall pharmaceutical expenditures. Moreover, while it may not be in Hong Kong's economic interest to provide for PTEs, as it will not by itself lead to increased R&D in the territory, the international trend toward PTE is clear. As Hong Kong prides itself as a jurisdiction with a high standard of IPRs and respect for the rule of law, it may be in its (perceived) reputational interest to enact some form of PTE. Moreover, if Hong Kong continues to negotiate FTAs, it is only a matter time before a partner requests or demands that the territory provide for PTE. It would be a better public policy outcome if the issues were discussed and debated internally before being imposed from an external source. For this reason, it is worth discussing several aspects of PTE to come up with general principles that should guide Hong Kong's potential (and perhaps eventual) adoption of the provision.

The most significant concern in PTE for Hong Kong would be that of overprotection, that is, providing extensions too easily and/or for too long a time period. Therefore, an important consideration must be protection against the creation of a regime that would provide protection for far too long, with the cost outweighing any potential benefits. For this reason, if Hong Kong were to consider adopting PTE, it should follow some general principles to ensure a proper balance of interests. While PTE provisions have become more extensive in scope and specific in details in recently concluded FTAs, variations within existing agreements may accommodate a balance of interests. In fact, most, if not all, of the principles that should guide Hong Kong can be drawn from provisions in existing FTAs.

The first issue to be decided, however, is whether to adopt an EU-style sui generis system of protection or a US-type system. While both are designed specifically to address failures in the patent system to differentiate pharmaceutical patents (with the extra hurdle of regulatory approval) from other patents, they go about it in very different ways. That being the case, in most respects a jurisdiction can reach the same outcome with either approach. There does not appear to be much difference in substance as opposed to form between the two systems.

The more important issues are found in the substance of the additional protection. Several issues must be addressed, and in order to highlight the most important issues that need to be considered and addressed, it is best to present them separately in a list.

- The duration of the PTE: What is the optimal duration and how should the duration of the PTE be determined? In line with prevailing practice of the EU and US domestic law, Hong Kong should limit a PTE to a period not exceeding five years in order to avoid prolonging the patent term and unfairly curtailing market access for generic medicines. In addition, Hong Kong should follow the US and EU approach of setting a maximum period of postmarketing authorization exclusivity. While that period is set at fourteen years in the United States and fifteen years in the EU (and Australia),[50] Hong Kong should thoroughly study the market before deciding on a figure for the desired effective term. It must be stated, however, that there does not appear any reason for Hong Kong

---

[50] The members of the Australian review agreed the term should be shortened, with two members recommending a ten-year period and one member proposing a twelve-year period of effective protection. See Australia Patent Review, at 84–85. Interestingly, Israel provides an extension for both basic and related pharmaceutical patents for up to five years and at the same time ensures that patents granted in "recognized countries" (currently the United States, Britain, Italy, Germany, Spain and France) are protected for at least fourteen years from the first marketing approval in the recognized country. See Israeli Patents Law, 5727–1967, S 64J.

to provide a longer period of protection than the United States and EU, but perhaps it may want to look at providing a shorter period given that whatever period is set, it will have little effect on overall investment incentives in the market.[51] Of course, it should also be noted that in reality reducing the effective term may result in little economic benefit as firms could simply adjust pricing in response.

- The PTE should not be automatic and should be limited: The system should make the PTE dependent on an application by the rights holder prior to the expiration of the basic patent and only on pharmaceuticals for the first marketing approval process. In addition, each new pharmaceutical product should benefit from only a single patent term adjustment/extension. While both the United States and EU limit eligibility for PTE, they do not always include such limitations in their respective FTAs. Hong Kong should ensure that such limitations form part of the domestic law.

- Eligibility for a PTE: PTE should be limited so as to apply only to patents covering a "new pharmaceutical product," defined as a product that at least contains a new chemical entity that has not been previously approved as a pharmaceutical product in the territory of the party. The PTE should therefore be granted on the new product per se, as opposed to a process to obtain a product or the use of a product. While PTE most often normally applies to any pharmaceutical product that is covered by a patent, narrowing the eligibility is a way to achieve the policy goals of encouraging the development of truly "innovative" pharmaceutical products without sacrificing too much consumer interest or access to

---

[51] A plethora of literature exists on the quest for an effective patent term, but consensus has not emerged. See, for instance, Fritz Machlup, "An Economic Review of the Patent System," Study of the Subcommittee on Patents, Trademarks, and Copyrights of the Committee on the Judiciary, United States Senate, 85th Congress, Second Session (1958); F.M. Scherer, "Nordhaus' Theory of Optimal Patent Life: A Geometric Reinterpretation," (1972) 62 *American Economic Review* 422; William Nordhaus, "The Optimum Life of a Patent: Reply" (1972) 62(3) *American Economic Review* 428; Louis Kaplow, "The Patent-Antitrust Intersection: A Reappraisal" (1984) 97 *Harvard Law Review* 1815; Richard Gilbert and Carl Shapiro, "Optimal Patent Length and Breadth" (1990) 21 *RAND Journal of Economics*, 106–12; and Suzanne Scotchmer, "Standing on the Shoulders of Giants: Cumulative Research and the Patent Law" (1991) 5 *Journal of Economic Perspectives* 29. See also Neel U. Sukhatme and Judd N. L. Cramer, "Who Cares about Patent Term? Cross-Industry Differences in Term Sensitivity" (2014), http://scholar.princeton.edu/sites/default/files/sukhatme/files/sukhatme_who_cares_about_patent_term_0.pdf, accessed 4 March 2017 (finding significant variances in the sensitivity of patent term across industries and supporting "conventional wisdom that pharmaceutical applicants are especially sensitive to patent term").

medicines. There is precedent for such a limitation, most prominently in the KORUS.[52] Therefore, PTE should be granted only for a new pharmaceutical product containing a "new chemical entity" and on the "first marketing approval" for the pharmaceutical product in the territory.

- Further conditional eligibility: In order to promote the availability of new pharmaceutical products in the jurisdiction, as a condition of eligibility for a PTE Hong Kong should require a patent holder/applicant to commence the process of obtaining marketing approval for the new pharmaceutical product within a certain number of years from the date of the first marketing approval of the same pharmaceutical product in another country. While the optimal period of time can be debated, it would seem a two- to three-year period would be sufficient to encourage quick registration in Hong Kong, meaning early access to drugs and then to generic equivalents.[53] Thus, if marketing approval in Hong Kong is not sought within the prescribed period, the product would not be eligible to receive the one-time PTE.

- Limitation on the grounds for an extension: The effective patent life may be curtailed by different types of regulatory delays in patent examination and drug marketing approval. Regulations should ensure that PTE is limited to particular types of delay and qualification criteria (e.g., what can constitute an "unreasonable" delay) and that time is subtracted from the extension for delays caused by the applicant themselves.

- Rights and limitations: The regulations must ensure that the rights and limitations in regard to scope and coverage of the extended patent are not greater or lesser than those of the original patent rights, with certain exceptions. One such exception, as explained above, is notion that a product is eligible for PTE only if an application for marketing approval is made within a set period of time following approval in another jurisdiction. A related exception Hong Kong should adopt is a "use it or lose it" safeguard that allows for the authorities to revoke the PTE should the pharmaceutical product not actually be marketed in the jurisdiction within a set number of years following the granting of marketing approval. Again, while the relevant time period can be debated, it would

---

[52] See, contra, Article 18.48(2) of the TPP, which simply refers to "a pharmaceutical product."

[53] While it can be debated whether Hong Kong is a large enough market for any incentive to be effective, the point here is for Hong Kong to take proactive steps to ensure that pharmaceuticals come to market as quickly as possible and to prevent overprotection. It should also be noted that pharmaceutical companies normally apply for marketing approval in Hong Kong earlier than other Asian markets due to pricing mechanisms; in essence, Hong Kong pays more than other regional markets and guides the regional price.

seem that a period of two years would be sufficient to discourage delays. Yet another exception can be taken from Australia, where during the period of the PTE the exclusive rights of the patentee are not considered to have been infringed where another person exploits the pharmaceutical substance for a purpose other than therapeutic use, or exploits any form of the invention that does not include the substance.[54]

4.4 Concluding Remarks

Patent term extension is designed to address the issue of regulatory delays either in the granting of a patent or in reviewing applications for market approval for pharmaceutical products. As a result of these regulatory delays, on average between eight and twelve years of the patent term has expired before the medicine is placed on the market. To counteract the effects of the regulatory delays and loss of monopoly selling period, an extension of patent term has been generally accepted by most industrialized countries – usually for a period of up to five years and under specific conditions – in order to facilitate the continued development of the innovative pharmaceutical industry.

While PTE is predicated on the idea that the branded pharmaceutical industry needs the additional period of monopoly selling rights in order to continue producing a steady pipeline of new and innovative medicines, public health activists strongly oppose PTE on the grounds that the extension delays access to cheaper medicines and simply provides for the extension of monopoly rents. Such criticism has intensified since the United States and EU began including PTE in their FTAs with trading partners. With the proliferation of FTAs, several separate ways to operationalize PTE have developed, with the US model providing extensions for unreasonable delays in the issuance of a patent and unreasonable curtailment of the effective patent term as a result of the marketing approval process. For its part, the EU formula offers essentially the same protection through a sui generis system that blends both processes.

Given the immense commercial and public interests involved in extending the regular patent term for pharmaceutical products, Hong Kong and other countries considering the adoption of a PTE system should be cautious and carefully consider the benefits of such a system against the detriments and balance the private interests with the public interests. It is abundantly clear that Hong Kong's adoption of PTE will

---

[54] Australian Patents Act 1990 (Ch), s 78.

do little to nothing to encourage major multinationals to increase R&D budgets or somehow become more innovative. Likewise, it is unlikely that the adoption of PTE will lead to investment in Hong Kong for either R&D or clinical trials. At the same time, it is debatable whether PTE will significantly raise costs. Regardless, as a jurisdiction that prides itself on rule of law and strong protection of IPRs, it may be in Hong Kong's long-term interest to consider the adoption of PTE. Looking into the future (albeit somewhat cynically, perhaps), if Hong Kong remains active in the negotiation of FTAs, it is only a matter of time before Hong Kong will as part of an FTA be required by its negotiating partner to adopt and implement PTE.

If, and perhaps when, Hong Kong does decide to adopt a system of PTE, it should look to the implementation of PTE in other jurisdictions as a guide. Such a comparative approach will offer a variety of policy options to shape the contours of the domestic PTE system. This chapter highlighted several principles and safeguards that Hong Kong should strongly consider adopting should it decide to adopt PTEs. If followed, Hong Kong will demonstrate that it is a good international citizen while at the same time guarding against overprotection.

PTEs can be implemented so as to ensure that Hong Kong pays for the innovative R&D (without risks inherent in conducting such R&D) only years after it has been undertaken and only if the drug becomes established in the market and its entry is delayed by a considerable period of time due to the patent application or marketing approval process. This seems to be in line with Hong Kong's view of itself as a strong protector of IP and good international citizen. On the other hand, there is no reason to believe that PTE would lead to increased pharmaceutical R&D in Hong Kong; for that, other more targeted incentives are needed.

5

Exceptions to Exclusive Rights

5.1 Introduction

Article 28 of the TRIPS Agreement confers exclusive rights on the patent holder, including making, using, offering for sale, selling or importing the protected product. These rights, however, are subject to exceptions contained in the Agreement. In other words, while the TRIPS Agreement grants substantive rights to a patent owner, it also allows but does not oblige Members to take advantage of exceptions to these rights. The two most notable exceptions discussed in this chapter are contained in Articles 30 and 31. Article 30 is a broadly worded provision allowing Members to provide exceptions to the patent owner's exclusive rights, provided that such exceptions are limited, do not unreasonably conflict with a normal exploitation of the patent and do not unreasonably prejudice the legitimate interests of the patent owner, taking account of the legitimate interests of third parties. Meanwhile, Article 31 relates to the issuance of compulsory licenses, with the mainly procedural provision permitting Members to allow third-party use of the patent without authorization of the rights holder.

Both exceptions play an important role in maintaining the balance between patent owners and broader societal interests. Both have also been the subject of controversy since the inception of the TRIPS Agreement, and the exact contours of these exceptions have yet to be fully defined. For this reason, great diversity exists in the domestic legislation of WTO Members – with some countries, most notably India and Argentina, pushing the boundaries of the exceptions while other Members take a more cautious approach. Hong Kong can generally be viewed as falling into the latter category, for reasons that appear to be more of benign neglect than design. This must change as the drafting of precise and clear provisions in domestic legislation allowing for possible exceptions to owner rights is critical in ensuring the system can properly function not only in normal circumstances but especially in case of emergency or in times of health crisis.

The Article 30 exception is inextricably linked to the issue of access to medicines. As mentioned elsewhere in this book, stringent testing requirements apply to new pharmaceuticals, while subsequent generic applicants are subject to simplified procedures. The safety and efficacy of the drug has been established and thus the generic must only submit data evidencing that their product is the bioequivalent ("biosimilar")[1] or chemical equivalent of the innovator drug, depending on the country at issue.[2] While the issue is more complicated for biological drugs (i.e., pharmaceuticals made from a living organism or its products), countries are devising regulations to facilitate the entry of biosimilars.[3] Owing to the abbreviated application process, the time period needed in order to secure marketing approval for a generic applicant is generally less than that of the original innovator. That said, depending on the jurisdiction and unique circumstances of each case, approval time may still be considerable.

If a generic producer must wait to apply for marketing approval until the expiration of the patent period, the time lag will delay the introduction of competitor products and result in additional monopoly rents paid to the patent owner. Simply, if a generic manufacturer cannot apply for marketing approval until the expiration of the term of patent(s) covering a pharmaceutical product, the patent owner will enjoy a prolonged period of de facto monopoly power. This de facto monopoly and corresponding monopoly rent will last for the time period it takes for the generic version of the product to gain market approval.

---

[1] Biosimilar products are "interchangeable" with licensed biological products, in the way that generic products are interchangeable with innovative drugs made from a chemical entity. See, for instance, the definition formulated by the US Food and Drug Administration at www.fda.gov/Drugs/DevelopmentApprovalProcess/ HowDrugsareDevelopedandApproved/ApprovalApplications/TherapeuticBiologic Applications/Biosimilars/. For a similar definition, see also Biosimilar Development, "About Biosimilar Regulations," www.biosimilardevelopment.com/doc/about-biosimilar- regulations-0001.

[2] In the United States, this means proving through means of tests on 24–36 healthy subjects that the generic product performs in the same manner as the innovator drug. See, e.g., US Food and Drug Administration, "Abbreviated New Drug Application (ANDA): Generics," www.fda.gov/Drugs/DevelopmentApprovalProcess/ HowDrugsareDevelopedandApproved/ApprovalApplications/AbbreviatedNewDrug ApplicationANDAGenerics/, accessed 6 March 2017.

[3] See Yaniv Heled, "Biologics, Biosimilars and Patents," in Bryan Mercurio and Daria Kim (eds.), *Contemporary Issues in Pharmaceutical Patent Law: Setting the Framework and Exploring Policy Options* (Routledge, 2017).

The "regulatory review" or "Bolar" exception under Article 30 is designed to eliminate the de facto monopoly period by allowing a generic producer to apply for marketing approval during the life the patent, without breaching the exclusive rights of the patent owner. In this regard, the regulatory review exception reduces the time it takes for a generic to enter the market, thereby allowing competition onto the market almost immediately following the expiration of a patent. Thus, the regulatory review exception serves the purpose of reducing the price of and increasing access to affordable pharmaceuticals by allowing the generic to "use" the patent for testing and the purposes of making an application for marketing approval from the relevant governmental agency. As is discussed in greater detail below, the panel in *Canada – Pharmaceutical Patents* held that Canada's regulatory review provision fell within the scope of the three-step test contained in Article 30 of the TRIPS Agreement.[4]

Anyone familiar with issues involving pharmaceuticals and the WTO over the last two decades would be familiar with the issue of compulsory licenses. The TRIPS Agreement allows for compulsory licenses to be issued for patented products and processes under limited circumstances and on satisfying certain conditions. These conditions have proven controversial as they limit usage of compulsory licenses. Thus, while the conditions guard against abuse, they also for example essentially prevent Members with insufficient or no manufacturing capacities from making use of the provision. The WTO addressed the issue of health and trade in the November 2001 WTO Ministerial Conference in Doha, which adopted a Ministerial Declaration on the TRIPS Agreement and Public Health reiterating and expressly stating that the TRIPS Agreement does not limit the grounds on which compulsory licenses may be granted and acknowledging the right of each Member to determine when a "national emergency" or "other circumstances of extreme urgency" exist in its territory.[5] The issue of the limitation regarding compulsory licensing was not resolved until a follow-up agreement in 2003, which provided for a "waiver" of certain conditions and thus allowed Members with insufficient or no manufacturing capacities to import pharmaceuticals under compulsory license.

---

[4] Panel Report, *Canada – Patent Protection of Pharmaceutical Products*, WT/DS114/R, adopted 7 April 2000.

[5] WTO, Doha Declaration on the TRIPS Agreement and Public Health, WT/MIN(01)/DEC/2, adopted on 14 November 2001, at 5(b) and 5(c).

This chapter proceeds as follows. Section 5.2 discusses Article 30, with particular focus on the experimental use or research exception, which includes the regulatory review exception. Section 5.3 discusses the Article 31 exception for compulsory licensing. Compulsory licenses have received considerable attention in the literature over the past two decades but are perhaps not as important in the Hong Kong context given the jurisdiction's perceived need to provide strong protection to IPRs. Nevertheless, reviewing the situation in Hong Kong and providing for adequate and effective laws should the need arise remains crucial for a properly functioning regulatory regime. Both sections will review the international framework and practice in other jurisdictions in order to formulate practical recommendations for Hong Kong.

5.2   The Exceptions

5.2.1   Article 30 – Experimental or Research Exception

The experimental use or research exception is a policy tool used by many countries in order to promote scientific research and technological development and to encourage inventive activities.[6] In most cases, the exception "enables researchers to examine the stated effects of patented inventions and improve such patented inventions without having to fear infringing the patent."[7] The rationale underlying the exception is that allowing experimentation and research on existing technologies without cost or impediment leads to the development of even more technological advancement, thereby furthering the aims of the patent system. Thus, one of the justifications (if not the main one) for the exception for experimental use is to promote scientific research and innovation. The panel in *Canada – Pharmaceutical Patents* discussed this point when stating:

> We may take as an illustration one of the most widely adopted Article 30-type exceptions in national patent laws – the exception under which use of the patented product for scientific experimentation, during the term of the patent and without consent, is not an infringement. It is often argued

---

[6] See, for instance, WIPO Standing Committee on the Law of Patents, "Exceptions and Limitations to Patent Rights: Experimental Use and/or Scientific Research," Document SCP/20/4, Twentieth Session (Geneva, 27–31 January, 2014), www.wipo.int/edocs/mdocs/patent_policy/en/scp_20/scp_20_4.pdf, accessed 4 March 2017, para. 6.

[7] WIPO Standing Committee on the Law of Patents, *Exclusions from Patentable Subject Matter and Exceptions and Limitations to the Rights*, Thirteenth Session (Geneva, 23–27 March 2009), p. 27, www.wipo.int/edocs/mdocs/scp/en/scp_13/scp_13_3.pdf, accessed 6 March 2017.

that this exception is based on the notion that a key public policy purpose underlying patent laws is to facilitate the dissemination and advancement of technical knowledge and that allowing the patent owner to prevent experimental use during the term of the patent would frustrate part of the purpose of the requirement that the nature of the invention be disclosed to the public. To the contrary, the argument concludes, under the policy of the patent laws, both society and the scientist have a "legitimate interest" in using the patent disclosure to support the advance of science and technology.[8]

The reasoning behind such an exception is in line with that of the patent system, which attempts to balance the needs of the inventors/patent holders with those of secondary innovators, end users and society at large. More specifically, the experimental use or research exemption can be traced to the ultimate aim of the patent system to provide incentives to invent in exchange for disclosure and the promotion of subsequent innovation and technological development. In this regard, free access to prior inventions and discoveries by subsequent researchers might be viewed as an effective means of promoting progress and technological development in some fields of research. Restraining this research avenue could invite peril. In a submission to an Australian report on patents and experimental use released in 2005, the Ludwig Institute for Cancer Research states:

> Curtailing the experimental use exemption could stifle innovation and slow the advance of technology. The practical effect of barring research would be to allow a patent holder to stop not only commercial competition, as is a proper right under the patent system, but also all research that might lead to such competition, as well as barring improvement, challenge or avoidance of a patented invention[9]

Likewise, the World Health Assembly recommended that countries adopt an experimental use exception in order to promote "greater access to knowledge and technology relevant to meet public health needs of developing countries" and that they address public health needs in a manner fully consistent with the TRIPS Agreement.[10]

---

[8] Panel Report, *Canada – Pharmaceutical Patents*, above n. 4, at 7.69.

[9] Australian Government Advisory Council on Intellectual Property, "Patents and Experimental Use" (October 2005), p. 14 (citing Ludwig Institute, Submission 24), www.ipaustralia.gov.au/sites/g/files/net856/f/acip_final_report_patents_and_experimental_use_archived.pdf.

[10] See Sixty-First World Health Assembly, "Global Strategy and Plan of Action on Public Health, Innovation and Intellectual Property," WHA61.21 para. 2.4, http://apps.who.int/medicinedocs/documents/s21429en/s21429en.pdf, accessed 6 March 2017.

In the absence of a clear experimental use exemption, it is advanced that users of the patent system incur unnecessary costs and societal costs, which include adverse effects on innovation, competition and, in regard to pharmaceutical inventions, public health. Of course, there are questions regarding the extent to which commercial interests should be able to make use of the exception or whether the exception is limited to noncommercial purposes (e.g., teaching). It is also debatable whether the exception should apply equally to all fields of technology. For instance, pharmaceutical research involves an immense capital investment and concomitant commercial risks, and some commentators believe that the legal regime should guard against free-riding on the substantial efforts of the primary researchers. This, however, raises further questions regarding the distinction between the use of inventions for the intended purpose and purely experimental use. The practical reality, however, is that the distinction between basic, "pure" research with no commercial implications (which most commentators believe should be freely accessible) and applied research, which most believe should be accessible only with the authorization of the patent holder, is not as clear as one might expect. Instead, the two categories are increasingly blurred in many fields of research, including pharmaceuticals.[11] Despite these challenges, the aim should be for jurisdictions to draft regulations granting strong patent protection but at the same time not allowing the patent system to stifle justified scientific research activities and ultimately scientific progress.

The experimental exception is a recognized and legitimate flexibility in the exclusive rights of a patent holder,[12] but nevertheless remains controversial. As should be clear from the above discussion, little consensus exists among countries on the scope and parameters of the exception.[13] In some jurisdictions the exception is narrowly crafted, whereas in others it appears quite broad. This leads to uncertainties and thus domestic legislation is at times attacked by critics. Despite – or perhaps because of – the differences, to date there have been few attempts to systematize and

---

[11] See Rebecca Eisenberg, "Patents and the Progress of Science: Exclusive Rights and Experimental Use" (1989) 56 *University of Chicago Law Review* 1017, 1018.

[12] See, e.g., WIPO, "Exceptions and Limitations to Patent Rights," above n. 6.

[13] See UK Department of Trade and Industry, "Patents for Genetic Sequences: The Competitiveness of Current UK Law" (2004), a study by the Intellectual Property Institute on behalf of the DTI, available at http://webarchive.nationalarchives.gov.uk/20060213221438/http://www.dti.gov.uk/5397_DTi_Patent_Study.pdf, at 6 ("there is evident uncertainty...about the extent of the patent research exemption, which is widely seen as problematic").

disseminate a best practices approach across countries.[14] Even FTAs do not attempt to clarify or elaborate in any way on the scope of the exception, instead preferring to merely repeat the language of Article 30 of the TRIPS Agreement verbatim.[15]

The laws in Hong Kong as currently drafted are vague and do not specifically provide for a number of recognized exceptions, most notably the regulatory review exception. To avoid legal uncertainty in the research sector, Hong Kong should carefully draft an experimental use provision that clarifies the extent to which research is exempted from patent infringement liability. This includes the addition of a clear provision on the consistency of generic use of a patented product for the purposes of obtaining marketing approval. In order to reach this conclusion, the section will first review the international framework, namely, through exploration of the Article 30 exception to the exclusive rights of the patent owner. The section then proceeds to examine the experimental use exception in the national laws of various countries and in FTAs with a view to finding potential sources of inspiration for Hong Kong to emulate. Finally, the section offers analysis and recommendations for Hong Kong.

International Obligations

The need to include exceptions to patent rights was generally recognized by the negotiating parties to the TRIPS Agreement. The parties differed, however, in the scope of the exceptions. While several countries supported a broad exception clause,[16] the United States preferred a more limited

---

[14] OECD, "Patents and Innovation: Trends and Policy Challenges" (DSTI/STP92003)27 13-Oct-2003 at 22, www.oecd.org/sti/sci-tech/24508541.pdf, accessed 6 March 2017. In *Canada – Pharmaceutical Patents*, Canada provided the panel with a list of what it deemed permitted experimental uses in accordance with Article 30: "(a) testing an invention to determine its sufficiency or to compare it to prior art; (b) tests to determine how the patented invention worked; (c) experimentation on a patented invention for the purpose of improving on it or developing a further patentable invention; (d) experimentation for the purpose of "designing around" a patented invention; (e) testing to determine whether the invention met the tester's purposes in anticipation of requesting a licence; and (f) academic instructional experimentation with the invention." The Panel did not engage with or comment on this list. Panel Report, *Canada – Pharmaceutical Patents*, above n. 4, at 75.

[15] For example, Article 17.9.3 of the US-Chile FTA provides that "[e]ach Party may provide limited exceptions to the exclusive rights conferred by a patent, provided that such exceptions do not unreasonably conflict with a normal exploitation of the patent and do not unreasonably prejudice the legitimate interests of the patent owner, taking account of the legitimate interests of third parties."

[16] See, e.g., "Guidelines and Objectives Proposed by the European Community for the Negotiation on Trade-Related Aspects of Substantive Standards of Intellectual Property Rights,"

exception.[17] The draft text of July 1990 included a broad, nonexhaustive list of exceptions, which included experimental purposes.[18] The final version of the experimental use or research exception, however, is formulated more generally and without any list of exempted acts. It appears as Article 30 of the TRIPS Agreement:

> Members may provide limited exceptions to the exclusive rights conferred by a patent, provided that such exceptions do not unreasonably conflict with a normal exploitation of the patent and do not unreasonably prejudice the legitimate interests of the patent owner, taking account of the legitimate interests of third parties.

This formulation is based on Article 9(2) of the Berne Convention, with a general three-step test to determine compatibility with the provision. Article 30 is thus forever intertwined with the Berne Convention, with the negotiating history of that earlier agreement remaining relevant to the interpretation of Article 30 as per both the Vienna Convention on the Law of Treaties (VCLT) and the specific incorporation of the Berne Convention into the TRIPS Agreement.[19] In the only WTO dispute to interpret the provision, the panel in *Canada – Pharmaceutical Patents* supported its interpretation of the TRIPS Agreement through explicit reference to the negotiating history of the Berne Convention.[20]

The panel in *Canada – Pharmaceutical Patents* was called on to determine whether two of Canada's pharmaceutical regulatory provisions were exceptions to patent rights covered by Article 30. The provisions were the so-called regulatory review (or Bolar) exception and the stockpiling exception, which are as follows:

7 July 1988, MTN.GNG/NG11/W/26 (section D.a.(i)); Uruguay Round – Group of Negotiations on Goods – Negotiating Group on Trade-Related Aspects of Intellectual Property Rights, Including Trade in Counterfeit Goods – Standards for Trade-Related Intellectual Property Rights – Submission from Canada, MTN.GNG/NG11/W/47, 25 October 1989; Uruguay Round – Group of Negotiations on Goods – Negotiating Group on Trade-Related Aspects of Intellectual Property Rights, Including Trade in Counterfeit Goods – Communication from Brazil, MTN.GNG/NG11/W/57, 11 December 1989.

[17] US Submission, MTN.GNG/NGII/W/70, 11 May 1990 (proposing to limit exceptions to compulsory licenses).

[18] Multilateral Trade Negotiations – The Uruguay Round, Group of Negotiations on Goods (GATT) Negotiating Group on Trade-Related Aspects of Intellectual Property Rights, including Trade in Counterfeit Goods, 23 July 1990 (W/76), para. 2.2.

[19] See TRIPS Agreement, Article 2.2.

[20] See Panel Report, *Canada – Pharmaceutical Patents*, above n. 4. In the context of copyright, see Panel Report, *United States – Section 110(5) of the US Copyright Act*, WT/DS160/R, adopted 27 July 2000.

Patent Act, Section 55.2(1):
It is not an infringement of a patent for any person to make, construct, use
or sell the patented invention solely for uses reasonably related to the development and submission of information required under any law of Canada,
a province or a country other than Canada that regulates the manufacture,
construction, use or sale of any product.

Patent Act, Section 55.2(2):
It is not an infringement of a patent for any person who makes, constructs,
uses or sells a patented invention in accordance with subsection (1) to
make, construct or use the invention, during the applicable period provided for by the regulations, for the manufacture and storage of articles
intended for sale after the date on which the term of the patent expires.

The panel determined that the three-step test contained in Article 30 is
cumulative and therefore each step is independent of the others, meaning
that in order to comply with Article 30, exceptions should (1) be "limited,"
(2) "not unreasonably conflict with a normal exploitation of the patent"
and (3) "not unreasonably prejudice the legitimate interests of the patent
owner, taking into account the legitimate interests of third parties."[21] The
panel then clarified:

> The three conditions must, of course, be interpreted in relation to each
> other. Each of the three must be presumed to mean something different
> from the other two, or else there would be redundancy. Normally, the order
> of listing can be read to suggest that an exception that complies with the
> first condition can nevertheless violate the second or third, and that one
> which complies with the first and second can still violate the third. The syn-
> tax of Article 30 supports the conclusion that an exception may be "limited"
> and yet fail to satisfy one or both of the other two conditions. The order-
> ing further suggests that an exception that does not "unreasonably conflict
> with normal exploitation" could nonetheless "unreasonably prejudice the
> legitimate interests of the patent owner."[22]

The panel found that the stockpiling exception was not "limited" simply
because it only applied to products that require regulatory approval (and a

---

[21] Ibid., para. 7.20. This finding has been criticized in the literature. See, e.g., the Max Planck
Institute for Innovation and Competition, "Declaration on Patent Protection. Regulatory Sovereignty under TRIPS," para. 8, www.mpg.de/8132986/Patent-Declaration.pdf,
accessed 4 March 2017 ("Contrary to what [the panel in *Canada – Pharmaceutical Patents*]
seemed to assume, the three conditions are not cumulative. The three-step test may be
understood to require a comprehensive overall assessment rather than a separate and independent assessment of each criterion. Failure to comply with one of the three conditions
need not result in the exception being disallowed").
[22] Ibid., para. 7.21.

further argument that the focus of inquiry should be on the right to "sell"). Instead, the panel found that the lack of limitations on the quantity of production and stockpiling during the six months immediately prior to the expiration of the patent resulted in a "substantial curtailment" of Article 27.1 and therefore could not fall within the meaning of "limited."[23] Since the stockpiling exception fell at the first hurdle, the panel did not review it under the two remaining steps of the test.[24]

On the contrary, the panel found that the regulatory exception is consistent with Article 30 – that is, Members can use a patented invention, without the consent of the patent holder, for testing required data in order to obtain marketing approval for pharmaceutical or other products. In regard to the first step, that the exception be "limited," the panel first had to determine the meaning of the word. In this regard, the panel stated:

> 7.30 The word "exception" by itself connotes a limited derogation, one that does not undercut the body of rules from which it is made. When a treaty uses the term "limited exception," the word "limited" must be given a meaning separate from the limitation implicit in the word "exception" itself. The term "limited exception" must therefore be read to connote a narrow exception – one which makes only a small diminution of the rights in question.

> 7.31 In the absence of other indications, the Panel concluded that it would be justified in reading the text literally, focusing on the extent to which legal rights have been curtailed, rather than the size or extent of the economic impact. In support of this conclusion, the Panel noted that the following two conditions of Article 30 ask more particularly about the economic impact of the exception, and provide two sets of standards by which such impact may be judged. The term "limited exceptions" is the only one of the three conditions in Article 30 under which the extent of the curtailment of rights as such is dealt with.

Thus, the panel focused on the extent of the curtailment of the rights, leaving the economic effect of the rights to be evaluated under the second and third steps of the test.[25] In addition, the panel stated that when

---

[23] Ibid., paras. 7.27–38.   [24] Ibid., para. 7.38.

[25] To some commentators, the panel's determination that "the economic impact of the exception must be evaluated under the other conditions of Article 30 unduly narrows down the scope of admissible exceptions" and could result in a scenario where the exception may not be applicable even when the rights owner is not negatively affected in economic terms. See, e.g., Carlos Correa, "The Bolar Exception: Legislative Models and Drafting Options," in Mercurio and Kim (eds.), *Contemporary Issues in Pharmaceutical Patent Law*. It should

evaluating the limiting conditions of a measure, "both the goals and the limitations stated in Articles 7 and 8.1 [as the objectives and principles of the TRIPS Agreement] must obviously be borne in mind, as well as other provisions of the TRIPS Agreement which indicate its objective and purposes."[26]

In regard to the second step, that the exception not unreasonably conflict with normal exploitation of the patent, the critical issues for the panel were determining what is "normal exploitation" of a patent and whether any such conflict (if any) is unreasonable. While scholars have offered several conflicting interpretations of "normal," the panel sought guidance from the dictionary and found "normal" to be "regular, usual, typical, ordinary, conventional."[27] The panel considered that "normal exploitation of the patent" referred to the "commercial activity by which patent owners employ their exclusive patent rights to extract economic value from their patent."[28] In so doing, the panel avoided having to weigh in on whether the term has empirical or normative connotations. Instead, the panel combined the two approaches and found that normal exploitation is "an empirical conclusion about what is common within a relevant community" and "a normative standard of entitlement."[29]

For the panel, the "protection of all normal exploitation practices is a key element reflected in all patent laws," and the "normal practice" is for patent owners "to exclude all forms of competition that could detract significantly from the economic returns anticipated from a patent's grant of market exclusivity."[30] The panel further elaborated that patent exploitation is not static and that for "effective exploitation" a patent owner must

---

be noted that the panel rejected Canada's submission for a broader interpretation of the first step. See *Canada – Pharmaceutical Patents*, above n. 4, para. 7.37.

[26] *Canada – Pharmaceutical Patents*, above n. 4, para. 7.26.   [27] Ibid., para. 7.54

[28] Canada argued that "exploitation" involved the extraction of commercial value by "working" the patent, by selling the product in a market from which competitors are excluded, by licensing others to do so or by selling the patent rights. The European Communities largely agreed, but differed in its interpretation of the term "normal." Ibid., para. 7.51.

[29] Ibid., para. 7.54.

[30] Ibid., para. 7.55. Correa strongly disagrees with the panel's reasoning: "The panel's reasoning is questionable. The right to exclude the use of the patented subject matter by third parties is not a form of exploitation of the patent, but a legal power established by law that may be exercised or not. The exploitation consists of the acts of making, using or commercializing the inventions without third parties' competition. In addition, the panel went too far in considering 'all forms of competition' since competition may legitimately proceed through the improvement of the patented technology. The normal exploitation of a patent should be deemed limited to uses of the invention that are shielded from competition by law." Correa, above n. 25.

"adapt to changing forms of competition due to technological development and the evolution of marketing practices."[31]

Applying the law to the facts of the case, the panel concluded that the
"additional period of *de facto* market exclusivity created by using patent
rights to preclude submissions for regulatory authorization should not
be considered 'normal.'"[32] The additional period of monopoly sales following the expiration of a patent during which time a generic must seek
marketing approval is not a "natural or normal" consequence of enforcing
patent rights, but rather an "unintended" consequence "of the conjunction
of the patent laws with product regulatory laws."[33] That is, patent owners
do not expect this additional period of monopoly sales, but it results by
operation of the regulatory laws regarding the sales of pharmaceuticals.

As to the third criterion that the exception does "not unreasonably prejudice the legitimate interests of the patent owner," the panel held that
"legitimate interest" is not limited to "legal interests" and must instead
be "defined in the way that it is often used in legal discourse – as a normative claim calling for protection of interests that are 'justifiable' in the
sense that they are supported by relevant public policies or other social
norms."[34] The panel further added that a definition equating "legitimate
interests" with legal interests makes no sense at all when applied to the
final phrase of Article 30 referring to the legitimate interests of third
parties.[35] As the last part of Article 30 – "taking account of the legitimate
interests of third parties" – is not included in Article 9(2) of the Berne
Convention or in Article 13 of the TRIPS Agreement, the panel concluded
by stating:

> Absent further explanation in the records of the TRIPS negotiations, how-
> ever, the Panel was not able to attach a substantive meaning to this change
> other than what is already obvious in the text itself, namely that the refer-
> ence to the "legitimate interests of third parties" makes sense only if the
> term "legitimate interests" is construed as a concept broader than legal
> interests.[36]

In the case at issue, the panel was not sympathetic that an additional
period of post-patent monopoly sales was a "legitimate interest," stating that the "interest claimed on behalf of patent owners whose effective period of market exclusivity had been reduced by delays in marketing

---

[31] Ibid., para. 7.55.   [32] Ibid., para. 7.57.   [33] Ibid.
[34] Ibid., para. 7.69.   [35] Ibid., para. 7.68.   [36] Ibid., para. 7.71.

approval was neither so compelling nor so widely recognized that it could be regarded as a 'legitimate interest' within the meaning of Article 30."[37]

The panel therefore found the Canadian regulatory review exception consistent within the scope of Article 30 and thus the TRIPS Agreement. In so doing, the panel did not accept the argument that the patent owner should have a de facto extension of its monopoly for delays resulting from the marketing approval process for generic pharmaceuticals. This decision has played a large role in the development of experimental use exceptions in a number of countries. The panel report does not, however, settle every issue and leaves significant scope for continuing discussion and debate on the breadth of the Article 30 exception.

Experimental Use Exception in Leading Jurisdictions

As mentioned above, the experimental use exception varies under national laws in terms of the scope of coverage, definition and types of justifiable experimentation and research activities.[38] This subsection cannot provide comprehensive coverage of the issue, but instead will canvass a variety of domestic laws so as to provide a framework from which Hong Kong can take guidance and construct a more tailored and appropriate law.

United States The United States is one of a handful of nations that does not enshrine the experimental use exemption in statutory law. Instead, the exception is firmly established as part of the common law. The experimental use exception has a long history in the United States, with Judge Story in the 1813 case of *Whittemore v. Cutter* holding that "it could never have been the intention of the legislature to punish a man who constructed such a machine merely for philosophical experiments, or for the purpose of ascertaining the sufficiency of the machine to produce its described

---

[37] Ibid., para. 7.82.

[38] See, e.g., the World Intellectual Property Organization, Exclusion from Patentable Subject Matter and Exceptions and Limitations to the Rights, SCP/13/3 (2009); Christopher Garrison, "Exceptions to Patent Rights in Developing Countries," Issue Paper 17, UNCTAD-ICTSD Project on IPRs and Sustainable Development (2006); Carlos Correa, "The International Dimension of the Research Exception," American Association for the Advancement of Science (January 2005), available at http://citeseerx.ist.psu.edu/viewdoc/download;jsessionid=9897DEF5F0DE7D22FDF1CCC6A2C09165?doi=10.1.1.207.4033&rep=rep1&type=pdf; Anthony Tridico, Jeffrey Jacobstein and Leythem Wall, "Facilitating Generic Drug Manufacturing: Bolar Exemptions Worldwide," *WIPO Magazine* (June 2014), www.wipo.int/wipo_magazine/en/2014/03/article_0004.html, accessed 4 March 2017.

effects."[39] The court, however, limited the scope of the exception to use done "merely for philosophical experiments, or for the purpose of ascertaining the sufficiency of the [patented invention] to produce its described effects."[40] The court in *Peppenhausen v. Falke* (1861) summarized the state of the law by stating:

> It has been held, and no doubt is now well settled, that an experiment with a patented article for the sole purpose of gratifying a philosophical taste, or curiosity, or for mere amusement, is not an infringement of the rights of the patentee.[41]

The Federal Circuit applies the exception in a "very narrow and strictly limited" manner,[42] sustaining it only when actions are performed "for amusement, to satisfy idle curiosity, or for strictly philosophical inquiry" and not when the infringing activities are "in keeping with the alleged infringer's legitimate business."[43] For instance, the court in *Madey v. Duke University* held that the experimental use of a patent furthers the university's "legitimate business" objectives, which include educating and enlightening students, faculty participating in research projects and furthering the university's reputation and ability to attract grants, students and faculty.[44] Such a narrow interpretation of the common law privilege limits the value of the exception and means that the exception is "rarely sustained."[45]

In addition to the common law, the United States has a number of statutory exceptions relating to experimental use. For the purposes of pharmaceutical research, the most relevant is the Bolar exception. This exception came about as a result of *Roche Products, Inc. v. Bolar Pharmaceutical Co.*, a 1984 case that tested the limits of the experimental use exception. In the case, Roche claimed Bolar infringed its patent on the drug Dalmane by conducting bioequivalence studies in order to apply for marketing approval from the FDA for a generic version of Dalmane (flurazepam).[46]

---

[39] *Whittemore v. Cutter*, 29 F. Cas. 1120, 1121 (C.C.D. Mass. 1813) (No. 17, 600).

[40] Ibid., at 1121. See also *Sawin v. Guild*, 21 F. Cas. 554 (C.C.D. Mass 1813) (No. 12, 391).

[41] *Peppenhausen v. Falke*, 19 F. Cas. 1048, 1049 (C.C.S.D.N.Y. 1861).

[42] *Madey v. Duke University*, 307 F. 3d 1351 (Fed. Cir. 2002), at 1361.

[43] Ibid., at 1352.   [44] Ibid., at 1362.

[45] Rebecca S. Eisenberg, "Proprietary Rights and the Norms of Science in Biotechnology Research" (1987) 97 *Yale Law Journal* 177, 220. For criticism of the *Madey* decision, see Lawrence M. Sung and Claire M. Maisano, "Piercing the Academic Veil: Disaffecting the Common Law Exception to Patent Infringement Liability and the Future of a Bona Fide Research Use Exemption after *Madey v. Duke University*" (2003) 9 *Journal of Health Care Law and Policy* 256.

[46] *Roche Products, Inc. v Bolar Pharmaceuticals Co.*, 572 F. Supp. 255 (E.D.N.Y. 1983).

At first instance, the US District Court for the Eastern District of New York ruled in favor of Bolar, holding no liability under the common law experimental use exemption doctrine. The US Court of Appeals for the Federal Circuit overruled the District Court primarily due to the "truly narrow" scope of the exception and the commercial nature of Bolar's activities:

> Bolar's intended "experimental" use is solely for business reasons and not for amusement, to satisfy idle curiosity, or for strictly philosophical inquiry. Bolar's intended use of flurazepam hcl to derive FDA required test data is thus an infringement of the [Roche] patent. Bolar may intend to perform "experiments," but unlicensed experiments conducted with a view to the adaptation of the patented invention to the experimentor's business is a violation of the rights of the patentee to exclude others from using his patented invention. It is obvious here that it is a misnomer to call the intended use *de minimis*. It is no trifle in its economic effect on the parties even if the quantity used is small. It is not a dilettante affair such as Justice Story envisioned. We cannot construe the experimental use rule so broadly as to allow a violation of the patent laws in the guise of "scientific inquiry," when that inquiry has definite, cognizable, and not insubstantial commercial purposes.[47]

In so holding, the Court also rejected Bolar's argument that public policy considerations justify experimental use during the life of the patent in order to facilitate the availability of generic drugs immediately upon the expiration. With some sympathy, the Court stated that it should be Congress and not the courts to create exceptions and change the law.[48]

In response, Congress took action later that same year and passed the Drug Price Competition and Patent Term Restoration Act (Hatch-Waxman Act).[49] Attempting to balance the protection of patented pharmaceuticals with more timely entry of generic drugs into the market, the Act reshaped the pharmaceutical market and relationship between branded and generic manufacturers in the United States. The relevant part of the Act states:

> [I]t shall not be an act of infringement to make, use, offer to sell, or sell within the United States or import into the United States a patented invention ... solely for uses reasonably related to the development and submission of information under a Federal law which regulates the manufacture, use, or sale of drugs or veterinary biological products.[50]

---

[47] *Roche Products, Inc. v. Bolar Pharmaceutical Co.*, 733 F.2d 858 (Fed. Cir. 1984), at 863.
[48] Ibid., at Section C.
[49] Drug Price Competition and Patent Term Restoration Act, Pub.L. No. 98–417, 98 Stat. 1585 (1984) 38 USC Section 271(e)(1)-(2) (2000).
[50] 35 USC §271(e)(1).

Thus, Section 271(e)(1) immunizes generic drug manufacturers from liability of patent infringement for "uses reasonably related to the development and submission of information under a Federal law which regulates the manufacture, use, or sale of drugs."[51] In other words, a generic manufacturer will not be held liable for patent infringement when it conducts bioequivalence studies "reasonably related" to obtaining FDA approval of an Abbreviated New Drug Application (ANDA). The Act is of critical importance as it provided generic manufacturers with the right to "use" patented subject matter for the purpose of gaining regulatory approval prior to the expiration of the relevant patent(s) in exchange for the opportunity of patent owners to seek a patent term extension for delays resulting from the approval process.[52] As a result, generics no longer need to conduct expensive and unnecessary clinical tests in order to apply for marketing approval, thus reducing the cost of pharmaceuticals to consumers.

The courts have interpreted the "reasonably related" component of the Bolar exception rather broadly. For instance, courts have held that Section 271(e)(1) covers medical devices, pharmaceuticals[53] and pre- and even postclinical studies undertaken with the intent of making a submission to the FDA even if the product/submission never materializes.[54] Moreover, courts do not look to the underlying purpose or intended consequences of a use, so long as the use is reasonably related to the FDA approval.[55] Essentially, the exception will be applied where the alleged infringer – as opposed to the court – reasonably believed that there was a decent prospect that the "use" in question would contribute to the generation of

---

[51] 35 USC §271(e)(1). The provision now also covers biological products and veterinary drugs. Generic Animal and Patent Term Restoration Act, Pub. L. No. 100–670, 102 Stat. 3971.

[52] For discussion and analysis of patent term extension, see Chapter 4.

[53] *Eli Lilly and Co. v. Medtronic* 496 US 661, 665–666 (1990) (Justice Scalia interpreted the phrase "a Federal law which regulates the manufacture, use, or sale of drugs" to mean the entire of Food, Drug and Cosmetic Act, which covers not only drugs but also medical devices and other products). As a result, most commentators would extend the Act to also cover such items as food and color additives. See John R. Thomas, "Scientific Research and the Experimental Use Privilege in Patent Law," CRS Report for Congress, 28 October 2004, 16.

[54] See *Merck KGaA v. Integra Lifesciences I, Ltd.*, 545 US 193, 202 (2005); see also *Momenta Pharma. v. Amphastar Pharm.*, 686 F.3d 1348, Section II (2012) ("the fact that Amphastar's testing is carried out to 'satisfy the FDA's requirements' means it falls within the scope of the safe harbor, even though the activity is carried out after approval").

[55] *AbTox, Inc. v Exitron Corporation*, 122 F.3d 1019, 1020 (Fed. Cir. 1997), modified 131 F. 3d 1009 (Fed. Cir. 1997).

information that was likely to be relevant in the FDA approval process.[56] In fact, even postapproval studies that could include "materials the FDA demands in the regulatory process" have been deemed to fall within the safe harbor provision.[57] Of course there are limits to the extent of the exception, and courts have held that studies with the patented compound for the purposes of developing a new patented drug are excluded from the scope of the Bolar exception.[58]

European Union The EU has for some time been grappling with the particularities of the experimental use exception. Attempts to add some clarity have met with limited success. One such attempt was the Community Patent Convention (CPC) 1975,[59] which included the following provision for experimental use:

> Article 31(b): The rights conferred by a Community Patent shall not extend to acts done for experimental purposes relating to the subject matter of the invention.

The CPC, however, was not ratified by the Member States and never came into effect.[60] That being the case, similarly worded provisions on experimental use can be found in the legislation of most EU Member States. However, the scope and extent of the exception is far from harmonized, with some members explicitly limiting it to noncommercial activities, whereas others allow acts that anticipate a future commercial exploitation. Legislation in some Member States is simply silent on this point.

Another point of differentiation among EU Member States is the meaning of the term "experiment" and the breadth and limits in regard to

---

[56] See also *Intermedics, Inc. v. Ventritex, Inc.*, 775 F. Supp. at 1280 (stating that the court should apply the exception "[w]here it would have been reasonable, objectively, for an accused infringer to believe that there was a decent prospect that the use in question would contribute (relatively directly) to the generation of information that was likely to be relevant in the processes by which the FDA would decide to approve the product"). See also *Abtox, Inc. v. Exitron Corp.*, 122 F.3d 1019 (Fed. Cir. 1997); *Glaxo, Inc. v. Novopharm, Ltd.*, 110 F.3d 1562 (Fed. Cir.1997); *Amgen, Inc. v. Hoechst Marion Roussel, Inc.*, 3 F. Supp. 2d 104, 106 (D. Mass. 1998).

[57] *Momenta Pharms., Inc. v. Amphastar Pharms.*, Inc., 686 F.3d 1348, 1359–60 (Fed. Cir. 2012).

[58] See, e.g., *Integra Lifesciences, I, Ltd. v. Merck*, 331 F.3d 860 (Fed. Cir. 2003); *PSN Ill., LLC v Abbott Labs. & Abbott Bioresearch Ctr., Inc.*, 2011 US Dist. LEXIS 108055(N.D. Ill. Sept. 20, 2011).

[59] Convention for the European Patent for the Common Market (Community Patent Convention), 1976 O.J. (l 17).

[60] An amended version of the CPC (1989) also failed to be ratified by at least four of the then-twelve EU Member States.

the exception. For instance, in the United Kingdom, Section 60(5) of the Patents Act 1977 provides for an exception for acts (a) done privately and for purposes that are not commercial and (b) for experimental purposes relating to the subject matter of the invention. However, the experimental use exception is limited to "experiments which generate genuinely new information," thus excluding tests designed to verify existing knowledge or acts undertaken by a generic applicant in order to obtain marketing approval.[61] Moreover, case law has also interpreted the phrase "relating to the subject matter of the invention" narrowly to mean "having a real and direct connection with that subject matter."[62]

In contrast, courts in Germany have given a broad interpretation to Section 11.2 of the German Patent Act 1981, which reads: "The effect of the patent shall not extend to ... acts done for experimental purposes relating to the subject matter of the patented invention." More specifically, the Federal Supreme Court has found the term "experiment" to include "checking of the utilisability of the subject-matter of the patented invention and checking possibilities of further development,"[63] regardless of "whether the experiments are used only to check the statements made in the patent or else to obtain further research results, and whether they are employed for wider purposes, such as commercial interests."[64] Thus, the scope of the German exception extends to commercial-oriented research as opposed to being limited to research of a purely scientific nature.[65]

Yet another point of difference within Europe is whether the experimental use exception applies only to research *on* or *into* a patented invention or whether research *with* or *using* the patented product is also covered.[66] While the majority of Member States limit application of the exception to the former, others follow the Belgian model, which covers

---

[61] *Stauffer Chemical Co. v. Monsanto Co.*, 623 F. Supp. 148 (E.D. Mo. 1985). See also *Micro-Chemicals Ltd. v. Smith Kline and French Inter-America Ltd.*

[62] *Smith Kline & French Laboratories Ltd.* v. Evans *Medical Ltd.* [1989] FSR 513

[63] *Klinische Versuche (Clinical Trials) I* RPC 623; Klinische Versuche (Clinical Trials) II *(Case XZR 68/94)* R.P.C.423, 433 [1998].

[64] *Klinische Versuche (Clinical Trials) I* RPC 623, 639 [1997], Federal Supreme Court of Germany.

[65] See William Cornish, "Experimental Use of Patented Inventions in European Community States," 29(7) IIC 735 (1998) (arguing that "[g]iven the forcefulness of the judgements . . . in Klinische Versuche I and II, there must be a strong likelihood that their outcome will be followed in courts elsewhere in the EC").

[66] See, e.g., Sean O'Connor, "Enabling Research or Unfair Competition? De Jure and De Facto Research Use Exceptions in Major Technology Countries," in Toshiko Takenka (ed.),

"acts accomplished for scientific purposes *on* and/or *with* the subject matter of the patented invention."[67]

Turning specifically to pharmaceuticals, the legality of the regulatory review exception was until recently in some doubt throughout the EU even though experimentation on an invention has generally been accepted. This is the case despite, as described above, that under certain circumstances acts done for commercial purposes in some Member States fell within the scope of the exception.[68] The regulation of the pre-patent-expiry development was not harmonized at the EU level, and while national legislation of EU Member States commonly provided for a general research exemption for "acts done for experimental purposes relating to the subject-matter of the patented invention... legal uncertainty existed whether it covered pre-patent expiry testing in the EU,"[69] and national courts differed in their interpretations.[70] The EU amended Directive 2001/83/EC to provide for enhanced certainty:

> Conducting the necessary studies and trials with a view to the application [for marketing approval] and the consequential practical requirements shall not be regarded as contrary to patent rights or to supplementary protection certificates for medicinal products.[71]

Patent Law and Theory: A Handbook of Contemporary Research (Edward Elgar, 2009) (surveying exceptions in technology-oriented jurisdictions and distinguishing between commercial R&D exceptions and government or public nonprofit research exceptions as well as exceptions for research conducted "on" the patented invention (i.e., studying the drug for purposes of creating a bioequivalent version) and research "with" a patented drug (i.e., using the drug to perform other research activities)).

[67] Belgian Patent Act of 1984, as amended by the Law of April 28, 2005, Article 28.1(b).

[68] See, Clinical Trials II, above n. 63.

[69] European Commission, "Pharmaceutical Sector Inquiry – Final Report" (8 July 2009), http://ec.europa.eu/competition/sectors/pharmaceuticals/inquiry/staff_working_paper_part1.pdf, at 122–23.

[70] See, e.g., *Monsanto v. Stauffer* (1985) R.P.C. 515 (C.A.) (UK Court of Appeal holding that the experimental use provision did not exempt trials by generic companies aimed at securing regulatory approval), subsequently followed in *Auchinloss v. Agricultural & Veterinary Supplies Ltd.* (1999) RPC 397. But see *Klinische* Versuche II, above n. 63 (German Supreme Court holding that test data generation for the purpose of obtaining regulatory marketing approval can qualify for the experimental use exemption if such tests also advanced the state of art in some way).

[71] Article 10(6) of the Directive 2001/83/EC of the European Parliament and of the Council of 6 November 2001 on the Community code relating to medicinal products for human use (as amended). See also Directive 2004/27/EC of the European Parliament and of the Council of 31 March 2004 amending Directive 2001/83/EC on the Community code relating to medicinal products for human use (Official Journal L 136, 30/4/2004 p. 34–57).

The Directive is clearly designed to provide an exception for the use of a patented invention made to comply with the requirements for obtaining marketing approval for generic medicines.[72] Unfortunately, due to vague drafting and lack of clarity surrounding the term "studies and trials," implementation of the Directive differs widely among EU Member States.[73] In essence, while some Members apply the exception narrowly to include only activities relating to marketing approval of generic medicines,[74] other Members also allow uses in trials related to the development of new products,[75] with some even allowing trials undertaken to comply with regulatory requirements abroad to fall within the scope of the exemption.[76] Case law in the EU to establish the contours of the provision is still developing,[77] and some Member States have been slow in updating the law. For instance, in the United Kingdom it was not until October 2014 that Section 60(5)(b) of the Patents Act was amended to specifically allow generic companies to use a patented product for testing or other activity for the purposes of providing information to the regulatory authorities who decide whether a drug should be given a marketing approval.

Finally, it is worth mentioning the possibility of extending the experimental use exception to cover clinical trials performed for purposes other than the approval of a generic version. The recent amendments to the UK Patents Act provide for such usage;[78] meaning uses of drugs in the

---

[72] This is confirmed through Article 27(d) of the Agreement on a Unified Patent Court (UPC), which states: "The rights conferred by a patent shall not extend to any of the following: (d) the acts allowed pursuant to Article 13(6) of Directive 2001/82/EC 1 or Article 10(6) of Directive 2001/83/EC 2 in respect of any patent covering the product within the meaning of either of those Directives."

[73] See generally András Kupecz et al., "Safe Harbors in Europe: An Update on the Research and Bolar Exemptions to Patent Infringement" (2015) 33 *Nature Biotechnology* 710.

[74] This group includes the United Kingdom, Belgium, Cyprus, Ireland, the Netherlands and Sweden.

[75] This group includes Austria, Bulgaria, the Czech Republic, Denmark, Estonia, Finland, France, Germany, Hungary, Italy, Latvia, Lithuania, Luxembourg, Malta, Poland, Portugal, Romania, Slovakia, Slovenia and Spain.

[76] This group includes Austria, Germany, Denmark and Italy.

[77] See, e.g., *Astellas Pharma Inc. Polpharma SA Pharmaceutical Works* (CSK 92/13); C-661/13, http://curia.europa.eu/juris/liste.jsf?language=en&num=C-661/13, accessed 4 March 2017.

[78] The Legislative Reform (Patents) Order 2014 entered into force as of 1 October 2014 and amended the Patents Act 1977. Section 6(D) reads: "For the purposes of subsection (5)(b), anything done in or for the purposes of a medicinal product assessment which would otherwise constitute an infringement of a patent for an invention is to be regarded as done for experimental purposes relating to the subject-matter of the invention." For background information, the description and assessment of the draft proposal, see Regulatory

course of clinical tests and studies carried out for the purposes of regulatory approval *other than proving bioequivalence of generic drugs* (e.g., as comparators for original drugs) are now explicitly exempted from patent infringement. Prior to the amendment in 2014, Section 60(5)(i) of the Patents Act exempted from infringement uses related to the regulatory approval of generic drugs; however, the Act "[did] not extend to innovative drugs."[79] The amendment now extends the exception in subsection (5)(b) to all acts done in or for the purposes of a medicinal product assessment (not only those for demonstrating bioequivalence to the approved drugs). Section 60(6D) now provides that "anything done in or for the purposes of a medicinal product assessment . . . is to be regarded as done for experimental purposes relating to the subject matter of the invention."

The amendment thus broadens the scope of the exception and is intended to promote clinical drug development in the United Kingdom. In this regard, the UK IPO stated:

> Many factors are taken into account by companies when deciding where to locate clinical trials; the risk of patent infringement being one of them . . . In its favour, the UK has a good healthcare and scientific infrastructure, world experts in particular conditions, specialised hospitals, good access to patients through the NHS network, and high levels of literacy and ethical standards. However, the narrow exceptions to patent infringement in UK law may put companies at a disadvantage compared to other countries with broader exceptions. Stakeholders have indicated that, everything else being equal, it is likely that trials would be located in a jurisdiction with more generous Bolar or research exceptions.[80]

Such reasoning lacks strong empirical basis[81] but has been persuasive to date. It will be interesting to see what effect the UK shift has on other European jurisdictions.

Reform Committee – First Report Draft Legislative Reform (Patents) Order 2014, www.publications.parliament.uk/pa/cm201415/cmselect/cmdelreg/331/33102.htm, accessed 6 March 2017.

[79] See UK Intellectual Property Office, "The Legislative Reform (Patents) Order 2014, Explanatory Document," at 1.5, available at www.parliament.uk/documents/DPRR/2014-15/LROs/Patents-Order-2014/Explanatory-Document-(Patents).pdf.

[80] Intellectual Property Office Explanatory document, above n. 79, para. 1.13 (citations omitted).

[81] Centre for Intellectual Property Policy, above n. 66, at 48. Following a study of the United States, Australia, Germany, the United Kingdom and France, this report concluded: "While the precise impact of experimental use exceptions on the vitality of health care related R&D industries remains elusive, a number of conclusions can be drawn. Most notably, . . . a comparative study of the strength of research-based industries in the courtiers discussed above relative to the scope of their respective experimental use exceptions suggests that

China   As of the latest revision to the Patent Law in 2008, China now explicitly provides for an experimental use exception and a more specific clause pertaining to the regulatory review exception. The experimental use exemption focuses on how a patented invention is used (i.e., experimentation on the patented invention per se or employing the patented invention as a means), rather than the purpose of the use (business or philosophical) as is the case in the United States.[82] Experimental use in China has generally been considered to refer to scientific research and experimentations carried out specifically on the patented technology as such, but not those that are conducted by exploiting the patented technology. This understanding is now reflected in a directive delivered by the Beijing Higher People's Court in 2013, entitled "Guidelines for Judgment of Patent Infringement."[83] Although not technically binding, the Guidelines are indicative of how courts will interpret the scope of experimental use and what is generally considered "good law" in the Chinese system.

In regard to the regulatory review provision, Article 69(5) of the Patent Law states that use "[f]or the purpose of providing the information needed for the administrative approval" shall not be deemed to be a patent infringement. While this is rather vague, China interprets the provision broadly. Such an interpretation has been confirmed by the State Intellectual Property Office (SIPO), which issued a binding directive entitled "Guidelines for Determination of Patent Infringement and Passing Off," stating that the exception is applicable not only to patents on drugs and medical devices as such, but also to those on an active ingredient of a drug, a process for preparing a drug, a process for preparing an active ingredient of a drug, parts specifically for use in a medical device and a method

there is no measured negative or positive correlation between investment in R&D and the breadth of experimental use exceptions."

[82] Patent Law of the People's Republic of China, Adopted at the 4th Meeting of the Standing Committee of the Sixth National People's Congress on 12 March 1984 and amended as of 27 December 2008, available from the All China Patent Attorneys Association at www.acpaa.cn/english/article/content/201510/121/1.html. Article 69 reads: "None of the following shall be deemed an infringement of the patent right: (4) Where any person uses the patent concerned solely for the purposes of scientific research and experimentation."

[83] See Article 123 Guidelines for Judgment of Patent Infringement, Beijing Higher People's Court, 2013, www.chinacourt.org/article/detail/2014/01/id/1175142.shtml, accessed 4 March 2017: "Using relevant patents solely for the purpose of scientific research and experiment shall not be deemed an infringement...Using relevant patents solely for the purpose of scientific research and experiment, refers to scientific research and experiment on the patented technical solution itself exclusively. Scientific research and experiment on the technical solution itself should be distinguished from using patented technical solution in scientific research and experiment."

of using a medical device.[84] Therefore, activities falling within the scope of the provision include (1) manufacture, use or import of a patented drug or patented medical apparatus by any person in order to acquire information necessary for seeking marketing approval; as well as (2) manufacture or import of the drug/apparatus by any person solely for others to acquire such information will be deemed as an exception to patent infringement.

Regulatory Review Exception – Other Jurisdictions Subsequent to the panel report in *Canada – Pharmaceutical Patents*, a number of countries adopted a regulatory review exception, which has now been widely adopted throughout the world. As expected, the scope of the provision differs between and among jurisdictions.[85] In some jurisdictions, the experimental use exception explicitly includes acts undertaken to obtain marketing approval, while in others the regulatory review exception is contained in a separate provision. In some jurisdictions, the experimental use exception has been given a broad interpretation so as to encompass acts by third parties to obtain regulatory approval, whereas others more narrowly interpret the provision.

Ironically, perhaps, the take-up rate for the exception is lowest in Africa where increased access to medicines is most needed. For instance, review of national legislation published in 2007 revealed that only three of the thirty-nine countries included specifically provided for a regulatory review exception (Kenya, Namibia and Zimbabwe).[86] While several countries have subsequently incorporated the exception, the take-up rate remains exceedingly low. Somewhat surprising too is the fact that several countries in Latin America and the Middle East introduced a regulatory review exception only as a result of an FTA with the United States, whose

---

[84] Section 7, Chapter Three, Part I Guidelines for Determination of Patent Infringement and Passing Off, www.sipo.gov.cn/tz/gz/201309/t20130925_819909.html, accessed 4 March 2017. Section 7(2) reads: "[T]he implemented medicine patents include not only the patents of the medicine itself, but also the patents of the active ingredients in the medicine, the patents of the preparation method of the medicine, and the patents of the preparation method of pharmaceutical active ingredients in the medicine; the implemented medicinal equipment patents include not only the patents of the medicinal equipment itself, but also the patents of special parts of the medical equipment, and the patents of the usage method of the medical equipment."

[85] See Tridico et al., above n. 38.

[86] Sisule Musungu, "Access to ART and Other Essential Medicines in Sub-Saharan Africa: Intellectual Property and Relevant Legislations," Report commissioned by United Nations Development Programme (UNDP), at 13, http://apps.who.int/medicinedocs/documents/s18248en/s18248en.pdf, accessed 6 March 2017.

negotiating template includes a narrow form of the exception. An example of such a provision is Article 17.9.4 of the US-Chile FTA, which states:

> If a Party permits the use by a third party of the subject matter of a subsisting patent to support an application for marketing approval or sanitary permit of a pharmaceutical product, the Party shall provide that any product produced under such authority shall not be made, used, or sold in the territory of the Party other than for purposes related to meeting requirements for marketing approval or the sanitary permit, and if export is permitted, the product shall only be exported outside the territory of the Party for purposes of meeting requirements for issuing marketing approval or sanitary permits in the exporting Party.

In fact, even India introduced a regulatory review exception only in 2002, taking inspiration from the US approach. The Indian exception, however, is wider of scope than the US provision, as it allows the experimental use exception to apply to the submission of information domestically or overseas, whereas the United States limits this exception for the submission of information domestically. Section 107A of the Indian Patents (Amendment) Act 2002 reads:

> Certain acts not to be considered as infringement. – For the purposes of this Act:
>
> (a) any act of making, constructing, using or selling a patented invention solely for uses reasonably relating to the development and submission of information required under any law for the time being in force, in India, or in a country other than India, that regulates the manufacture, construction, use or sale of any product;
> (b) importation of patented products by any person from a person who is duly authorised by the patentee to sell or distribute the product, shall not be considered as an infringement of patent rights.[87]

What this diversity of approach indicates is that while the experimental use exception is an acceptable means of achieving the balance of rights and obligations needed to promote technological innovation and dissemination, the nuances regarding scope and breadth have been left to jurisdictions. This leads to uncertainty and accusations of going beyond the parameters of Article 30 of the TRIPS Agreement. While some favor a narrow exception, others argue for a broader approach.[88] For Hong Kong, the

---

[87] The Patents (Amendment) Act, 2002, No. 38, §44, Acts of Parliament, 2002 (India).

[88] See, e.g., Shamnad Basheer and Prashant Reddy, "The 'Experimental Use' Exception through a Developmental Lens," (2010) 50(4) *IDEA* 831, 834 and 872 ("TRIPS was premised on the promise of transfer of technology. Given that there is no meaningful way of obligating developed countries to transfer technology, TRIPS should at the very least

limits may not matter as in practice it is not likely to push the boundaries of the international order. The more important issue for the jurisdiction is providing clarity to existing law.

Policy and Legal Considerations for Hong Kong   Hong Kong's experimental use exception is outdated and does not serve the purpose for which it is intended. The provision should be reviewed and updated. In so doing, Hong Kong should take a holistic approach to the experimental use exception and be mindful not to unduly limit its scope and potential importance in the community. Hong Kong should thus follow the advice of Sean O'Connor, who opined that "policymakers should be aware of the full range of research use exceptions – from exceptions for competitive commercial R&D to very narrowly tailored de facto research use exceptions for government research – and employ models that match broad research, public domain, and competition policies in their country."[89] At present, and like many other jurisdictions, Hong Kong's legislation limits the scope of the exception in such a way as to curtail the usefulness of the provision. More specifically, Section 75 of the Patents Ordinance (Cap 514), entitled "Limitation of effect of patent," sets out the experimental use exemption:

> The rights conferred by a patent shall not extend to (a) acts done privately for non-commercial purposes; (b) acts done for experimental purposes relating to the subject-matter of the relevant patented invention.

Modeled after Section 42 of the Irish Patents Act 1992, the section has not been updated despite an amendment to the Irish Patents Act in 2006 implementing the EU directive on the regulatory review exception.[90] Section 42 of the Irish Patents Act now includes subsection (g), "Limitation of effect of patent," providing:

> The rights conferred by a patent shall not extend to –
> (g) acts done in relation to the subject matter of the relevant patented invention which consist of:
> (i) acts done in conducting the necessary studies, tests and trials which are conducted with a view to satisfying the application requirements ... for a marketing authorisation in respect of a medicinal product for human use.

enable countries to ramp up technological capabilities by themselves. One way of doing so is by having a robust experimental use exception, enabling such countries to work with registered patents, understand and absorb underlying technology").

[89] See O'Connor, above n. 66.
[90] More specifically, Directive 2001/83/EC as amended by Directive 2004/27/EC, above n. 71.

In order to avoid legal uncertainty, Hong Kong should carefully draft a regulation that makes the delineations of the experimental use exemption clear. It should also seek to draft the provision in terms as wide as possible; given its lack of domestic pharmaceutical industry, the objective should be to provide access to affordable medicines as quickly as possible. Before making further recommendations on a potential course of action, however, it is useful to review the two main issues in crafting a regulatory review exception. First, the provision should improve availability of affordable drugs by facilitating the timely entry of generic competition into the marketplace. Second, the provision should provide certainty regarding which uses (related to regulatory approval) fall within the scope of the exception and which can potentially constitute patent infringement.

With these overarching issues in mind, and with the aims and objectives of Hong Kong at the forefront, the following analysis considers specific matters relating to the regulatory review exception.

Covered Products: One of the first issues that must be considered is whether the exception will apply to all products subject to regulatory approval or should be more limited, such as applying only to patented pharmaceutical products or to related products and medical devices.[91] There does not seem to be an overriding justification to limit the exception only to health-related or pharmaceutical products. In fact, doing so may be inconsistent with Article 27.1 of the TRIPS Agreement's prohibition on discrimination in regard to the field of technology.[92] Thus, at a minimum the regulatory review exception should cover pharmaceutical products and related medical devices.

Permitted Acts: Prior to seeking marketing approval from the regulatory authority, a generic applicant normally must "use" the patented product in a variety of ways. This includes working with samples of the patented product. The applicant may produce the sample or obtain it through purchase and importation. While most regulatory review provisions do not specifically allow for all such possibilities, some in fact do clearly set out which acts are permissible under the exception. An example in this regard is Section 69A of the South African Patent Act (as amended in 2002), which provides:

---

[91] The United States, as described above in n. 55, extends the exception to related products and medical devices. Other jurisdictions limit the exception to pharmaceutical products. See, e.g., Australian Patents Act 1990, Section 119A (explicitly excluding medical and therapeutic devices from the scope of the exception).

[92] But see *Canada – Pharmaceutical Patents*, above n. 4, para. 92.

(1) It shall not be an act of infringement of a patent to make, use, exercise, offer to dispose of, dispose of or import the patented invention on a non-commercial scale and solely for the purposes reasonably related to the obtaining, development and submission of information required under any law that regulates the manufacture, production, distribution, use or sale of any product.

(2) It shall not be permitted to possess the patented invention made, used, imported or acquired in terms of subsection (1) for any purpose other than for the obtaining, development or submission of information as contemplated in that subsection.

This provides certainty to both patent owners and generic producers regarding the scope of their rights. The provision is also drafted to ensure that importation of the patented product (or active ingredient) comes within the scope of the exception. Failure to include importation in the scope of the exception would in effect mean that few if any companies manufacturing generics in Hong Kong could make use of the provision, resulting in a de facto prohibition on applications for marketing approval of generics during the life of the patent. Hong Kong should thus follow this approach and set out exactly which acts fall within the scope of the provision.

Another point worth mentioning is South Africa's broad wording in regard to the purpose of the exception. Note here that the South African provision applies to "any law that regulates" as opposed to the more narrowly worded "acts for regulatory approval," "acts solely for uses reasonably related to regulatory approval" or "acts exclusively aiming at regulatory approval,"[93] which are used in other jurisdictions. Here again, Hong Kong would be wise to follow South Africa and draft a broad provision in order to guard against litigation and unnecessarily narrow interpretation of the exception.

Limitation to Generics or a Broader Exception: An important consideration is whether to have the regulatory review provision apply only where marketing approval for a *generic* product is sought or to widen the scope of the provision and have it also apply to research that could lead to the development of a *new* product. A number of laws do not address the issue or distinguish it based on ultimate aim of the researcher.[94] This seems like

---

[93] See WIPO, "Exceptions and Limitations to Patent Rights," above n. 6, para. 132.

[94] See, e.g., Thailand Patent Act B.E. 2522 (1979) as Amended by the Patent Act (No. 2) B.E 2535 (1992) and the Patent Act (No. 3) B.E. 2542 (1999), Article 36.4 (providing the patentee's exclusive rights shall not apply to any act concerning an application for drug

the correct approach, as a company cannot guarantee that testing will be successful or that circumstances dictate filing for marketing approval in every case. As detailed above, such a broad approach is in line with the judicial application and interpretation of US law.

Likewise, most countries do not stipulate whether the regulatory review exception applies only to preclinical studies or also applies to subsequent clinical studies (including postclinical testing). The US approach of extending the exception to all studies so long as there is a reasonable basis to believe that those studies will produce information relevant to an application to be filed with the regulatory authority seems again to be the correct approach. If the studies may be useful or required by the regulatory authority, there is no reason to distinguish between the stages of trials or when the studies are conducted.

Temporal Limitations: Most countries do not address the issue, but some limit the exception to a certain time frame prior to the expiration of the patent.[95] There does not seem to be any justification for a temporal restriction. In fact, such a restriction limits the ability of a generic to challenge the validity of the patent by bringing a drug to market within a few years of the normal expiration of the patent.

Submissions in Other Jurisdictions: Some jurisdictions limit the regulatory review exception to acts undertaken with respect to an application for marketing approval in their respective country, whereas others allow the exception to cover acts undertaken for submission in another jurisdiction. An example of the latter includes India, where Section 107(a) of the Patents Act covers acts relating to the development and submission of information required by law "in India or in a country other than India."[96] Many others with similar provisions, such as Brazil, have a similar interest in encouraging generic production within their jurisdictions.[97] While

---

registration or to the applicant intending to produce, distribute or import the product after the expiration of the patent term). See also Argentine Law 24.766 on Confidential Information of December 1996, Article 8.

[95] Mexican Industrial Property Law (as amended up to 9 April 2012), www.wipo.int/wipolex/en/details.jsp?id=11711 (limiting the exception to within three years of expiration).

[96] Section 107A(a) of the Patents Act 1970 (incorporating all amendments until 23 June 2017).

[97] See, e.g., Brazil Law No. 9.279, May 14, 1996 (Industrial Property Law) as amended by Law 10.196 of 14 February 2001, Article 43 (VII) (applying "to acts performed by non-authorized third parties, regarding patented inventions, which aim exclusively [at] the production of information, data and test results directed to procure commerce registration, in Brazil or any other country, to allow the exploitation and commercialization of the patented product, after the termination of the terms provided in article 10").

this is not particularly relevant to Hong Kong, there are reasons to recommend that the territory allow acts undertaken for submission in another jurisdiction. Correa succinctly makes the point:

> There is no solid justification for a limitation regarding submissions in foreign countries. The legitimate interests protected under a patent granted in the country where trials take place are not affected by acts made in another jurisdiction. Patents are of territorial nature. Whether the submission of information in a foreign country, before the expiry of a patent granted there, is admissible or not is a matter solely subject to the law of that country.[98]

Correa's point is valid and there is no solid justification to limit the scope of the provision to within the territory. Moreover, as Hong Kong occasionally discusses becoming a pharmaceutical hub, it should ensure that its laws allow this to occur. Thus, Hong Kong should follow the Indian model of applying the exception to acts undertaken for submission in another jurisdiction.

Concluding Comments on Article 30

By paying attention to the details of its regulatory review exception, Hong Kong can benefit from the experience of other jurisdictions, and the time taken to complete the marketing approval process can potentially be reduced. Hong Kong should therefore craft a provision that is both more specific and broader than that of Ireland's, taking into account its position as a pharmaceutical importer with little to no branded operations currently operating in the territory.

Of course, the regulatory review exception is only the starting point and does not resolve many of the important questions regarding the scope of the broader experimental use provision. For instance, it is debatable whether Hong Kong should continue with its narrow interpretation of the exception limiting its use to noncommercial purposes or broaden the interpretation (as is the case in Germany). Without an amendment specifically for a regulatory review exception, it would seem sensible for Hong Kong to broaden the scope of the general experimental use provision. However, the easier and more targeted approach would simply be to add the regulatory review amendment, such as that of the Irish provision highlighted above. In this respect, the integrity of a limited and narrow experimental use provision remains intact with clarity and explicit recognition

---

[98] See Correa, above n. 25.

of specific necessary acts from pharmaceutical companies as a result of health and safety regulations. That being the case, limiting the exception to noncommercial use narrows the scope of the exception and does not allow users to take advantage of the full extent of Article 30 of the TRIPS Agreement. The limitation is unnecessary and not in line with the health or competition policies of the jurisdiction. Thus, Hong Kong should remove the noncommercial use limitation so as to broaden the scope of the provision while at the same time ensuring that its law remains in line with the parameters set by Article 30 of the TRIPS Agreement.

Hong Kong should also clarify whether the exception covers "experimenting with" or "experimenting on" patented inventions. In the United Kingdom, "experimenting with" inventions falls within the experimental use exception, whereas "experimenting on" inventions is outside the scope of the provision. As a net importer of patented inventions, one could argue that Hong Kong's provision ought to be wide enough to permit entities to experiment on patented inventions with a view toward improving or even inventing around such patents. It could therefore follow Belgium in drafting a provision with wide scope. However, Hong Kong also must be mindful of the expectations of the global business community, including the pharmaceutical industry, and of its perceived place in the region as an IP hub and therefore not deviate too much from world legal standards. Moreover, the jurisdiction hosts very little pharmaceutical research and development. Given this, it does not seem appropriate for Hong Kong to push the boundaries, and thus the jurisdiction should limit the exception to "experimenting with" patented inventions.

5.2.2   Article 31 Exceptions

Compulsory licensing refers to the exploitation of a patent without the patent holder's consent on the authorization of a national authority. Such authorization can be granted to a third party or to a government entity. In the context of pharmaceuticals, compulsory licenses are most often issued to a third party when the price and/or availability of the pharmaceutical product constrains access by citizens in the relevant market.[99]

The vast majority of WTO Members legislatively allow for the government and/or third parties, under certain circumstances and conditions,

---

[99] Carlos M. Correa, "Implications of Doha Declaration on the TRIPS Agreement and Public Health," Health Economics and Drugs EDM Series no. 12, June 2002 (WHO/EDM/PAR/2002,3), at 15, http://apps.who.int/medicinedocs/pdf/s2301e/s2301e .pdf, accessed 15 January 2016.

to use a patented invention without the authorization of the right holder via a compulsory license. Similar to the experimental use exception, the exact circumstances, boundaries and limits of the legislation differ among and between the jurisdictions, as the interests of various stakeholders may diverge between jurisdictions. What remains constant, however, is the core basis for the exception – that is, to prevent abuse of the monopoly power granted by a patent right and to help "ensure that the patent system contributes to the promotion of innovation in a competitive environment and to the transfer and dissemination of technology, meeting the objectives of the system and responding to the public interest at large."[100] The compulsory license is also viewed as a "safeguard" ensuring that a government can adequately and effectively respond to a national security or health emergency or crisis.[101] Compulsory licenses differ from other exceptions in that the government and/or third party is not allowed to freely exploit the patented invention. Rather, exploitation is limited to the terms of the license, and patent owners maintain the right to remuneration for such use.

While activists have for some time viewed compulsory licenses as an effective way to provide access to essential medicines throughout the developing world, the truth is that the mechanism is not a panacea. On the contrary, the value of the law *as such* is of more benefit as it serves to encourage voluntary licenses and price reductions.[102] Thus it is the *threat* of a compulsory license that is a valuable bargaining chip to be used to extract concessions from the rights holder; whereas the *use* of a compulsory license is fraught with challenges. For example, while a voluntary license comes with technical knowledge and know-how, a compulsory license comes with no such assistance. Where undisclosed or technically advanced know-how is required in order to fully exploit the patented invention, the compulsory license cannot achieve the goals of reducing price and increasing access. The issuance of a compulsory license is therefore only really effective when the technology is already known and only access to it is required and the technical competence needed to exploit the technology is not advanced or difficult to replicate.[103] Another potential

---

[100] WIPO, "Economics of IP and International Technology Transfer," Fourteenth Session of the Committee on Development and Intellectual Property (CDIP), Geneva, 10–14 November 2014. Document CDIP/14/INF/7, 18 September 2014, at 79.

[101] Ibid.

[102] See, e.g., Jayashree Watal, *Intellectual Property Rights in the WTO and Developing Countries* (Oxford University Press, 2001), at 328.

[103] Ibid.

consequence of issuing a compulsory license could be reprisals from the patent owner or its home government. Reprisals can come in many forms, but to date include the delay in registration of other products by the patent owner (thus keeping them off the host country market) and the reduction of governmental aid and other assistance.

The remainder of this section introduces the international framework on compulsory licenses before reviewing how this framework has been put in place domestically in select jurisdictions. The section then reviews the current framework in Hong Kong before concluding with recommendations to update and amend the legislation in order to more fully meet the needs of the territory.

International Context

The international community has long recognized the legitimacy of compulsory licenses. Compulsory licensing features in the Paris Convention with Article 5(A)(2) explicitly granting signatories "the right to take legislative measures providing for the grant of compulsory licenses to prevent the abuses which might result from the exercise of the exclusive rights conferred by the patent, for example, failure to work." With Article 2(2) of TRIPS importing the obligations Members have under the Paris Convention,[104] this clause of the Paris Convention is to be read as if it is contained in the TRIPS Agreement itself.[105] In this regard, the TRIPS Agreement builds on, rather than replaces, the earlier convention. With respect to compulsory licenses, Article 31 of the TRIPS Agreement provides for a more comprehensive procedural structure that conditions the use of compulsory licenses in a number of respects. The conditions include the following:[106]

---

[104] The most reasonable viewpoint is that the WIPO treaties were incorporated as they stood at the date of the TRIPS Agreement – 1994. For a concurring opinion, see Joost Pauwelyn, *Conflict of Norms in Public International Law: How WTO Law Relates to Other Laws of International Law* (Cambridge University Press, 2003), p. 265; Suzy Frankel, "WTO Application of the 'Customary Rules on Interpretation of Public International Law' to Intellectual Property" (2005–2006) 46 *Virginia Journal of International Law* 365, 409.

[105] Article 2.2 of the TRIPS Agreement reads: "Nothing in Parts I to IV of this Agreement [i.e. including Part II(5) – Patents] shall derogate from existing obligations that Members may have to each other under the Paris Convention, the Berne Convention, the Rome Convention and the Treaty on Intellectual Property in Respect of Integrated Circuits."

[106] These conditions must be read together with the related provisions of Article 27.1, which require that patent rights be enjoyable without discrimination as to the field of technology or whether products are imported or produced locally. In the context of Article 30, see *Canada – Pharmaceutical Patents*, above n. 4, paras. 7.88–91.

(a) authorisation of such use shall be considered on its individual merits;

(b) such use may only be permitted if, prior to such use, the proposed user has made efforts to obtain authorisation from the right holder on reasonable commercial terms and conditions and that such efforts have not been successful within a reasonable period of time. This requirement may be waived by a Member in the case of a national emergency or other circumstances of extreme urgency or in cases of public non-commercial use. In situations of national emergency or other circumstances of extreme urgency, the right holder shall, nevertheless, be notified as soon as reasonably practicable. In the case of public non-commercial use, where the government or contractor, without making a patent search, knows or has demonstrable grounds to know that a valid patent is or will be used by or for the government, the right holder shall be informed promptly;

(c) the scope and duration of such use shall be limited to the purpose for which it was authorised, and in the case of semi-conductor technology shall only be for public non-commercial use or to remedy a practice determined after judicial or administrative process to be anti-competitive;

(d) such use shall be non-exclusive;

(e) such use shall be non-assignable, except with that part of the enterprise or goodwill which enjoys such use;

(f) any such use shall be authorised predominantly for the supply of the domestic market of the Member authorising such use;

(g) authorisation for such use shall be liable, subject to adequate protection of the legitimate interests of the persons so authorised, to be terminated if and when the circumstances which led to it cease to exist and are unlikely to recur. The competent authority shall have the authority to review, upon motivated request, the continued existence of these circumstances;

(h) the right holder shall be paid adequate remuneration in the circumstances of each case, taking into account the economic value of the authorisation;

(i) the legal validity of any decision relating to the authorisation of such use shall be subject to judicial review or other independent review by a distinct higher authority in that Member;

(j) any decision relating to the remuneration provided in respect of such use shall be subject to judicial review or other independent review by a distinct higher authority in that Member; [and]

(k) Members are not obliged to apply the conditions set forth in subparagraphs (b) and (f) where such use is permitted to remedy a practice determined after judicial or administrative process to be anti-competitive. The need to correct anti-competitive practices may be taken into account in determining the amount of remuneration in such cases. Competent authorities shall have the authority to refuse termination of authorisation if and when the conditions which led to such authorisation are likely to recur.

It is beyond the scope of this chapter to review all the conditions, but it is worth singling out one subsection for special mention. Subsection (f) has played a major role in the controversy over patents and access to medicines, as it restricts the issuance of a compulsory license to that of "predominantly for the supply of the domestic market of the Member authorizing such use," meaning that a Member must have the means within its jurisdiction to produce the product itself or it cannot get the benefit of this provision. As explained below, the resolution to the problem faced by Members with insufficient or no manufacturing capacities came in the early 2000s.

The WTO reiterated and supplemented the TRIPS Agreement in November 2001 with the Doha Declaration on the TRIPs Agreement and Public Health (Doha Declaration),[107] and while the legal status of the Declaration remains undetermined, it is clearly a document that directly addresses the impact of the international intellectual property regime on the public health.[108] The Doha Declaration recognizes that "[e]ach member has the right to grant compulsory licenses and the freedom to determine the grounds upon which such licenses are granted"[109] and provides that the TRIPS Agreement "can and should be interpreted and

---

[107] WTO Declaration on the TRIPs Agreement & Public Health (WT/MIN(01)/DEC/W/2) adopted on 14 November 2001, available at www.wto.org/english/thewto_e/minist_e/min01_e/mindecl_trips_e.htm.

[108] For more discussion on the legal status of the Doha Declaration, see Bryan Mercurio and Mitali Tyagi, "Treaty Interpretation in WTO Dispute Settlement: The Outstanding Question of the Legality of Local Working Requirements" (2010) 19(2) *Minnesota Journal of International Law* 275, 312–13 ("the Declaration is not technically an authoritative interpretation under Article IX(2) of the Marrakesh Agreement, [but] has the *look* and *effect* of an authoritative interpretation"); James Gathii, "The Legal Status of the Doha Declaration on TRIPS and Public Health under the Vienna Convention on the Law of Treaties" (2002) 15 *Harv. JL & Tech.* 291; Andrew D. Mitchell and Tania Voon, "Patents and Public Health in the WTO, FTAs and Beyond: Tension and Conflict in International Law" (2009) 43 *Journal of World Trade* 571, 581.

[109] WTO Declaration, above n. 107, para. 5(b).

implemented in a manner supportive of WTO Members' right to protect public health and, in particular, to promote access to medicines for all."[110] Further, the Declaration reinforces the notion that Members can take measures to forestall or limit public health crises by stating that each has the right to determine what constitutes a national emergency or other circumstances of extreme urgency, with the explicit understanding that public health crises, including but not limited to those relating to HIV/AIDS, tuberculosis, malaria and other epidemics, can represent a national emergency or other circumstances of extreme urgency.[111]

The Doha Declaration failed in one respect as agreement was not reached on how Members with insufficient or no manufacturing capacities could make use of the compulsory license provisions in Article 31 of the TRIPS Agreement. Instead, paragraph 6 of the Declaration "recognize[s] that WTO members with insufficient or no manufacturing capacities in the pharmaceutical sector could face difficulties in making effective use of compulsory licensing under the TRIPS Agreement... [and] instruct[s] the Council for TRIPS to find an expeditious solution to this problem and to report to the General Council before the end of 2002."

The "paragraph 6 solution" in fact was not reached until August 2003, when Members agreed on a "waiver" to the limitation on the export of pharmaceuticals under compulsory license to LDC Members and other Members with insufficient or no manufacturing capacities. Officially the "Decision of the General Council of August 30, 2003 on the Implementation of Paragraph 6 of the Doha Declaration on the TRIPS Agreement and Public Health" sets out a scheme to facilitate the exportation and importation of pharmaceuticals under compulsory license. The scheme is detailed and requires the importing and exporting Member to adhere to several procedural steps. For instance, the importing Member must notify the TRIPS Council of the names and expected quantities of the products needed, either confirm that it is an LDC or have established that it has insufficient or no manufacturing capacities in the pharmaceutical sector for the products in question and confirm that, if the product is patented in its territory, it has granted or intends to grant a compulsory license in accordance with Article 31 of the TRIPS Agreement.[112]

---

[110] Ibid., para. 4.   [111] Ibid., para. 5.

[112] See WTO, Implementation of Paragraph 6 of the Doha Declaration on the TRIPS Agreement and Public Health, Decision of the General Council of 30 August 2003, WT/L/540 and Corr.1, 1 September 2003, para. 2(1).

For its part, the exporting Member must confirm that the particulars of the intended importing Member are in order and that it has granted or intends to grant a compulsory license for only the amount necessary to meet the needs of the eligible importing Member; that the product is clearly identified as being produced under this special system, such as through specific labeling or marking; that the product is distinguishable through special packaging and/or special coloring/shaping;[113] and that prior to shipment certain required information has been posted on a website.[114]

While the particulars of the waiver have been criticized and the system has been formally used only once since its inception,[115] the Decision of the General Council of 6 December 2005 made the waiver a permanent amendment to the TRIPS Agreement (to replace the Decision of the General Council of 30 August 2003) on acceptance by two-thirds of the WTO membership – this occurred on 23 January 2017.[116]

Since the establishment of the TRIPS regime, certain countries have also included provisions regarding compulsory licensing of patents in FTAs.[117] In most cases, the FTA will restrict the issuance of a compulsory license to a limited set of circumstances. The United States is the leading proponent of such limitations, with its FTAs often providing that a compulsory license can only be issued to remedy an anticompetitive practice, for noncommercial use, in situations of national emergency or other circumstances of extreme urgency or on the grounds of failure to

---

[113] There is a caveat here, being "provided that such distinction is feasible and does not have a significant impact on price." Ibid., para. 2(b)(ii).

[114] Ibid., para. 2(b).

[115] For a brief description of the implementation, operation and use of the system, see World Trade Organization, World Intellectual Property Organization and World Health Organization, "Promoting Access to Medical Technologies and Innovation: Intersections between Public Health, Intellectual Property and Trade" (2012), Annex II, at 222–30, www.wto.org/english/res_e/booksp_e/pamtiwhowipowtoweb13_e.pdf. For criticism of the waiver, see, e.g., Médecins Sans Frontières (MSF), "Neither Expeditious, nor a Solution: The WTO August 30th Decision Is Unworkable" (MSF, 2006).

[116] See WTO, "Amendment of the TRIPS Agreement: Decision on 6 December 2005," WT/L/641 (8 December 2005). For background, see www.wto.org/english/tratop_e/trips_e/amendment_e.htm.

[117] It should also be noted that Article 1709.10 of the NAFTA set out conditions to the issuance of compulsory licenses, such as that the license be nonexclusive and nonassignable, predominantly to supply the domestic market; that efforts be made to obtain authorization from the right holder; that adequate remuneration be paid to the rights holder; and that the licensee is not authorized to use of the subject matter of a patent to exploit another patent except where allowed to remedy a violation of domestic competition laws.

meet working requirements, provided that importation shall constitute working.[118]

The Application of Compulsory License Schemes

Domestic legislation provides various grounds for granting compulsory licenses for patents and specifies factors and conditions when such provisions apply. Most of these are drawn directly from the text of Article 31 of the TRIPS Agreement. There are differences among jurisdictions, however, and as highlighted above can be (re)shaped through FTA commitments. Among the most common triggers for the issuance of a compulsory license are the following:

- Non-working or insufficient working: Domestic provisions clarify the circumstances and criteria for when a patent holder's activities constitute "non-working" of the patent, as well as determinants of the "sufficiency" of working a patent. The issue of "non-working" is contentious, as some interpret the phrase to mean that local "working" of the patented product is required, whereas others view importation and availability of the patented product as fulfilling the requirement. This issue has been subject to a WTO claim brought by the United States against Brazil, with the complaint challenging Brazil's legislation allowing for a compulsory license if the patent is not "worked" in the territory of Brazil as inconsistent with Articles 27 and 28 of the TRIPS Agreement and Article III of the GATT 1994.[119] The parties reached a mutually agreeable solution and the claim never went to a panel. Noteworthy is the fact that Brazil did not agree to amend its legislation as part of the settlement.[120]

---

[118] See Article 4.20 of the US-Jordan FTA. See also Article 17.9.7 of the US-Australia FTA; Article 16.7.6 of the US-Singapore FTA. It should be noted that a number of other FTAs – including most of those negotiated by European Free Trade Association and the EU – do not restrict compulsory licensing and explicitly recognize the principles established in the Doha Declaration. See, e.g., Article 11.5 of the Switzerland-China FTA; Article 6.2.5 of the EFTA-Peru FTA; Article 6.2.5 of the EFTA-Colombia FTA; Article 147(B) of the EU-CARIFORUM EPA; Article 10.34 of the EU-Korea FTA.

[119] Brazilian legislation defined "failure to be worked" as "failure to manufacture or incomplete manufacture of the product" or "failure to make full use of the patented process." See Brazil – Measures Affecting Patent Protection – Request for Consultations by the United States (WT/DS199/1, G/L/385, IP/D/23) (8 June 2000).

[120] See Brazil – Measures Affecting Patent Protection – Notification of Mutually Agreed Solution (WT/DS199/4, G/L/454, IP/D/23/Add.1), para. 3 (19 July 2001) ("Should the U.S. withdraw the WTO panel against Brazil concerning the interpretation of Article 68, the Brazilian Government would agree, in the event it deems necessary to apply Article 68 to

- Anti-competitive practices: Domestic legislation usually allows for the issuance of a compulsory license to remedy breaches of competition law, often as a remedy in cases brought before a domestic competition authority or through judicial action in relation to an abuse of monopoly power.[121]
- Public interest: Domestic legislation commonly allows for the issuance of a compulsory license in situations of emergency or crisis. Most often associated with national health emergences, nonavailability of patented products and excessive pricing, which reduces availability in the market, these justifications are generally accepted as being compatible with Article 31 of the TRIPS Agreement.[122] This is, however, not always the case and can lead to controversy and potential WTO disputes. These issues will be further explored below.
- Dependent and blocking patents: Many jurisdictions allow for the issuance of a compulsory license in situations where one patent (a so-called dependent patent) cannot be exploited without infringing another patent ("blocking" patent). Pursuant to Article 31 of the TRIPS Agreement, a compulsory license can be granted only if the second invention is an important technical advance of considerable economic significance and where a compulsory license is granted to the holder of a dependent patent.[123]

There being no database or official repository, the actual number of compulsory licenses issued globally is difficult to ascertain. According to one study, between 1995 and 2011 twenty-four compulsory licenses were issued in seventeen countries covering forty pharmaceutical

---

grant compulsory license on patents held by the U.S. companies, to hold prior talks on the matter with the U.S. Government. These talks would be held within the scope of the U.S. – Brazil Consultative Mechanism, in a special session scheduled to discuss the subject").

[121] TRIPS Agreement, Articles 8(2) and 40(1) and (2).

[122] This is not limited to pharmaceuticals. For instance, the United States has issued compulsory licenses for patents relating to pollution control devices under the Clean Air Act and those involving nuclear materials. See, e.g., the Clean Air Act, United States Code Title 42, Chapter 85, §7608.

[123] For jurisdictions providing for the issuance of a compulsory license on the grounds of non-working or insufficient working, public interest, anticompetitive practices and dependent patents, see World Intellectual Property Organization, "Exclusions from Patentable Subject Matter and Exceptions and Limitations to the Rights," SCP/13/3, at 36–47 (2009). For a detailed cross-country overview of compulsory license provisions in a variety of jurisdictions, see the World Intellectual Property Organization, "Study on Exceptions and Limitations to Patent Rights," SCP/17/3, Annex II (2011).

product patents.[124] The most notable compulsory license occurred in 2007 when Rwanda made use of the waiver and notified the WTO of its importation of 260,000 packs of Apo-Triavir (a generic version of a patented HIV/AIDS drug) manufactured in Canada by Apotex Inc.[125] The process took some time, as both Rwanda and Canada had to comply with the procedural conditions of the waiver but ultimately allowed for the export of pharmaceuticals under compulsory license. Another notable case occurred in 2012 when Indonesia issued a compulsory license for governmental use on seven HIV and hepatitis medicines, with only a 0.5 percent royalty on generic sales payable to the rights holder.[126] Likewise, in 2006 and 2007, Thailand issued compulsory licenses for governmental use on Merck's antiretroviral efavirenz (Stocrin),[127] Abbott's antiretroviral lopinavir/ritonavir (Kaletra) and Sanofi-Aventis' heart disease drug clopidogrel (Plavix) with only a 0.5 percent royalty on generic sales (while the United Nations Development Program (UNDP) recommends that rates normally be set at 4 percent).[128] In response, Thailand suffered repercussions as Abbott withdrew certain products from the Thai market and it would no longer register new drugs in Thailand. Thailand responded by initiating a competition law complaint against Abbott.[129] Malaysia

---

[124] Reed Beall and Randall Kuhn, "Trends in Compulsory Licensing of Pharmaceuticals since the Doha Declaration: A Database Analysis" (2012) *PLoS Med* 9(1), http://journals .plos.org/plosmedicine/article?id=10.1371/journal.pmed.1001154#ack, accessed 4 March 2017.

[125] For details, see Matthew Rimmer, "Race against Time: The Export of Essential Medicines to Rwanda" (2008) 1(2) *Pub Health Ethics* 89; Matthew Rimmer, "The Jean Chretien Pledge to Africa Act: Patent Law and Humanitarian Aid" (2005) 15 (7) *Expert Opinion on Therapeutic Patents* 889; International Center for Trade and Sustainable Development, "Rwanda Tests Public Health Waiver" (October 2007) 11(6)*Bridges News*, http://ictsd.org/ i/news/bridges/4095/, accessed 4 March 2017.

[126] The pharmaceuticals included the HIV antiretroviral efavirenz (Sustiva) (previously subject to a compulsory license dating from 2007), abacavir (Ziagen), didanosine (Videx), combination lopinavir and ritonavir (Kaletra), tenofovir (Viread), the combination of tenofovir and emtricitabine (Truvada) and the combination of efavirenz, emtricitabine and tenofovir (Atripla). See Act Up Paris, "Indonesia Issues Compulsory Licences against Seven HIV, Hepatitis Drugs" (October 2012), www.actupparis.org/spip.php?article4984.

[127] Washington College of Law, Program for Information Justice and Intellectual Property, "Timeline for Thailand's Compulsory Licenses," www.wcl.american.edu/pijip/ documents/timeline.pdf, accessed 6 March 2017.

[128] Siraprapha Rungpry and Edward J. Kelly, "Compulsory Licensing Developments in Thailand" (2008) 16 *Asialaw IP Review*, www.tilleke.com/sites/default/files/compulsory_ licensing_developments_TH.pdf, accessed 4 March 2017.

[129] Sean Flynn, "Appeal of Thailand Commission Order on Abbott's Refusal to Sell AIDS Medications in Thailand" (2008), www.wcl.american.edu/pijip/thai_comp_licenses.cfm, accessed 4 March 2017.

similarly issued compulsory licenses on three patented HIV/AIDS medicines for governmental use in 2003, purportedly importing generic versions of the patented products from India. While the price of the pharmaceuticals dropped by 81 percent (from US$315 to US$58 per month) and the number of HIV/AIDS patients treated in government hospitals and clinics increased from 1,500 to 4,000,[130] it is debatable whether the savings of US$642,500 is worth the potential reprisals by the branded industry and other governments.

Brazil has been among the most effective countries in using the better option of threating the issuance of compulsory license only to negotiate discounts from branded pharmaceutical companies. Most notably, in 2003 Brazil negotiated price reductions on Bristol-Myers Squibb's atazanavir by 76 percent and Merck's efavirenz by 25 percent, and in 2004 it negotiated with several pharmaceutical companies (Hoffmann-La Roche, Gilead and Abbott) to reduce the price of the five most expensive antiretrovirals by between 10 and 76 percent.[131] South Africa has adopted a similar tactic and has been successful in using the threat of compulsory license together with competition law to force price reductions on branded pharmaceuticals. Notable cases include voluntary licenses following investigations in 2002–2003 by the South African Competition Commission against GlaxoSmithKline and Boehringer Ingelheim concerning excessive pricing practices for several pharmaceuticals (ritonavir, lamivudine, ritonavir/lamivudine and nevirapine).[132]

Regardless of approach, the first step in the process is to design and draft laws that enable the issuance and use of compulsory licenses. India has taken the lead in formulating clear principles behind the patent system, and where these are not met, a compulsory license can be issued. More specifically, Article 83 of the Indian Patents Act sets out the general principles applicable to the grant of compulsory licenses and other actions under Chapter XVI of the Act:

---

[130] Chee Yoke Ling, "Malaysia's Experience in Increasing Access to Antiretroviral Drugs: Exercising the 'Government Use' Option" (2006) Intellectual Property Rights Series 9 Third Work Network 14, www.twn.my/title2/IPR/pdf/ipr09.pdf, accessed 6 March 2017.

[131] Washington College of Law, Program for Information Justice and Intellectual Property, "Timeline on Brazil's Compulsory Licensing," www.wcl.american.edu/pijip/download .cfm?downloadfile=9C0107B5-DE2F-4E48-6CE8D03F4933FCD4, accessed 15 January 2017.

[132] James P. Love, "Recent Examples of the Use of Compulsory Licenses on Patents" (2007) *Knowledge Ecology International*, Research Note 2, p. 16, www.keionline.org/misc-docs/ recent_cls_8mar07.pdf, accessed 4 March 2017.

(a) patents are granted to encourage inventions and to secure that the inventions are worked in India on a commercial scale and to the fullest extent that is reasonably practicable without undue delay;

(b) patents are not granted merely to enable patentees to enjoy a monopoly for the importation of the patented article;

(c) the protection and enforcement of patent rights should contribute to the promotion of technological innovation and to the transfer and dissemination of technology, to the mutual advantage of producers and users of technological knowledge and in a manner conductive to social and economic welfare, and to a balance of rights and obligations;

(d) patents granted shall not impede protection of public health and nutrition and should act as instrument to promote public interest specially in sectors of vital importance for socio-economic and technological development of India;

(e) patents granted shall not in any way prohibit the Central Government to take measures to protect public health;

(f) patent rights shall not be abused by the patentee or by persons deriving the title or interest on the patent from the patentee, and he shall not resort to practices which unreasonably restrain trade or adversely affect the international transfer of technology; and

(g) patents are granted to make the benefit of the patented invention available at reasonably affordable prices to the public.

India backs this up with a broad framework that details when and under what circumstances a compulsory license can be issued, with Section 84 of the Indian Patents Act stating:

(1) At any time after the expiration of three years from the date of the [grant] of a patent, any person interested may make an application to the Controller for grant of compulsory licence on patent on any of the following grounds, namely:

(a) that the reasonable requirements of the public with respect to the patented invention have not been satisfied, or

(b) that the patented invention is not available to the public at a reasonably affordable price, or

(c) that the patented invention is not worked in the territory of India.

In 2012, and with some controversy, India issued its first post-TRIPS compulsory license. In a meticulous decision India's Controller General issued a compulsory license in favor of Natco to manufacture and sell a generic version of Nexavar (a kidney/liver cancer drug known by the generic name of sorafenib tosylate) at a rate of Rs 8800 for a monthly dose (120 tablets), with a 6 percent royalty on the net sales payable to Bayer. The license also requires Natco to donate medicine to 600 patients in need per year. In so deciding, the Controller found the following: (1) The reasonable requirements of the public with respect to Nexavar were not met since Bayer supplied the drug to only 2 percent of potential patients; (2) Bayer's selling price of 2,800 lakhs per month was excessive and therefore not a "reasonably affordable price"; and (3) since Bayer did not manufacture the Nexavar in India, it did not sufficiently "work" the patent in India.

While every aspect of the decision is controversial and can be debated, the third criterion is of particular interest. To many commentators, Article 27 of the TRIPS Agreement would not allow Members to discriminate between locally produced and imported products. Thus, the Controller's statement "that 'worked in the territory of India' means manufactured to a reasonable extent in India" may not be in line with the TRIPS Agreement. While I have argued elsewhere that India's position is in fact TRIPS compliant,[133] the issue is far from settled. Another interesting aspect of this judgment is that since approximately 90 percent of all pharmaceutical patents are only imported into and not manufactured in India, the decision leaves the vast majority of pharmaceuticals liable to the issuance of a compulsory license. A diverse range of jurisdictions, including Brazil and as will be detailed below Hong Kong, contain similar provisions and reliance on imported pharmaceuticals.

Hong Kong

In Hong Kong, a compulsory license can be granted if at any time after three years from the grant of the standard patent one or more of the following applies:

(a) where the patented invention is capable of being commercially worked in Hong Kong, that it is not being so worked or is not being so worked to the fullest extent that is reasonably practicable;

(b) where the patented invention is a product, that a demand for the product in Hong Kong is not being met on reasonable terms;

---

[133] Mercurio and Tyagi, above n. 108, 326 (arguing that Article 5(2) of the Paris Convention must be read together with the TRIPS Agreement as per Article 31 of the VCLT and that the object and purpose of the TRIPs Agreement and the principles of good faith mean that domestic legislation providing for local working requirements does not unjustifiably discriminate against other Members in violation of Article 27 of the TRIPS Agreement).

(c) where the patented invention is capable of being commercially worked in Hong Kong by manufacture, that it is being prevented or hindered from being so worked
  (i) in the case of a product, by the importation of the product; or
  (ii) in the case of a process, by the importation of a product obtained directly by means of the process or to which the process has been applied;

(d) that by reason of the refusal by the proprietor of the patent to grant a licence or licences on reasonable terms:
  (i) the working or efficient working in Hong Kong of any other patented invention which involves an important technical advance of considerable economic significance in relation to the patent is prevented or hindered; or
  (ii) the establishment or development of commercial or industrial activities in Hong Kong is unfairly prejudiced; or

(e) that by reason of conditions imposed by the proprietor of the patent on the grant of licences under the patent, or on the disposal or use of the patented product or on the use of the patented process, the manufacture, use or disposal of materials not protected by the patent or the establishment or development of commercial or industrial activities in Hong Kong, is unfairly prejudiced.[134]

In addition, Section 66(1) directs the court to have the following purposes in mind when determining whether to issue a compulsory license:

(a) that inventions which can be worked on a commercial scale in Hong Kong and which should in the public interest be so worked shall be worked there without undue delay and to the fullest extent that is reasonably practicable;

(b) that the inventor or other person beneficially entitled to a patent shall receive reasonable remuneration having regard to the nature of the invention;

(c) that the interests of any person for the time being working or developing an invention in Hong Kong under the protection of a patent shall not be unfairly prejudiced.

On its face, the compulsory license provision in Hong Kong is extremely broad and more in line with what one would expect from a developing

---

[134] Section 64(2).

industrial country such as India and Brazil.[135] The provision is drafted so as to explicitly allow for a compulsory license if the product is not being "commercially worked in Hong Kong" and for reasons of technology transfer. While the consistency of these provisions with Article 31 of the TRIPS Agreement is questionable, the reality is that Hong Kong will not utilize the provisions in the foreseeable future. The most applicable provision in relation to pharmaceuticals and Hong Kong is subsection (b), which allows for a compulsory license if "demand for the product in Hong Kong is not being met on reasonable terms." This places the government in a better bargaining position with pharmaceutical companies as it can always threaten to issue a compulsory license should price demands not be reduced.

In order for a compulsory license to be granted, Hong Kong also requires several mainly procedural steps to be fulfilled. These steps are, for the most part, mandated by and set out in Article 31 of the TRIPS Agreement. For instance, Section 64(5) obliges applicants for a compulsory license to make "reasonable efforts to obtain authorization ... on reasonable commercial terms and conditions" and the license will be granted only if "such efforts have not been successful within a reasonable period of time." Moreover, and again in accordance with the international framework, Hong Kong law provides that the license shall be nonexclusive and nonassignable.[136]

Likewise in line with the Doha Declaration on TRIPS and Public Health and the subsequent paragraph 6 solution and Decision of the General Council of 6 December 2005, the Patents Ordinance contains provisions relating to emergency situations and public health crises. More specifically, in regard to the former, Section 68 empowers the Chief Executive to declare a "extreme emergency" whenever he or she "considers it to be necessary or expedient in the public interest for the maintenance of [or securing sufficient] supplies and services essential to the life of the community," and Section 69 allows the government to "do any act in Hong Kong in relation to the invention as appears ... to be necessary or

---

[135] For a comparison of compulsory licensing provisions in the United States, Canada, China and India, see Maggie Huang, "Grounds for Compulsory Patent Licensing in United States, Canada, China, and India," Centre for Internet & Society, http://cis-india.org/a2k/blogs/grounds-for-compulsory-patent-licensing-in-us-canada-china-and-india, accessed 4 March 2017.

[136] See Section 64(7), with there being one minor exception to nonassignability.

expedient in connection with the urgency giving rise to the declaration under Section 68."[137]

In regards to the latter, amendments in 2007 gave the Chief Executive the power under Section 72B to make a "declaration of extreme urgency for public health problem" when he or she "considers it to be necessary or expedient in the public interest to do so to address any public health problem or threatened public health problem in Hong Kong."[138] Furthermore, under Section 72C during a period of extreme urgency a nonexclusive "import compulsory licence" allowing the marketing, stocking and using of the product may be granted if the government determines that "the pharmaceutical industry in Hong Kong has no or insufficient capacity to manufacture a patented pharmaceutical product to meet the needs for the product in Hong Kong." Section 72D backs up this section with a list of procedural hurdles in line with the paragraph 6 solution, including notification requirements, that the scope of the exception is limited to the terms of the license, that the patented pharmaceutical product that is imported under the license shall not be exported out of Hong Kong and that the patented pharmaceutical be clearly identifiable as being imported under the license through specific labeling or marking and distinguished from the same branded product (i.e., special packaging, color or shape). Remuneration provisions are also in accordance with the paragraph 6 solution.[139] It is worth noting that Hong Kong has declared that it "will only use the compulsory licensing system as an importer in situations of national emergency or circumstances of extreme urgency."[140]

---

[137] Remuneration is to be agreed by the government and patent owner or, if necessary, by the court. Section 69(4).

[138] For background, see Patents (Amendment) Bill 2007, Legislative Council Brief, Patents Ordinance (Chapter 514) CIB CR 06/08/11, including background information and the text of the Patents (Amendment) Bill (Annex A) and the Administration's Response to the Submissions Made by Deputations to the Bills Committee on the Patents (Amendment) Bill 2007, LC Paper No. CB(1)2191/06-07(01), www.legco.gov.hk/yr06-07/english/bc/bc02/papers/bc020719cb1-2191-1-e.pdf, accessed 4 March 2017.

[139] See Section 72E.

[140] Report of the Bills Committee on Patents (Amendment) Bill 2007, Paper for the House Committee meeting on 2 November 2007, LC Paper No. CB(1)154/07-08, Ref: CB1/BC/2/06, www.legco.gov.hk/yr06-07/english/bc/bc02/reports/bc021121cb1-191-e .pdf, accessed 4 March 2017, see in particular para. 4. See also Hong Kong's declaration to the WTO at the time of the paragraph 6 solution. For the complete list of Members declaring that they would use the system as importers only in situations of national emergency or other circumstances of extreme urgency as well as the list of Members declaring that they would not use the system, see WTO, Compulsory Licensing of Pharmaceuticals

Hong Kong has also legislated to effectuate the paragraph 6 solution in the export of patented pharmaceutical products under a compulsory license. These provisions mirror to a large extent the import provisions explained above and are in line with the procedural mandate of the paragraph 6 solution.[141]

Concluding Comments on Article 31

Hong Kong is unlikely to issue a compulsory license on pharmaceuticals absent a public health emergency or crisis. Moreover, if Hong Kong did issue a compulsory license, it almost inevitably would have to import the product at issue – meaning the local industry would not benefit from the issuance of the compulsory license. Therefore, questions of using compulsory licensing as a means to enable the transfer of technology, innovation and local production are essentially a nonissue in Hong Kong. At the same time, Hong Kong should be aware of the social costs to pharmaceutical patents and view the compulsory licenses as a tool to control healthcare costs and promote a coherent approach to pharmaceutical patent policy. The circumstances of Hong Kong demand that it remains vigilant and maintains policy options – Hong Kong is densely populated, and it and the region are prone to pandemics, thus necessitating that potential life-saving medicines can be easily acquired or produced in a short period of time, or even stocked and stored in large quantities before any outbreak.

The laws in Hong Kong in regard to compulsory licensing seem suitable for the purpose and are not in need of much change. The laws are broad, and the territory has put in place legislation to effectuate the importation or exportation of pharmaceuticals in line with the conditions set out in the WTO waiver/amendment. In this regard, the laws as such provide ample room for Hong Kong to negotiate for price reductions or voluntary licenses should it so desire. There is a question, however, whether Hong Kong should amend the law so as to make importation into the territory equate with "working," as the current law may offend notions of adequate IPR protection and is arguably inconsistent with Article 27.1 of the TRIPS Agreement. This change would not reduce the ability of Hong Kong to react in times of health emergency or crisis.

---

and TRIPS (Oct. 2005), www.wto.org/English/tratop_e/trips_e/public_health_faq_e .htm, accessed 4 March 2017.

[141] Section 72L–72S.

6

Test Data Exclusivity

6.1 Introduction

As explained in previous chapters, the originator of a drug must first apply for regulatory approval with a national drug regulatory authority to ensure that the drug is safe, effective and of sufficient quality before distributing a drug on the market. The regulatory authority acts on the information submitted by the applicant, which includes clinical trial and other relevant data and information, but does not undertake clinical trials or otherwise test the drugs. When a generic manufacturer later applies for marketing approval for the same drug, the regulatory authority does not require it to submit data of its own tests, but rather allows the applicant to prove that the drug it seeks to distribute is of the same quality and therapeutically equivalent to the previously approved drug. Thus, while the originator must demonstrate safety and efficacy through the production of costly and time-consuming test data, the generic applicant essentially "free rides" on the R&D. Generic applications are usually approved on the basis of comparative studies known as bioequivalence information, which simply demonstrate that the applicant can meet the same safety and efficacy standards as the originator pharmaceutical.[1] Referred by some as springboarding, this process not only facilitates the entry of generic competition into the marketplace, but allows those companies to save millions of dollars in tests, and thus the final product is made available on the market at a fraction of the originator's price.[2]

---

[1] For reference, see the guidelines for the United States and EU, respectively: US Food and Drug Administration, "Abbreviated New Drug Application (ANDA): Generics" (2014), www.fda.gov/Drugs/DevelopmentApprovalProcess/HowDrugsareDevelopedandApproved/ApprovalApplications/AbbreviatedNewDrugApplicationANDAGenerics/, accessed 22 February 2017; European Medicines Agency, "Guideline on the Investigation of Bioequivalence" (2010) 4, www.ema.europa.eu/docs/en_GB/document_library/Scientific_guideline/2010/01/WC500070039.pdf, accessed 22 February 2017.

[2] Jerome H. Reichman, "Rethinking the Role of Clinical Trial Data in International Intellectual Property Law: The Case for a Public Goods Approach" (2002) 13(1) *Marquette*

Test data exclusivity is a sui generis right that protects data generated by the holder from being referred to or used by another person or company for a specific period of time. Test data exclusivity precludes the regulatory authority from even accepting applications from generic applicants, which rely on the test data until the exclusivity period ends. By contrast, in what is referred to as "market exclusivity," the regulatory authority is prevented from granting marketing approval until the exclusivity period ends. Test data exclusivity is the stronger form of protection, as it provides an additional period of de facto exclusivity equal to the time it takes the regulatory authority to consider the application and grant the marketing approval.

Test data exclusivity is not traditionally a recognized IPR and can be categorized more as a quasi-IPR that attaches irrespective of whether the product is subject to patent protection. Test data exclusivity provides the holder with limited term protection against others using or referencing its preclinical, clinical trial or other data in an application for marketing approval or from the drug regulatory authority relying in its own right on the originator's test data for approval of a generic pharmaceutical product. In this regard, test data exclusivity is an automatic right and a negative right – it essentially acts as a right to exclude others from using as opposed to a right to use.[3]

The objective of test data exclusivity is to compensate the manufacturer of a new product (and hence allow them to protect their investment) for time and money invested in inventing, testing and bringing the product to market. The costs involved in this process are hugely expensive, and therefore it makes sense to ensure that the fruits of the investment are not simply handed over to generic competitors. This need to incentivize clinical trials and the generation of test data is of course balanced by other interests, such as the right to health and information. The question is whether patent rights alone are sufficient compensation and protection or if an additional layer of rights is warranted. Proponents of test data exclusivity argue that patent rights do not always apply and may not ensure an effective term of protection for the generation of test data such

---

Intellectual Property Law Review 1, 9 ("the costs of clinical trials are high, growing higher, and have lately become potentially unsustainable").

[3] But see International Federation of Pharmaceutical Manufacturers and Associations (IFPMA), "Encouragement of New Clinical Drug Development: The Role of Data Exclusivity" (2000) 5, www.eldis.org/go/home&id=29224&type=Document#.WLpaTxKGNcA, accessed 4 March 2017 (stating that test data exclusivity "provides a limited duration of time during which only the owner or generator of . . . preclinical and clinical trial data can *use* it for purposes of marketing authorization").

that innovators are rewarded and encouraged to continue creating new products. Thus, additional sui generis rights must apply in tandem with patent rights. In this regard, test data exclusivity prevents generic manufacturers from making "unfair commercial use" of such data (i.e., free riding on the research of the innovator company) for a set period of time that effectively ensures a minimum period of marketing exclusivity for the originator/innovator company.[4] On the other hand, critics view test data exclusivity as merely another method utilized by the branded industry to prolong the period of marketing exclusivity and maximize profits to the detriment of public health.

Section 6.2 of this chapter reviews the international framework regulating test data exclusivity. It begins with a review of the TRIPS Agreement before analyzing the evolution of test data exclusivity in domestic legislation and through the proliferation of FTAs. Section 6.3 critically reviews Hong Kong's commitment to apply test data exclusivity and offers recommendations for how the jurisdiction can limit the negative effects of such protection through targeted legislative drafting and interpretation. Part IV concludes.

6.2   The International Framework

6.2.1   The TRIPS Agreement

Test data is recognized as a category of intellectual property in Article 1.2 of the TRIPS Agreement. To many commentators, referring to test data protection as an IPR is misplaced. Prior to the TRIPS Agreement, very few countries provided for any form of test data or market exclusivity and even fewer would have recognized it as an IPR. Regardless, after much discussion and debate, test data protection was included in the TRIPS Agreement and thus now forms part of the international framework.[5] More specifically, Article 39(3) of the TRIPS Agreement states:

---

[4] Test data exclusivity does not prevent generic manufacturers from conducting their own tests, submitting the results to the regulatory authorities and obtaining marketing approval on the basis of these tests. However, requiring generic manufacturers to redo toxicological and clinical tests is unnecessary, wasteful, financially prohibitive and arguably unethical as such tests would be of limited value to society, as safety and efficacy have already been determined, and would at the same time expose animal and/or human lives to unnecessary dangers. For more on human rights aspects of such tests, see Xavier Seuba, "Pharmaceutical Test Data Protection and Human Rights," in Peter K. Yu and Molly Land (eds.), *Reshaping Intellectual Property Law through a Human Rights Lens* (forthcoming), https://papers.ssrn .com/sol3/papers.cfm?abstract_id=2670225, 12–15.

[5] For background position papers during the negotiations, see, e.g., "Statement of Views of the European, Japanese and United States Business Communities" (1988); US Draft Text, 28

> Members, when requiring, as a condition of approving the marketing of pharmaceutical or of agricultural chemical products which utilize new chemical entities, the submission of undisclosed test or other data, the origination of which involves a considerable effort, shall protect such data against unfair commercial use. In addition, Members shall protect such data against disclosure, except where necessary to protect the public, or unless steps are taken to ensure that the data are protected against unfair commercial use.[6]

In essence, the vaguely worded provision requires WTO Members to protect the submission of undisclosed test data of pharmaceutical and agrochemical products that contain new chemical entities (left undefined, and thus differing interpretations may be permissible) and involve considerable effort against unfair commercial use.[7] Test data protection is thus a reward for the production of data in accordance with standard protocols and procedure, rather than the normal reward for creativity of innovation.[8] In this regard, test data protection is similar to the EU's protection of databases rather than a typical IPR.

Article 39(3) requires two distinct obligations: protect data against *unfair commercial use* and against *disclosure*,[9] unless it is necessary to protect the public or unless steps are taken to protect against unfair commercial use. While the obligation against disclosure by the heath authorities is relatively straightforward, the requirement to protect against "unfair commercial use" is opaque. In what can only be termed "constructive ambiguity," the drafters of the TRIPS provided no guidance or other information as to the meaning of the term. Thus, it is unclear how protection should occur, what the limit of such protection is or what the time period is for

---

October 1987, Article 31(1); EC Draft Text, MTN.GNG/NG11/W/68, 29 March 1990, Article 28; Switzerland Draft Text, NG11/W/73, 14 May 1990, Article 241(1); Communication from India, MTN.GNG/NG11/W/37, 10 July 1989, p. 18.

[6] Protected data includes health and safety testing in regard to humans, animals and plants, as well as environmental impact tests and other information the relevant authorities may require that includes manufacturing, storage and packaging tests. See Carlos M. Correa, "Unfair Competition under the TRIPS Agreement: Protection of Data Submitted for the Registration of Pharmaceuticals" (2002) 3(1) *Chicago Journal of International Law* 69, 73.

[7] Article 39 does not use the terms "trade secret" or "undisclosed information" perhaps because "[t]he difficulty of finding a common and acceptable understanding of what those notions mean favoured the adoption of a more neutral terminology, which does not characterize the contents of the information, but only its 'undisclosed' nature." See the United Nations Conference on Trade and Development and the International Centre for Trade and Sustainable Development, *Resource Book on TRIPS and Development* (Cambridge University Press, 2005), 521.

[8] On this point, see Correa, above n. 6, 72.

[9] Thus, information that is in the public domain is not within the scope of the protection.

such protection. The question at the forefront of this debate is whether and to what extent Article 39(3) requires Members to preclude their drug regulatory authorities from using and relying on test data submitted by the originator in the examination of a generic product for a certain period of time. This question should be resolved through recourse to the VCLT, namely, Articles 31 and 32, which dictate that the interpretation should first and foremost be in good faith in accordance with the ordinary meaning to be given to the terms of the treaty in their context and in the light of its object and purpose of the agreement.

Most governments and commentators do not believe that the provision requires test data exclusivity. In this view, there is nothing in Article 39(3) that requires WTO Members to prevent the health authorities from allowing generic applicants to rely on test data submitted by the originator in order to obtain marketing approval.[10] To those holding this view, WTO Members must merely adequately protect eligible "undisclosed test or other data" against "unfair commercial use" and "disclosure" by providing in their laws protection against misappropriation of test data.[11] In this regard, it is not unnecessarily "unfair" for the generic manufacturer to benefit from use of the preexisting test data but rather a "legitimate exploitation of an externality created during legitimate competition in the

---

[10] See UNCTAD, "The TRIPS Agreement and Developing Countries," p. 48 (UN, UNCTAD/ITE/1 1996), http://unctad.org/en/docs/ite1_en.pdf ("authorities are not prevented … from using knowledge of such data, for instance, to assess subsequent applications by third parties for the registration of similar products").

[11] In this way Article 39(3) is viewed not as a guard against generic applicants but as a requirement on the regulatory agency to protect originator-submitted test data against "unfair commercial use." See Carlos M. Correa, "Protection of Data Submitted for the Registration of Pharmaceuticals: Implementing the Standards of the TRIPS Agreement" (South Centre, 2002); Carlos M. Correa, "Data Exclusivity for Pharmaceuticals: TRIPS Standards and Industry's Demands in Free Trade Agreements," in Carlos M. Correa (ed.), *Research Handbook on the Protection of Intellectual Property under WTO Rules: Intellectual Property in the WTO*, vol. 1 (Edward Elgar, 2010), 713. See also TRIPS Council, "TRIPS and Public Health," Submission by the African Group, Barbados, Bolivia, Brazil, Dominican Republic, Ecuador, Honduras, India, Indonesia, Jamaica, Pakistan, Paraguay, Philippines, Peru, Sri Lanka, Thailand and Venezuela (IP/C/W/296) (29 June 2001), para. 39, www.wto.org/english/tratop_e/trips_e/paper_develop_w296_e.htm, accessed 22 February 2017 ("[T]he Agreement clearly avoids the treatment of undisclosed information as a 'property' and does not require granting 'exclusive' rights to the owner of the data"). For concurring views, see UNCTAD, "The TRIPS Agreement and Developing Countries" (1996), above n. 10; World Health Organization, "Report of the Commission on Intellectual Property Rights," Innovation and Public Health (CIPIH) (2006), 143, www.who.int/intellectualproperty/documents/thereport/ENPublicHealthReport.pdf?ua=1, accessed 4 March 2017.

market."[12] Another argument proponents of this view make is based on the connection between Article 39(3) and Article 39(1) of TRIPS with reference to Article 10 *bis* of the Paris Convention. The former seeks to guard against "unfair commercial practices," which does not mean the same thing as "unfair competition" in the market in the absence of exclusive rights, as used in Article 39.1 TRIPS with a reference to Article 10 *bis* of the Paris Convention on the Protection of Industrial Property.[13] Proponents of such a view argue that interpreting Article 39(3) as requiring test data exclusivity would render moot Article 39(1). Furthermore, proponents of this view argue that Article 39 only illustrates and provides examples of but does not add to Article 10 *bis* of the Paris Convention.[14]

Moreover, while it is clear that the use of the test data will provide a benefit to the generic company, it is less clear whether such governmental use should be deemed "commercial." Governmental use is not normally associated with commerce, but rather is administrative in nature. In other words, the purpose of Article 39(3) is to prevent the unfair use of data by competitors – through, for instance, dishonest practices – not to restrain use by governments in assessing a subsequent application for marketing approval.[15] In fact, one can even question whether the regulatory authority or even the generic applicant engages in "use" of the data – certainly, the regulatory authority does not use the data when granting marketing authorization on the basis of approval in another jurisdiction.

A further argument against an interpretation requiring test data exclusivity is that during the course of the negotiations, this quasi-IPR was

---

[12] Correa, above n. 6, 77.

[13] Paris Convention on the Protection of Industrial Property (WIPO) of 20 March 1883, as amended, www.wipo.int/treaties/en/text.jsp?file_id=288514. In particular, Article 39(1) reads: "In the course of ensuring effective protection against unfair competition as provided in Article 10 *bis* of the Paris Convention (1967), Members shall protect undisclosed information in accordance with paragraph 2 and data submitted to governments or governmental agencies in accordance with paragraph 3."

[14] Correa, above n. 6, 78.

[15] Those holding this view include Carlos M. Correa, *Trade Related Aspects of Intellectual Property Rights* (Oxford University Press, 2007), 391; CIPIH, above n. 11, 124; Panel of Eminent Experts on Ethics in Food and Agriculture, Report of Eminent Experts on Ethics in Food and Agriculture, Third Session 23 (14 September 2005), www.fao.org/docrep/010/a0697e/a0697e00.HTM, accessed 4 March 2017; Human Rights Council, "Promotion and Protection of All Human Rights, Civil, Political, Economic, Social and Cultural Rights, Including the Right to Development," Report of the Special Rapporteur on the Right of Everyone to the Enjoyment of the Highest Attainable Standard of Physical and Mental Health (A/HRC/11/12) (31 March 2009), para. 79, www2.ohchr.org/english/bodies/hrcouncil/docs/11session/A.HRC.11.12_en.pdf, accessed 15 May 2017.

discussed, debated and rejected by the negotiating parties.[16] More specifically, the negotiating parties rejected a US proposal and subsequent bracketed text in the Brussels Draft tabled at the Brussels Ministerial Meeting 1990, which would have obligated protection of all test data without approval of the right holder for a period of not less than five years (the US proposal also allowed for payment of reasonable compensation). Instead, Members agreed in the TRIPS Agreement to provide more limited protection to "unfair commercial practices." Thus, as Reichman succinctly states, "the collocation of clinical test data within the provisions regulating unfair competition negated any inference that the TRIPS drafters had imposed an exclusive intellectual property right on this subject matter and indirectly confirmed the implications to be drawn from the deletion of the U.S.-EU bracketed proposal between 1990 and 1991."[17] In another publication, Reichman adds that "to ignore the clear evolution of the text in favour of quasi-exclusive rights in regulatory data, in a form that was proposed but ultimately excised from the 1994 Final Act, would in effect amount to imposing unbargained-for trade concessions under a discredited 'TRIPS plus approach' that has no legal foundation whatsoever."[18] Such a view is sensible and has textual support, as Article 3.2 of the WTO's Dispute Settlement Understanding (DSU) provides that "[r]ecommendations and rulings of the DSB [Dispute Settlement Body] cannot add to or diminish the rights and obligations provided in the covered agreements."

Again, the question becomes what is a legitimate benefit to a generic manufacturer and what is a benefit based on an "unfair commercial practice" – the point being, it is not the existence of the benefit that matters for Article 39(3) but whether the benefit was fair or unfair. The distinction is unstated in TRIPS and thus a reasonable interpretation would provide Members with some discretion on the matter.

On the other hand, the United States, EU and others hold a much different position and maintain that Article 39(3) requires test data exclusivity.[19]

---

[16] See UNCTAD-ICTSD, above n. 7, at 522–26.   [17] Reichman, above n. 2, 18–19.

[18] Jerome H. Reichman, "The International Legal Status of Undisclosed Clinical Trial Data: From Private to Public Goods," in Pedro Roffe, Geoff Tansey and David Vivas-Eugui (eds.), *Negotiating Health: Intellectual Property and Access to Medicines* (Earthscan, 2006) 140.

[19] See generally Bruce N. Kuhlik, "The Assault on Pharmaceutical Intellectual Property" (2004) 71 *University of Chicago Law Review* 96; International Federation of Pharmaceutical Manufacturers and Associations (IFPMA), "Data Exclusivity: Encouraging Development of New Medicines" (July 2011), www.ifpma.org/wp-content/uploads/2016/01/IFPMA_2011_Data_Exclusivity__En_Web.pdf, accessed 4 March 2017; IFPMA, above n. 3.

To these parties, Article 39(3) mandates test data exclusivity. For instance, on the coming into force of TRIPS the US Trade Representative stated that Article 39(3) means:

> [T]he data will not be used to support, clear or otherwise review other applications for marketing approval for a set amount of time unless authorized by the original submitter of the data. Any other definition of this term would be inconsistent with logic and the negotiating history of the provision.[20]

More specifically, these parties argue that the drafters intentionally used differing language in Article 39(1) and Article 39(3) – simply stated, "unfair competition" does not equate to "unfair commercial use." In Article 39(1), the reference to Article 10 *bis* of the Paris Convention relates to behavior among competitors, with the article defining unfair competition as "any act of competition contrary to honest practices in industrial or commercial matter." This has been referred to as "practices such as false allegations on competitors' products or services, acts which may cause confusion about the origin and nature of products or services, undue advantage of the goodwill of another's enterprise, parasitism, etc. as regulated in the EC's Member States' national laws."[21] By contrast, Article 39(3) refers not to the behavior among competitors but to a governmental function of protecting certain types of test data so as not to provide unfair competitive advantages to generic manufacturers seeking

---

[20] Office of the General Counsel, US Trade Representative, "The Protection of Undisclosed Test Data in Accordance with TRIPS Article 39.3," unattributed paper for submission in bilateral discussions with Australia (May 1995). This view, however, can be contrasted with that of the US Government Accountability Office, which later admitted to "different interpretations of the obligations under TRIPS 39(3), and exactly what practices can be considered a fulfillment of this obligation." US Government Accountability Office, "U.S. Trade Policy Guidance on WTO Declaration on Access to Medicines May Need Clarification," GAO Report 07–1198 (2007), www.gao.gov/products/GAO-07-1198. The EU, which reads Article 39(3) as establishing test data exclusivity, has also stated: "It must be admitted that the following of Article 39.3 does not, from a prima facie reading, appear to impose data exclusivity during a certain period of time. This lack of clarity is the obvious result of a difficult negotiation process where divergences of views arose between developing and industrialized countries as to the necessity of EC/US like type of data protection as well as among industrialized countries on the length of the data exclusivity period." See European Commission, "Legal Issues Related to Compulsory Licensing under the TRIPS Agreement: An EU Contribution" (2006), http://trade.ec.europa.eu/doclib/docs/2006/may/tradoc_122031.pdf, accessed 22 February 2017.

[21] See European Union Commission, *Questions on TRIPs and Data Exclusivity – An EU Contribution* (Brussels, 2001), p. 2 note 3; European Commission, "Legal Issues," at note 18.

marketing approval their products.[22] To this group, therefore, there is little other choice but for drug marketing authorities to refuse to accept or rely on test data submitted by the originator in an application for generic marketing approval.[23] Finally, this group generally believes that because the TRIPS Agreement does not set any time limit to the period of exclusivity, Article 39(3) would not prevent a country from providing test data exclusivity for an unlimited period of time.[24]

Article 39(3) has never been interpreted by the WTO DSB, although in 2000 the United States did file a complaint against Argentina in relation to the provision.[25] The countries reached a mutually agreeable solution in 2002 and a panel was never established.[26] Argentina did not amend its laws as part of the solution or enact test data exclusivity.

Commentators have attempted to find a middle ground position between the two extremes outlined above, but these proposals lack a strong textual basis. For instance, Taubman argues that based on legitimate expectations of IP protection and a "fair relationship between competitors" any interpretation of Article 39(3) that would result in competitors using or benefiting from test data should be deemed "unfair and fit to be legally suppressed" if such use/benefit would be "likely systemically to deter submission and future production of such data."[27] Taubman believes this reading of Article 39(3) "reconciles utilitarian policymaking

---

[22] The EU perhaps overstates its case by making statements such as: "Both the logic and the negotiation history of Article 39.3 of TRIPs leave no doubt that providing data exclusivity for a certain period of time was the envisaged way to protect data against unfair use as prescribed by Article 39.3." European Union Commission, *Questions on TRIPs and Data Exclusivity*, at 3; European Commission, "Legal Issues," 20.

[23] The EU suggests but essentially dismisses the possibility of a payment by the generic manufacturer to the originator so as to ensure against "unfair commercial use." Ibid.

[24] It is worth noting that the TRIPS Agreement does not set out the temporal starting point for data exclusivity (if in fact it applies) – left unstated is therefore whether the date of filing or the date of marketing approval is the relevant point in time or whether this is left to the discretion of Members who only have to provide effective data exclusivity period for a long enough period to be considered sufficient protection against unfair commercial use.

[25] World Trade Organization Dispute Settlement Body, Argentina – Patent Protection for Pharmaceuticals and Test Data Protection for Agricultural Chemicals (WT/DS171) and Argentina – Certain Measures on the Protection of Patents and Test Data (WT/DS196), Notification of Mutually Agreed Solution According to the Conditions Set Forth in the Agreement, Document WT/DS171/3, WT/DS196/4, IP/D/18/Add.1, IP/D/Add.2 (20 June 2002).

[26] Ibid.

[27] Antony Taubman, "Unfair Competition and the Financing of Public Knowledge Goods: The Problem of Test Data Protection" (2008) 3 *Journal of Intellectual Property Law & Practice* 591, 601 and 606.

with legitimate claims of limited exclusive rights, because they are strictly limited by public interest, and are defensible in terms of actual public welfare, while offering data originators fair commercial opportunities."[28] Correa disagrees, pointing to the fact that such an interpretation is not in line with the VCLT and existing WTO jurisprudence, which states that "legitimate expectations" can only be found in the text (and negotiating history indicates the negotiating parties did not accept a period of exclusivity for test data but rather an unfair competition rule). Moreover, Correa further points out that 85 percent of the global market for prescription drugs is in the developed world, and therefore whether a developing country applies test data exclusivity would not deter investment in test data.[29] Other commentators argue that Article 39(3) sets up (or should set up) a system of compensation,[30] whereby generic manufacturers must compensate the originator of the test data for use within a set period of time. Regardless of the potential merits of such a system, there is no textual basis for a compensatory system in Article 39(3). To the contrary, the US proposal including compensation as an option does not appear in the final text, indicating that Members considered and rejected such an approach.

6.2.2   Domestic Legislation

When included as part of domestic legislation, test data exclusivity differs in application among its adherents. In all countries with test data exclusivity, the regime is meant to strike a balance between the economic interests of the R&D-based pharmaceutical industry, on the one hand, and ethical considerations and the interests of the generic producers, on the other hand.[31] But there is no consensus on the outcome of this balance, with

---

[28] Ibid., at 606.

[29] Carlos M. Correa, "Test Data Protection: Rights Conferred under the TRIPS Agreement and Some Effects of TRIPS-Plus Standards," in Rochelle C. Dreyfuss and Katherine J. Strandburg (eds.), *The Law and Theory of Trade Secrecy: A Handbook of Contemporary Research* (Edward Elgar, 2011), 574–75.

[30] Aaron Fellmeth, "Secrecy, Monopoly, and Access to Pharmaceuticals in International Trade Law: Protection of Marketing Approval Data under the TRIPS Agreement" (2004) 45 *Harvard International Law Journal* 443, 478–500; Shamnad Basheer, "Protection of Regulatory Data under Article 39.3 of TRIPS: The Indian Context" (London: Intellectual Property Institute, 2006), 4–5; Correa, above n. 6, 78–79.

[31] Although it must be stated that Congress justified the introduction of marketing exclusivity to encourage "the development and testing of unpatentable pharmaceuticals," apparently with the burgeoning market for biologics in mind. See *Allergan Inc. v. Alcon Labs.*, 324 F.3d 1322, 1325 (Fed. Cir. 2003), *cert. denied*, 540 US 1048 (2003). Likewise, in the EU the fact that some countries in the common market did not adequately protect pharmaceutical

differences even appearing in the two most ardent proponents of test data exclusivity, the EU and United States, with the former protecting data for up to eleven years,[32] while the latter offers five years' protection.[33] Others applying five years' protection include Australia and New Zealand,[34] while Japan and China provide six years' protection and Switzerland grants a ten-year period of exclusivity. Likewise, regimes differ on the rigidity of test exclusivity and on the scope of exceptions.[35]

It is worth noting again that test data exclusivity is viewed in these countries as a reward for the production of data that are useful to society. The sui generis right provides protection separate from and regardless of patent protection. But it does not automatically provide the beneficiary with any additional profits beyond that of the patent. In the majority of instances, the period of test data exclusivity runs concurrently with and ends prior to the expiration of patent protection. In fewer cases, test data exclusivity does indeed extend beyond the period of patent protection, such as when marketing authorization is only sought well into the period

patents – namely, Spain and Portugal – played a large part in the adoption of test data exclusivity.

[32] The EU provided for test data exclusivity in 1987 and currently operates one of the more stringent regimes. The EU provides for an eight-year period of test data exclusivity plus an additional two years' market exclusivity and an additional one year for new indications that show significant clinical benefits over existing therapies. EU Directive 2004/27/EC of 31 March 2004 amending Directive 2001/83/EC on the Community code relating to medicinal products for human use.

[33] Test data exclusivity for pharmaceuticals first appeared in 1984 when the United States expanded its protection regime for pesticides (dating from 1972), providing for five years of exclusivity for new pharmaceutical chemical entities and three years for new clinical research and/or indications for pharmaceutical drugs. The regime has since expanded to provide for a period of four years' test data exclusivity and a concurrent period of twelve years' market exclusivity for biologic products. See US Biologics Price Competition and Innovation Act of 2009, www.fda.gov/downloads/Drugs/ GuidanceComplianceRegulatoryInformation/UCM216146.pdf, accessed 8 March 2017.

[34] Therapeutic Goods Legislation Amendment Act 1998 (No. 34, 1998), www.legislation.gov .au/Details/C2004A05345, accessed 8 March 2017. Australia amended its legislation to provide exclusivity as a result of pressure stemming from the US listing under Special Section 301 of the US Trade Act.

[35] In *Bayer v. Canada* (Attorney General) 243 NR 170 (1999), the General Court of Appeal held that the health authority does not request or examine undisclosed information during an application by a generic for marketing approval, but rather ensures the generic product is the same as the original – thus, the data are not used and the exclusivity period is irrelevant. However, if the health authority uses the data when assessing the generic application, it would be bound to protect such information for the five-year period as per Canadian law and NAFTA. The TRIPS consistency of this ruling is not beyond question. See Basheer, above n. 30, 31.

of patent or when the product has not received patent protection. It is in these cases where test data exclusivity can negatively impact on the costs of pharmaceuticals, but for the data exclusivity a generic competitor could be on the market. The impact of such provisions thus differs from product to product depending on the time period when the data exclusivity extends beyond patent protection.

Despite the potential to raise the cost of and delay access to medicines, test data exclusivity is now part of the national legal system of more than fifty countries,[36] and the list grows every year. Test data exclusivity is far from the new international standard, however, and many countries remain committed to resisting its spread. Among this group of countries is Argentina, which crafted its regime so as to avoid even the most stringent interpretation of Article 39(3) and industry pressure. More specifically, Argentina maintains a restrictive approach requiring the submission of test data only for the registration of new chemical entities. Moreover, where pharmaceutical products already on the market in Argentina or in other jurisdictions meet certain predefined standards, the health authority can rely on the prior registration and avoid the need for the submission of test data.[37]

Test data exclusivity is now regularly included as a matter of course in FTAs concluded by the United States, EU and European Free Trade Association (EFTA). Test data exclusivity has even been included in accession commitments of a number of countries wishing to accede to the WTO, including most notably China and perhaps, rather oddly, Cambodia (an LDC).[38] The next subsection reviews the commitments made in FTAs and

---

[36] IFPMA, above n. 19.

[37] Ley de Confidencialidad Sobre Informacion y Productos que Esten Legitimamente Bajo Control de una Persona y se Divulgue Indebidamente de Manera Contraria a los Usos Comerciales Honestos, No. 24.766 of 1996, http://servicios.infoleg.gob.ar/infolegInternet/anexos/40000-44999/41094/norma.htm. For a comment on Law 24.766, see also International Association for the Protection of Intellectual Property (AIPPI) Question Q215, Argentina, Protection of trade secrets through IPR and unfair competition law (22 March 2010), https://aippi.org/download/commitees/215/GR215argentina.pdf, accessed 8 March 2017. See also Case 5619/05, Novartis Pharma AG c. Monte Verde SA s/ varios propiedad intelectual, Sentencia de la Sala III de la Excelentísima Cámara nacional de Apelaciones de la nación Argentina, 1 February 2011 (holding that test data exclusivity runs counter to the right to life and right to health).

[38] Working Party on the Accession of China, "Report on the Working Party on the Accession of China" (WT/ACC/CHN/49) (1 October 2001), para. 284, https://docsonline.wto.org/dol2fe/Pages/SS/DirectDoc.aspx?filename=t%3A%2Fwt%2Facc%2Fchn49.doc&; see also Working Party on the Accession of Cambodia, "Report of the Working Party on the Accession of Cambodia" (WT/ACC/KHM/21) (15 August 2003), para. 205, https://docsonline

templates of demandeur countries so as to illustrate the trend of increasing protection beyond that which is required by the TRIPS Agreement.

6.2.3 The Expansion of Test Data Exclusivity in Free Trade Agreements

The incorpation of test data exclusivity in FTAs began in 1994 with the NAFTA. More specifically, Article 1711 of NAFTA provides for a period of five-year data exclusivity from the date of marketing approval,[39] but also provides that a party can approve a drug by "relying" on the date of marketing approval of another party, in which case the period of exclusivity would run concurrently with that of the original party.[40] This approach subsequently served as the original post-TRIPS template for test data exclusivity in FTAs.[41]

In the past decade the reach of test data exclusivity has changed immensely with its inclusion in IP chapters of FTAs negotiated by, among others, the United States, EU and EFTA. In most cases, the demandeur requests and/or requires the partner country to match the level of protection in its domestic law. For example, US FTAs generally match its domestic standard by seeking a five-year period of exclusivity for a new pharmaceutical product (ten years for a new agricultural chemical product). For instance, Article 17.10.1(a) of the Australia-United States FTA (AUSFTA) reads:

> If a Party requires, as a condition of approving the marketing of a new pharmaceutical product, the submission of undisclosed test or other data concerning safety or efficacy of the product, the Party shall not permit third persons, without the consent of the person who provided such information, to market a same or similar product on the basis of (1) such

---

.wto.org/dol2fe/Pages/FormerScriptedSearch/directdoc.aspx?DDFDocuments/t/WT/ACC/KHM21.doc, accessed 8 March 2017.

[39] North American Free Trade Agreement (NAFTA), Article 1711(5)–(6), www.nafta-secalena.org/Home/Legal-Texts/North-American-Free-Trade-Agreement, accessed 8 March 2017.

[40] Article 1711.7 of NAFTA reads: "Where a Party relies on a marketing approval granted by another Party, the reasonable period of exclusive use of the data submitted in connection with obtaining the approval relied on shall begin with the date of the first marketing approval relied on." Similar language is used in certain US intellectual property rights agreements. See US Department of Commerce, International Trade Administration – Enforcement and Compliance, http://tcc.export.gov/Trade_Agreements/Intellectual_Property_Rights/index.asp, accessed 22 February 2017.

[41] This model was also adopted (but later abandoned) by the Andean Group in 1993. Andean Community, Decision No. 344 Establishing the Common Regime on Industrial Property of October 21, 1993, www.wipo.int/wipolex/en/details.jsp?id=9454, accessed 8 March 2017.

information or (2) the approval granted to the person who submitted such information for at least five years from the date of marketing approval in the Party.[42]

Several issues are worth noting. First, unlike the TRIPS Agreement, the wording of the FTA provision relates to marketing exclusivity but acts to prohibit third parties (i.e., generic manufacturers) from relying on test data for a period of time and gaining marketing approval. Second, and again unlike the TRIPS Agreement, the provision delineates the time period for such test data exclusivity – in the above example, five years from the date of marketing approval for the originator product.[43] Third, while the starting point for the period of data exclusivity is unstated in the TRIPS Agreement, the FTA makes clear that the starting date is not the date of filing the request but rather the date of marketing approval in the country. The fourth issue to note is the subtle deviation in wording from the TRIPS Agreement, which requires protection of a product "which involves a considerable effort" and containing "new chemical entities," arguably enlarging protection to every "new pharmaceutical product," which perhaps includes, for instance, a new application or method of a known chemical entity, new dosage, combinations, administration, indications and the like.[44] The effect of this linguistic shift is immense, as it allows an applicant for a new pharmaceutical product to obtain protection even in the case of old and well-known products (irrespective of whether any effort was spent in generating the data).[45]

In some FTAs, such as the US-Jordan FTA and the KORUS FTA, there is an additional provision that limits test data exclusivity to a period of three

[42] See also US FTAs with Singapore (Article 16.8.1), Bahrain (Article 14.9.1) and Oman (Article 15.9.1), and CAFTA-DR-US (Article 15.10.1).

[43] The exception to US FTA practice are the FTAs with Peru, Colombia and Panama, which do not provide a set period of protection but only state that protection must be for a "reasonable period" of time.

[44] But see that the term "new product" is loosely defined as "one that does not contain a chemical entity that has previously been approved by the Party." AUSFTA, Article 17.10.1(d). See also US FTAs with Morocco (Article 15.10.1); Central America FTA–Dominican Republic (Article 15.10.1(c)), Bahrain (Article 14.9.1(c)), Oman (Article 15.9.1(c)) and KORUS (Article 18.9.1(c)). See also the US-Jordan FTA (Article 4.22 (note 10)) and others that include "protection for new uses for old chemical entities for a period of three years" within the definition of "new chemical entity."

[45] For criticism, see Frederick M. Abbott, "The Doha Declaration on the TRIPS Agreement and Public Health and the Contradictory Trend in Bilateral and Regional Trade Agreements," Quaker United Nations Office Occasional Paper 14 (April 2004), 8, http://quno.org/resource/2003/9/doha-declaration-trips-agreement-and-public-health-and-contradictory-trend-bilateral, accessed 22 February 2017.

years from the date of obtaining marketing authorization for pharmaceutical products that contain a chemical entity that has been approved earlier for marketing in another pharmaceutical product (whereas for pharmaceutical products that do not contain a previously approved chemical entity the term of protection is five years from the date of obtaining marketing authorization).[46]

Most US FTAs contain an additional provision that explicitly states that the period of test data exclusivity period remains intact even after the expiration or invalidation of the patent. Article 17.10.3 of the AUSFTA provides an example of the US template in this regard:

> When a product is subject to a system of marketing approval ... and is also subject to a patent in the territory of that Party, the Party shall not alter the term of protection that it provides ... in the event that the patent protection terminates on a date earlier than the end of the term of protection.[47]

The reason for this provision is both simple and clear – test data exclusivity is regarded as a right separate from and in addition to patent rights. Thus, the expiration or invalidation of patent rights has no effect on test data exclusivity.

Several US FTAs also effectively prohibit generic manufacturers from using evidence of registration of the originator drug in another country to prove the safety and efficacy of their version so long as the originator applies for marketing approval within five years of registering the product in a country other than a party to that particular FTA.[48] In other words, a generic manufacturer is prevented from relying on the data used in the originator's application for marketing approval in another country for a certain time period even where the originator has not sought marketing approval in that jurisdiction; thus, the jurisdiction does not have access to that particular drug until the expiration of the data exclusivity period. Depending on how the originator times its entry into the market, the effect

---

[46] See, e.g., KORUS FTA, Article 18.9.2(a) and Article 18.9.1(a) in conjunction with 18.9.1(c), respectively. While neither party currents implements such practice, the KORUS also provides five years of test data exclusivity where the generic applicant seeks as a basis for registration information or evidence of prior marketing approval in such other territory. Ibid., at Article 18.9.1(b).

[47] See also US FTAs with Singapore (Article 16.8.1), Morocco (15.10.1, note 11), Oman (Article 15.9.3) and the KORUS FTA (Article 18.9.4).

[48] These provisions are found in US FTAs with Singapore (Article 16.8.2), AUSFTA (Article 17.10.1(c)), Morocco (Article 15.10.1), CAFTA-DR-US (Article 15.10.1(b)), Bahrain (Article 14.9.1(b)), Oman (Article 15.9.1(b)) and KORUS (Article 18.9.1(b)).

of the provision could result in ten years of test data protection. For example, an originator could wait almost five years after registering a drug in one of the FTA countries before submitting the marketing approval application in another FTA-member country. It would then be entitled to five years of exclusivity from that date in the secondary country.

The United States softened its approach in FTAs with Peru, Colombia and Panama in a manner that may hasten the registration of pharmaceuticals in these secondary markets. More specifically, if any of these countries uses US FDA approval as the basis for granting marketing approval in their jurisdiction to US originators, the period of exclusivity is to run concurrently with the period in the United States so long as approval is granted within six months of the date of application. Thus, no matter when the test data is registered in the FTA-partner country, the exclusivity period will expire when it expires in the United States.[49] These agreements also contain an explicit exception to test data exclusivity for measures to protect public health in accordance with the Doha Declaration and subsequent implementing protocols.

The "pullback" seen in the above FTAs did not last, as is evident in the recently negotiated (but not in force) TPP, with the "megaregional" FTA reverting to the protection commonly seen in US FTAs. More specifically, the TPP provides for the protection of undisclosed test data for "new pharmaceutical product[s]" (as opposed to new chemical entities) for a period of five years from the date of approval in another jurisdiction[50] with protection extending even if the jurisdiction grants marketing approval on the basis of registration in another territory.[51] In addition, the TPP is the first US agreement to specifically include biologics through a complicated formula that ultimately provides eight years' protection.[52]

---

[49] The latter exception also appears in the KORUS FTA (Article 18.9.3).

[50] See the Tran Pacific Partnership, Article 18.47(1)(a), available at the New Zealand Foreign Affairs and Trade website, www.mfat.govt.nz/en/about-us/who-we-are/treaties/trans-pacific-partnership-agreement-tpp/text-of-the-trans-pacific-partnership, accessed 8 March 2017.

[51] Ibid., at 18.47(1)(b).

[52] Ibid., at 18.51. There, the United States has proposed a twelve-year data exclusivity term for biologics to match its domestic legal framework, and the failure to achieve this period has caused much discussion and debate among US industry and politicians. See Zachary Brennan, "Final TPP Agreement Draws Ire from Both Sides over Biologics Exclusivity" (Regulatory Affairs Professional Society (RAPS), 5 October 2015), www.raps.org/Regulatory-Focus/News/2015/10/05/23325/Final-TPP-Agreement-Draws-Ire-from-Both-Sides-over-Biologics-Exclusivity/; Jenny Leonard, "Hatch: TPP Biologics Commitments Would Not Require Side Letters" (9 September 2016) 34(35) Inside U.S. Trade,

The other two major proponents of test data exclusivity are the EU and EFTA. While earlier FTAs negotiated by these trade blocs followed the United States in adopting a five-year protection periods,[53] the negotiating strategy later shifted upward in the EU and EFTA FTAs to a period of protection of eight years for pharmaceutical products.[54] The language used in the provision, however, more closely resembles Article 39(3) of the TRIPS Agreement than the standard US provision. For instance, Article 20(29) of the CETA provides protection for a period of eight years from the date of the granting of the originator's marketing approval against disclosure for "new chemical entities ... if the origination of such data involves considerable effort, except where the disclosure is necessary to protect the public or unless steps are taken to ensure that the data are protected against unfair commercial use."[55]

More recent EFTA FTAs shift to a new model that instead of setting a period of protection applies a cost-sharing or compensatory liability scheme. For example, Annex XIII, Article 3 of the EFTA-Korea FTA states:

> The Parties shall prevent applicants for marketing approval for pharmaceutical and agricultural chemical products from relying on undisclosed test or other undisclosed data, the origination of which involves a considerable effort, submitted by the first applicant to the competent authority for marketing approval for pharmaceutical and agricultural chemical products, utilizing new chemical entities, for an *adequate number of years* from the date of approval, except where approval is sought for original products. *Any party may instead allow in their national legislation applicants to rely on such data if the first applicant is adequately compensated* [emphasis added].[56]

https://insidetrade.com/inside-us-trade/hatch-tpp-biologics-commitments-would-not-require-side-letters; "Brown: Administration Will Hold Ground on Biologics, Hatch TPP Support Inevitable" (28 June 2016) *Inside U.S. Trade*, https://insidetrade.com/daily-news/brown-administration-will-hold-ground-biologics-hatch-tpp-support-inevitable. Links accessed 22 February 2017.

53 See, e.g., EU FTAs with Korea (Article 10.36) and Peru-Colombia (Article 231); EFTA FTAs with Colombia (Article 6.11.2).

54 See, e.g., EFTA agreements with Hong Kong (Annex XII, Article 4.2), Montenegro (Annex VI, Article 6.2) and Serbia (Annex VI, Article 5.2).

55 Generic applicants can, however, make use of test data after a period of six years. CETA, 20.29. The CETA does not require changes to existing Canadian law. Government of Canada, Regulations amending the Food and Drug Regulations (Data Protection), *Canada Gazette* Part II, vol. 140, 2006, 1493–502.

56 See also Article IV, Annex V of the EFTA–Lebanon FTA, which grants a period "'of least six years [protection], except where approval is sought for original products, *or unless the first applicant is adequately compensated*'" (emphasis added).

Two things are worth noting. First, the EFTA FTAs are fairly stringent in that they usually require data exclusivity (as opposed to market
exclusivity),[57] provide for eight years' protection and contain few exceptions. In many respects, the EFTA position is even more onerous and less
flexible than US FTAs. Second, EFTA FTAs are noteworthy in that they
provide for an alternative to exclusivity in the form of a compensatory
option requiring "adequate" compensation. The provision highlighted in
the extract above is similar, but slightly more onerous than the EFTA-
Tunisia FTA, which requires five years' protection or adequate compensation and also includes two safeguards in that the provision explicitly
provides that the parties could disclose data "as far as necessary, to protect public health against harmful effects of the products" and that the
term of protection "not exceed the period applying to the identical product in the country of origin or in the exporting country."[58] Perhaps even
more interestingly, the EFTA-Korea protects undisclosed test data involving new chemical entities that involved considerable effort for "an adequate number of years" – thus, the agreement leaves the term of protection
to the "relevant laws and regulations of the Parties."[59] The provision also
allows for "adequate compensat[ion]" in lieu of exclusionary protection.[60]

The shift to a cost-sharing compensatory approach is interesting for
many reasons, not least because in a number of ways it replicates the
debate between Taubman and Correa noted earlier in this chapter. While
such a method accomplishes the goal of rewarding current and encouraging future standardized tests and the production of societally useful data, it
is debatable whether "adequate compensation" from a developing country
would make much difference to the equation. On the other hand, payment
of even a token amount would recognize the costs involved in the production of the data and shield against attacks of the generic unfairly benefiting
through misappropriation of information.

What is clear is that the misappropriation approach as argued by many
developing countries at the WTO is failing at the bilateral and regional
levels. Both developed and developing countries are agreeing to recognize and protect test data for a set period of time. The question becomes
whether a compensatory, cost-sharing approach as that of the EFTA model

---

[57] This is in contrast to EU FTAs, which normally require market exclusivity as opposed to
the more stringent data exclusivity or a combination of the two, with data exclusivity for
five years and an additional period of market exclusivity. See, e.g., EU FTAs with Georgia
(Article 187(5)) and Moldova (Article 315(5)).

[58] EFTA-Tunisia FTA, Annex V, Article 4.

[59] EFTA-Korea FTA, Annex XIII, Article 3, including note 2.   [60] Ibid.

would be a better or fairer result than the more blunt exclusive property approach as seen in the US and EU models.[61] Several issues would need to be taken into account in answering that question, namely, how does one calculate adequate compensation?[62] Would cost figures need to be calculated as well as potential loss of profit? How can the system be designed to provide compensation but not unduly burden generic applicants at the risk of increasing the price of the medicine? How would the system apply in regard to the issuance of a compulsory license?

6.3 Test Data Exclusivity in Hong Kong

For many years, Hong Kong not only did not provide for test data exclusivity but approved applications from generic manufacturers simply where similar products had been approved or commercialized in another jurisdiction. This is no longer the case and now Hong Kong provides test data exclusivity for a period of eight years as provided in the Guidance Notes on Registration of Pharmaceutical Products/Substance, which reads:

> Clinical and scientific documentation substantiating the safety and efficacy of the product (except for generic products applications received on or after 1 Oct 2012 and their originator products have been registered in Hong Kong for *over 8 years* . . .) [emphasis in original].[63]

Hong Kong only recently raised its term of protection from a period of five to eight years. The reason for the increase in the term of protection is Annex XII, Article 4, of the HK-EFTA FTA (2011), which requires:

1. The Parties shall protect undisclosed information in accordance with Article 39 of the TRIPS Agreement.

---

[61] Reichman, above n. 2, 31–33; see also Robert Weissman, "Data Protection: Options for Implementation," in Pedro Roffe, Geoff Tansey and David Vivas-Eugui (eds.), *Negotiating Health: Intellectual Property and Access to Medicines* (Earthscan, 2006), 151–78.

[62] Reichman, above n. 2, 35 ("a reasonable royalty model could be adopted . . . which would oblige generic producers to pay a flat percentage of gross sales, or a flat percentage above marginal costs of production, as a tithe for the right to rely on the originators' test data results for a specified period of time, to last no longer than five years"). The lingering question is how to ensure this does not provide for under- or overcompensation.

[63] The Department of Health of the HKSAR Government, "The Guidance Notes on Registration of Pharmaceutical Products/Substances," Note 8 (D)(i) (December 2012), http://drugoffice.gov.hk/eps/do/en/doc/guidelines_forms/guid.pdf, accessed 22 February 2017. For drug registration requirements, see the Pharmacy and Poisons Regulations (Cap 138A), L.N. 163 OF 1975, last amended L.N. 145 of 1978, Part VIII.

2. For pharmaceuticals, including chemical entities and biologics . . . that require marketing approval by a competent authority, the Parties shall prevent applicants for marketing approval for such products from relying on, or referring to, undisclosed test data or other data submitted to the competent authority by the first applicant for a period, counted from the date of marketing approval, of at least eight years for pharmaceuticals . . .

3. Reliance on or reference to such data may be permitted:

(a) in order to avoid unnecessary duplication of tests of agrochemical products involving vertebrate animals, provided that the first applicant is adequately compensated; or

(b) where a written consent from the first applicant is presented.

Several issues are worth noting. First, the provision is not limited to "new chemical entities" but to "pharmaceuticals." In this regard, it is unlike and goes beyond the typical EFTA agreement in a manner that is more restrictive.[64] Second, while the eight-year term of test data exclusivity is in line with EFTA agreements, it is beyond those of the United States and therefore to the extreme end of exclusivity. Third, the protection applies to chemical entities and biologics, making this agreement one of the first globally to explicitly protect biologics. Fourth, the provision allows for adequate compensation instead of the eight-year waiting period but only applies it to certain agrochemical products. Here again, this is a departure from EFTA practice, which regularly applies this provision to pharmaceuticals. Overall therefore this provision is more restrictive than the usual EFTA template on test data exclusivity.

Moreover, it is worth highlighting that the agreement requires test data exclusivity as opposed to market exclusivity. This means that in practice, the period of market exclusivity extends beyond the eight-year period. This is the case since the regulatory review process in Hong Kong takes on average up to one year to complete, meaning the effect of data exclusivity actually will actually extend market exclusivity to an average of nine years.[65]

---

[64] The only way around this is to rather creatively read Article 4(1), which states that "[t]he Parties shall protect undisclosed information in accordance with Article 39 of the TRIPS Agreement," in such a way as to restrict application of the provision to chemical entities.

[65] The regulatory agency does not release records on this matter. The author established the stated period of time through informal conversations and interviews with pharmaceutical company representatives and lawyers who represent applicants and have experience with the system.

According to Shaikh's ranking of thirty-five FTAs involving twenty-three jurisdictions according to their "access to medicine," the HK-EFTA FTA ranks fairly low at twenty-fourth – with strong scores for proximity to Article 39(3) of TRIP and strength of test data exclusivity but weak on duration of test data exclusivity and inclusion of exceptions/access enabling provisions.[66] Even more worrying, however, is that in the survey of domestic laws on test data exclusivity Hong Kong ranked dead last among the twenty-three jurisdictions surveyed.[67] Thus, and rather curiously, Hong Kong's domestic legislation lacks many of the exceptions and flexibilities that are included in the HK-EFTA FTA. While it is in Hong Kong's interest to provide for an access-oriented regime, it is in fact proving to be the most restrictive regime of any jurisdiction.

Having agreed to a period of eight years of restrictive data exclusivity in the EFTA FTA, there is little Hong Kong can now do in regard to length of protection. Why Hong Kong would agree (or even demand) such a provision is unknown, but it makes little sense for the jurisdiction. Most notably, the main justification for test data exclusivity protection is to ensure that there is a sufficient period of marketing exclusivity to allow the originator drug companies to recoup R&D costs. This justification is of little relevance to Hong Kong, for a number of reasons. First, given the size of the market, it is unlikely that its protection of test data (or otherwise) would affect the decision-making of a company on whether it should proceed with clinical tests. Second, such protection will not stimulate the development of a pharmaceutical industry or in any way benefit Hong Kong companies. Third, the extended period of protection is burdensome for the healthcare budget.

Moreover, and as importantly, the extended period of exclusivity appears unwarranted in Hong Kong given that generic applicants often delay regulatory filings until even after the patent term has expired.[68] The requirement will also likely extend protection well beyond the expiration of the patent, as Hong Kong is rare in requiring that prior to filing an application for marketing approval containing a new chemical or

---

[66] Owais Hassan Shaikh, "Index of Data Exclusivity and Access (IDEAS): An Analysis of Test Data Exclusivity Provisions in Free Trade Agreements and National Laws," in Bryan Mercurio and Daria Kim (eds.), *Contemporary Issues in Pharmaceutical Patent Law: Setting the Framework and Exploring Policy Options* (Routledge, 2017).

[67] Ibid.

[68] See Aidan Hollis and Paul Grootendorst, "The Price of Exclusivity: The Economics of Patent Extensions and Data Protection," in Mercurio and Kim (eds.), *Contemporary Issues in Pharmaceutical Patent Law: Setting the Framework and Exploring Policy Options*.

biological entity, the product must have received prior registration in at least two specified countries.[69] This indicates that Hong Kong identifies itself as a secondary market for innovative drugs and not as a market that drives innovative products. Even more, it does not appear that Hong Kong undertook any economic or health impact analysis prior to its implementation of an eight-year period of test data exclusivity. Hong Kong is not alone in this regard, as there is a dearth of empirical evidence on the effect of test data exclusivity in general. That being said, the evidence that does exist indicates that test data exclusivity extends the period of effective protection for originator drugs, thereby delaying generic competition, and increases the cost of drugs to consumers and governmental purchasers.[70] The evidence also reveals that test data exclusivity has not led to an increase in pharmaceutical-related foreign direct investment (FDI) and that it may actually result in the delay of registration of drugs in secondary markets.[71]

This last point – that test data exclusivity could delay drug registration in secondary markets – has been understudied in the literature but may be more important than the impact on the introduction of generic pharmaceuticals. This is not only because originators can delay their application for marketing approval in such markets, but also because some FTAs restrict generic manufacturers from referencing the marketing approval from another jurisdiction. In the past, such references have been used by marketing authorities to approve generic drugs even in the absence of registration by the originator in the relevant market. In the restrictive FTAs, however, the result could be that the drug is not available in the

---

[69] "The Guidance Notes on Registration of Pharmaceutical Products/Substances," Note 8 (D)(g), above n. 63.

[70] Oxfam International, "All Costs, No Benefits: How TRIPS-Plus Intellectual Property Rules in the US-Jordan FTA Affect Access to Medicine," Oxfam Briefing Paper, March 2007, www.oxfam.org/sites/www.oxfam.org/files/all%20costs,%20no%20benefits.pdf, accessed 22 February 2017, pp. 9 and 14 (finding a substantial decrease in generic competition for drugs launched between 2001 and 2006 and an increase of pharmaceutical spending of between $6 and $22.04 million in Jordan due to the implementation of test data exclsuivity).

[71] Ibid. See also Ellen R. Shaffer and Joseph E. Brenner, "A Trade Agreement's Impact on Access to Generic Drugs" (2009) 28(5) *Health Affairs* 957, http://content.healthaffairs .org/content/28/5/w957.abstract, accessed 22 February 2017(discussing delays in the registration of drugs in Guatamala); M. E. C. Gamba, F. R. Buenaventura and M. D. V. Serrano, "Impacto de 10 años de protección de datos en medicamentos en Colombia" (2012) *Serie Buscando Remedio* 2, http://web.ifarma.org/images/files/buscandoremedio/ BuscandoRemedio_2.pdf, accessed 22 February 2017 (discussing the impact of test data exclusivity in Colombia).

jurisdiction for a considerable length of time. This is particularly the case where neither the domestic law nor the FTA requires the originator to apply for marketing approval within a certain period of time following the first approval or filing in another jurisdiction. The benefit of such practice for the originator is that it can delay the introduction of the drug into a lower-priced market until its period of exclusivity (and with it, higher prices and profits) ends in the primary markets.

In order to prevent gaming of the system in such a manner, secondary jurisdictions should require both in domestic law and as a safeguard in FTAs a provision that requires originators to submit applications for marketing approval within a certain period of time – e.g., six months – following submission or approval in another jurisdiction. In the Hong Kong context, the jurisdiction should amend existing the regulations so as to require originators to apply for registration within a certain time frame after gaining marketing authorization in the original market (or receiving approvals in two jurisdictions to mimic existing rules regarding submission) in order to be able to make use of the full eight-year protection period. Should an originator not meet the timeline, then test data exclusivity should run from the time of the date of the first grant of marketing approval. Because such a requirement does not exist in the EFTA-Hong Kong FTA, an amendment to that treaty would also be required.

Hong Kong should also take numerous other steps to minimize the potential harm that test data exclusivity could bring to the health system while maintaining good-faith compliance with its international commitments. For instance, one important step Hong Kong could take to liberalize and simplify its regime is by granting marketing approval to pharmaceuticals that have been approved in other select jurisdictions, perhaps by amending the existing rule such that when a product has been registered in two listed jurisdictions, marketing approval is automatically granted on application in Hong Kong. In this regard, Hong Kong would not "use" or "require" any originator data in the granting of marketing approval, and thus Article 39(3) of the TRIPS Agreement would not apply.[72]

Hong Kong could also amend the regulations such that when it requires the submission of test data, it will explicitly limit protection of the test data to that which is necessary in order to gain marketing approval. This

---

[72] Reichman, above n. 2, 19 ("WTO Members have no duty to 'require...the submission of undisclosed test or other data' and they may rely upon the health and safety decisions of other jurisdictions, or on the published medical literature, or a combination of both, without incurring liability under Article 39.3").

limitation would be in accordance with Article 39(3) of the TRIPS Agreement, which requires protection for data that are *necessary* for marketing approval. Where companies voluntarily submit information or submit excess information that is not needed for the granting of marketing approval, such information should not be subject to the data exclusivity regime. Such an interpretation should also be consistent with Article 4(1) of Annex XII of the HK-EFTA FTA, which calls on the Parties to "protect undisclosed information in accordance with [TRIPS] Article 39."

Furthermore, as the phrase "considerable effort" in Article 39(3) of the TRIPS Agreement is vague and undefined, Hong Kong could seek to define it in the legislation and interpret it not only in economic terms but so as to include technical and scientific terms. In this regard, while "considerable" may not be capable of being defined, it would be clear that the standard is high.

In addition, although Hong Kong is not likely to issue a compulsory license on a pharmaceutical, it nevertheless should give itself the flexibility to do so should the need arise (in line with Article 39(3) of the TRIPS Agreement). In this regard, it should provide an exception clause to test data exclusivity in both domestic legislation and in the text of its FTAs in the event of an emergency or other crisis that necessitates the issuance of a compulsory license. The reason an exception clause is necessary is that test data exclusivity could impede a generic manufacturer from obtaining marketing approval, even when acting in accordance with a compulsory license. Simply stated, a manufacturer granted authority to produce a generic drug under compulsory license must still obtain marketing approval prior to producing and placing the drug on the market. If test data exclusivity prevents it from using the originator's data and obtaining the registration, it cannot actually fulfill the terms of the compulsory license and supply the needed drug.[73]

Moreover, Hong Kong should seek an interpretation or amendment to the HK-EFTA FTA and legislatively provide for the possibility of a generic applicant providing "adequate compensation" in lieu of providing

---

[73] In the face of mounting criticism, the United States argued that "if circumstances ever arise in which a drug is produced under a compulsory license, and it is necessary to approve that drug to protect public health or effectively utilize the TRIPS/health solution, the data provisions in the PTA would not stand in the way." Such a response is somewhat problematic, however, as the legal status of "side letters" is unclear and the wording invites dispute between the parties as to what is "necessary." See Letter from USTR General Counsel John K. Veroneau to Congressman Sander M. Levin, 19 July 2004 (in the context of the US-Morocco FTA).

a blanket eight years of exclusive protection. Although generic manufacturers may not take advantage of this option, providing for the possibility is prudent, in line with the majority of EFTA's FTAs and would at least provide an avenue for early access to medicines for consumers.

Finally, and in order to better protect originators, Hong Kong should legislatively provide that a generic manufacturer or other third party cannot use pharmaceutical test data as evidence in an independent submission for marketing approval if the data had been acquired through dishonest commercial practice. In so doing, Hong Kong could take a position on the interpretation of Article 39(3) of TRIPS.[74]

6.4 Conclusion

Test data exclusivity is a reward for the creation of standardized and better data that is beneficial to society. It is separate from and often runs concurrently with patent protection. On the one hand, test data exclusivity makes sense so as to encourage R&D and the proliferation of test data, even where the likelihood of the originator receiving a patent is unlikely or nonexistent. In this regard, it seems unfair that a third party can "free ride" and immediately use the originator's data to produce a rival medicine. On the other hand, test data exclusivity can serve to delay the entry of generic competition onto the market. Where no patent exists or expires during the term of test data exclusivity, it acts as a de facto patent to ensure a minimum period of monopoly for the originator. In some agreements, countries can be prohibited from using test data submitted in another jurisdiction even where the originator has not sought registration in that market.

There is no consensus on the correct interpretation of Article 39(3) of the TRIPS Agreement, and efforts to further define the provision at the WTO so as to provide for test data exclusivity have been rejected by developing counties. While the trend is for providing test data exclusivity in FTAs, this is being demanded by a handful of developed countries and accepted by others as part of a more comprehensive trade bargain – it cannot be said that subsequent state action has not risen to the level where test data exclusivity can be viewed as the new norm or standard. Therefore, the majority view is also likely the correct interpretation of Article 39(3) of the TRIPS Agreement and the most in line with the VCLT – the provision protects against governmental authorities disclosing

---

[74] Such a view would be in line with the majority of WTO Members and commentators. See, e.g., ICTSD-UNTAD, above n. 7, 11–12; Correa, above n. 29, 576–77.

confidential data, with exceptions for the issuance of a compulsory license and to remedy anticompetitive practices.

Test data exclusivity may not be required by the TRIPS Agreement but it has worked its way into the domestic legislation of a number of jurisdictions. This includes Hong Kong, which agreed to eight years' test data exclusivity as part of the HK-EFTA FTA. Test data exclusivity in Hong Kong and other small jurisdictions seems misplaced, as surely these markets are too insignificant to influence or determine the decision to proceed with trials and other data-generating activities. Of course, one could still argue that a third party should not be able to "free ride" anywhere in the world, not just in the larger developed country markets. This argument is of course moot, as Hong Kong is now required to protect test data irrespective of whether it benefits the jurisdiction. That being the case, Hong Kong could take several steps to safeguard the healthcare system and limit the potential negative effects of test data exclusivity. If such steps are not taken, test data exclusivity will be an expensive and needless burden on an already stretched system.

7

Patent Linkage

7.1 Introduction

Patent linkage refers to the practice of national pharmaceutical registration authorities "linking" the granting of marketing approval – that is, the right to market a drug – with the patent status of an originator drug. The most common form of patent linkage prevents the relevant registration authority from granting marketing approval (i.e., registration of a generic drug for sale on the market) while there is a valid a patent in place covering the drug. Without patent linkage, the registration authority confines its assessment to ascertaining whether the pharmaceutical under investigation is safe and effective. Simply stated, without patent linkage the patent status of a drug is irrelevant to the marketing approval process. The registration authority ensures the safety and efficacy of the drug at issue while the patent act sets out the rights of the patent holder.[1] Of course, the granting of marketing approval does not in any way override patent rights, and a generic pharmaceutical company would infringe those rights by bringing the drug to market while a valid patent remains in force.

---

[1] The Canadian Supreme Court noted the inherent tension between the regimes in *AstraZeneca Canada Inc. v. Canada (Minister of Health)*, [2006] 2 S.C.R. 560, 2006 SCC 49 (Can.) at 12:

> The [patent linkage regulations] lie at the intersection of two regulatory systems with sometimes conflicting objectives. First, is the law governing approval of new drugs, which seeks to ensure the safety and efficacy of new medications before they can be put on the market... [This] process culminates (if successful) in the issuance of [marketing approval] to an applicant manufacturer by the Minister of Health on the advice of his officials in the Therapeutic Products Directorate. The... objective is to encourage bringing safe and effective medicines to market to advance the nation's health. The achievement of this objective is tempered by a second and to some extent overlapping regulatory system created by the Patent Act... Under that system, in exchange for disclosure to the public of an invention, including the invention of a medication, the innovator is given the exclusive right to its exploitation for a period of 20 years.

Patent linkage extends the monopoly selling period of an originator's pharmaceutical in the market by a period equal to the time it takes for a generic manufacturer to gain regulatory approval, usually between six and twenty-four months in developed markets. This extension of monopoly protection beyond the statutory period of the patent is unique to pharmaceutical products (and agrochemicals), where the additional step of gaining approval from a regulatory authority is necessary prior to marketing the product.

The TRIPS Agreement does not mandate, prohibit or even mention patent linkage. This is not because the topic was unknown during the Uruguay Round. To the contrary, the negotiating parties were aware of but chose not to include such protection in the international agreement. By not mentioning the subject, TRIPS neither requires nor prohibits patent linkage. Patent linkage is therefore a "TRIPS-Plus" provision that is beyond the mandate and scope of the WTO.[2] The one caveat to this is that certain newly acceded Members of the WTO agreed to patent linkage (and test data exclusivity) as part of their WTO accession package.[3]

While the purpose of patent linkage is "to provide monopoly rights to private firms in exchange for new and innovative drugs while at the same time facilitating the timely entry of generic drugs,"[4] public health advocates view it as simply a means for extending monopoly pricing, delaying access to more affordable medicines and extending market exclusivity

---

[2] For a discussion on TRIPS-Plus provisions, see Michael Handler and Bryan Mercurio, "Intellectual Property," in Simon Lester, Bryan Mercurio and Lorand Bartels (eds.), *Bilateral and Regional Trade Agreements: Commentary and Analysis*, 2nd edition, pp. 324–63 (Cambridge University Press, 2016).

[3] See WTO, Report of the Working Party on the Accession of Cambodia, WT/ACC/KHM/21 (2003) at 44. Commitments made in an Accession Protocol are binding and subject to the dispute settlement mechanism. See also Appellate Body Report, *China – Measures Related to the Exportation of Rare Earths, Tungsten and Molybdenum* (AB-2014-3; AB-2014-5; AB-2014-6–WT/DS431/AB/R; WT/DS432/AB/R; WT/DS433/AB/R), 7 August 2014 at 5.1–73; Appellate Body Report, *China – Measures Related to the Exportation of Various Raw Materials* (WT/DS394/AB/R; WT/DS395/AB/R; WT/DS398/AB/R) 30 January 2012 at 270–307; Appellate Body Report, *China – Measures Affecting Imports of Automobile Parts* (WT/DS339/AB/R; WT/DS340/AB/R; WT/DS342/AB/R), 15 December 2008 at 210–45; Appellate Body Report, China – Measures Affecting Trading Rights and Distribution Services for Certain Publications and Audiovisual Entertainment Products (WT/DS363/AB/R), circulated 21 December 2009, at 113.

[4] Ron A. Bouchard, Richard W. Hawkins, Robert Clark, Reidar Hagtvedt and Jamil Sawani, "Empirical Analysis of Drug Approval-Drug Patenting Linkage for High Value Pharmaceuticals" (2010) 8 *Northwestern Journal of Technology and Intellectual Property* 174, 181 note 44 (citing numerous Canadian Government Regulatory Impact Analysis Statements).

beyond that of the originating patent.[5] Regardless of position, it is clear that patent linkage is representative of a novel evolution of the protective framework for pharmaceutical products that impacts on the availability and cost of medicines and related products.[6]

The chapter proceeds as follows: Section 7.2 reviews the historical development of patent linkage in the United States and its spread to other jurisdictions. The section also analyses the situation in Hong Kong, which does not provide for patent linkage but has faced attempts by the industry to provide for the protection via judicial interpretation. Section 7.3 critically evaluates both the reasons why Hong Kong should not adopt patent linkage and considerations to take in case the jurisdiction ever contemplates its adoption. Section 7.4 concludes.

7.2 International Framework and Effect of Patent Linkage

7.2.1 Domestic Legislation: The Beginnings

Patent linkage first appeared in the United States as part of the Hatch-Waxman Act (1984)[7] as and part of a "grand bargain" intended to stimulate the development of innovation and availability of new medicines while at the same time facilitate the timely entry of generic competition into the market. Until the introduction of the Hatch-Waxman Act, the FDA essentially treated undisclosed clinical trial and other data submitted by a pharmaceutical company/originator in an application for marketing approval as a trade secret.[8] With the FDA considering such information confidential, competitors did not have access to and therefore could not rely on the

---

[5] Ibid., at 176–77. See generally Ron A. Bouchard, Jamil Sawani, Chris McLelland, Monika Sawicka and Richard W. Hawkins, "The Pas de Deux of Pharmaceutical Regulation and Innovation: Who's Leading Whom?" (2009) 24 *Berkeley Technology Law Journal* 1461.

[6] See Ron A. Bouchard et al, "Global Pharmaceutical Linkage Regulations: A Proposed Analytical Framework" (2011) 12(2) *Minnesota Journal of Law, Science & Technology* 1, 42.

[7] See Drug Price Competition and Patent Term Restoration Act of 1984, 98 P.L. 417 (24September 1984); 21 USCA 355 – New Drugs, at (c)(3)(D), reprinted in 21 CFR §314.108 (1993).

[8] See ibid., 21 USC 355(b)(1)(A). For background on reform attempts from the 1960s to 1980s, see Ellen J. Flannery and Peter Barton Hutt, "Balancing Competition and Patent Protection in the Drug Industry: The Drug Price Competition and Patent Term Restoration Act of 1984" (1985) 40(3) *Food Drug Cosmetic Law Journal* 269; Ronald L. Desrosiers, "The Drug Patent Term: Longtime Battleground in the Control of Health Care Costs" (1989) 24 *New England Law Review* 115. For a modern review of the Act, see Robert A. Armitage, "The Hatch-Waxman Act: A Path Forward for Making It More Modern" (2014) 40 *William Mitchell Law Review* 1200.

data when seeking to obtain marketing approval for generic versions of the patented pharmaceutical. While this did not bar generic applicants from conducting their own clinical trials, the time and expense of conducting such duplicative trials as well as the unlikelihood of recouping the R&D costs (not to mention the ethical concerns of repeating trials to achieve an already established result) meant in reality that competitors could not apply for marketing approval during the term of patent protection. With undisclosed data submitted to the FDA treated as a trade secret, the originator received monopoly power not only for the life of the patent, but also for a period of time thereafter as generic competitors prepare and apply for marketing approval.

The Hatch-Waxman Act allowed for quicker and easier entry into the market as generic companies can "use" a patented drug in order to seek marketing approval from the FDA before the expiration of patent protection[9] and without having to conduct clinical trials; instead, generic companies merely have to prove the bioequivalence – that is, potency and availability in the body – of their version of the pharmaceutical with the originator product.[10] While the Act does not allow generic competition on the market during the term of patent protection, it does provide a financial sweetener to facilitate early entry of generics into the market by granting a generic company that successfully challenges the validity of a patent with its own six-month period of market exclusivity.[11]

The Hatch-Waxman Act thus "linked" the patent status of a pharmaceutical (under the Patent Act) to marketing approval (under the Food, Drug, and Cosmetic Act).[12] Consequently, the FDA is now prohibited from granting marketing approval to a generic product so long as the originator company filing a New Drug Application (NDA) "listed" or "registered" at least one patent contained in the approved drug in the "Approved Drug Products with Therapeutic Equivalence" (commonly referred to as the "Orange Book").[13] While the FDA must now consider matters outside

[9] 35 USC 271 – Infringement of Patent at (e)(1) (2000 & Supp. 2005). The US Supreme Court has consistently expanded the boundaries of the exemption. See, e.g., *Eli Lilly and Co. v. Medtronic*, 496 US 661 (1990); *Merck KgaA v. Integra Lifesciences I, Ltd.*, 545 US 193 (2005); *Momenta Pharm. v. Amphastar Pharm*, 686 F.3d 1348 (2012).

[10] Generic manufacturers also have to demonstrate that the product was manufactured according to good manufacturing practice (GMP). See 21 CFR pt. 211 – Current Good Manufacturing Practice for Finished Pharmaceuticals (2007).

[11] 21 USC 355 above n. 7 at (j)(5)(B)(iv) (2000 & Supp. V 2005).

[12] 35 USC 1–376 (2006); Federal Food, Drug, and Cosmetic Act, 21 USC 301–97 (2006).

[13] 21 USC 355 above n. 7 at (j)(7)(A) (2006).

the scope of the safety and efficacy of a pharmaceutical product, the burden is not great as the agency simply relies on the information provided in the NDA to restrain approval of generic drugs.

Under the Hatch-Waxman Act, an Abbreviated New Drug Application (ANDA) facilitates the entry of generics into the market. However, ANDA applicants must certify that (1) the drug has not been patented; (2) the patent has expired; (3) the generic drug will not be placed on the market until the patent expires or (4) the patent is not infringed on or is invalid. Referred to as paragraph I, II, III and IV certifications, the first three are straightforward, whereas a paragraph IV certification is more complex. In a paragraph IV certification the ANDA applicant must notify the innovator company of its filing and describe the reasons why the patent will not be infringed or is invalid or unenforceable. Following receipt of the notice, the originator is given forty-five days to file a lawsuit for infringement (submission of a paragraph IV certificate to the FDA triggers an infringement for purposes of the Federal Court). If the originator begins proceedings, FDA approval is stayed for thirty months. Thus, the mere *claim* that a valid patent exists on the drug triggers an *automatic* thirty-month injunction. When this period expires, the FDA can issue tentative marketing approval allowing an ANDA applicant to enter the market, yet most do not actually market the product until resolution of the litigation in order to avoid what could be significant liability for damages if the court ultimately finds a patent infringement.

The Hatch-Waxman Act undoubtedly facilitated the entry of generic pharmaceuticals into the market – generics accounted for 18.6 percent of drugs sold in the United States in 1984 and 86 percent in 2015. At the same time, the Act has allowed for gaming and anticompetitive behavior, and serious questions have been raised in regard to both the economic and health benefits of the "grand bargain." Foremost among the concerns are the delayed introduction of generic competition resulting from multiple patents over one drug and the resulting evergreening strategies of the branded industry as well as agreements whereby potential generic applicants agree not to compete with the branded drug in exchange for monetary remuneration.[14]

---

[14] See, e.g., Federal Trade Commission, "Generic Drug Entry Prior to Patent Expiration: An FTA Study" (July 2002); European Commission, "Pharmaceutical Sector Enquiry: Final Report" (8 July 2009), para. 383; Mathew Avery, "Continuing Abuse of the Hatch-Waxman Act by Pharmaceutical Patent Holders and the Failure of the 2003 Amendments" (2008–2009) 60 *Hastings Law Journal* 171; Andrew A. Caffrey and Jonathon M. Rotter, "Consumer Protection, Patents and Procedure: Generic Drug Market Entry and the Need to

7.2.2   The Spread of Patent Linkage

In recent years, patent linkage has spread throughout the world. While most countries have introduced provisions as part of FTAs with the United States, some have adopted patent linkage without any external pressure. Patent linkage now exists in a diverse range of countries, including China, Japan, Mexico, South Korea, Singapore and Canada. In contrast, the EU considers patent linkage to be unlawful.[15]

Patent linkage provisions are not uniformly drafted and implemented. While a simple version of patent linkage could merely require that an applicant for marketing approval notify the patent owner of the application or limit the filing of applications to a specific time period prior to the expiration of the relevant patent (i.e., within two years of the expiration of the patent), the more common version not only includes a notification requirement, but also precludes the granting of marketing approval for a generic drug while the relevant patent remains in force (i.e., until it expires

Reform the Hatch-Waxman Act" (2004) *Virginia Journal of Law and Technology* 1; C. Scott Hemphill and Mark A. Lemley, "Earning Exclusivity: Generic Drug Incentives and the Hatch-Waxman Act" (2011) 77 *Antitrust Law Journal* 947; Monika Sawicka and Ron A. Bouchard, "Empirical Analysis of Canadian Drug Approval Data 2001–2008: Are Pharmaceutical Players 'Doing More with Less'?" (2009) 3 *McGill Journal of Law and Health* 87; Bouchard et al., above n. 5; Edward Hore, "Patently Absurd: Evergreening of Pharmaceutical Patent Protection under the Patented Medicines (Notice of Compliance) Regulations of Canada's Patent Act" (2004), www.canadiangenerics.ca/en/news/docs/patently_absurd_04.pdf, accessed 22 February 2017.

[15] See Article 81 of Regulation (EC) No. 726/2004 of the European Parliament and of the Council of 31 March 2004, setting out Community procedures for the authorization and supervision of medicinal products for human and veterinary use and establishing a European Medicines Agency. See also Article 10.6 and 126 of Directive (EC) No. 2001/83 of 6 November 2001, on the Community code relating to medicinal products for human use. See further, EC Final Report, above n. 14, para. 872 ("the task of marketing authorisation bodies is to verify whether a medicinal product is safe, effective and of good quality. Their main function is to ensure that the pharmaceutical products reaching the market are not harmful to public health. Other factors, such as the patent status of the product, should therefore not be taken into account when assessing the risk/benefit balance of a medicine"). See also European Commission, "Pharmaceutical Sector Inquiry: Preliminary Report," DG Competition Staff Working Paper (28 November 2008), 113, http://ec.europa.eu/competition/sectors/pharmaceuticals/inquiry/preliminary_report.pdf, accessed 5 March 2017. That being the case, patent linkage has crept into the laws and regulations of several Member States in what has been referred to as "ghost linkage." See ibid. at 14, 113 and table 22; see also European Generic Medicines Association, "Patent-Related Barriers to Market Entry for Generic Medicines in the European Union: A Review of Weaknesses in the Current European Patent System and Their Impact on the Market Access of Generic Medicines," 23–24 May 2008, www.ieis.org.tr/ieis/assets/media/EGA%20-%20IP_Barriers_web.pdf, accessed 13 March 2017.

or is invalidated) or even outright prohibits a registration authority from reviewing an application while a patent remains in force. In some countries (including the United States), patent linkage requires the registration authority to maintain a registrar of patents and essentially verify the patent status of any drug during the registration process.

It also must be stressed that while patent linkage may have made sense in the US context as part of a "grand bargain," most countries do not share the same legal and political framework. That is, context matters and what may be beneficial for one jurisdiction may be harmful for another with a different legal and social starting point. Perhaps the starkest contrast was the introduction of patent linkage in Canada. Canada adopted a model largely based on the US template in 1993 in anticipation of the coming into force of the NAFTA.[16] In Canada, patent linkage did not facilitate the entry of generics into the market but rather effectively killed one of the most pro-generic regimes in the developed world.[17] Until the introduction of patent linkage, Canada was home to a number of successful generic manufacturers[18] and Canadians enjoyed some of the most affordable drug prices among the developed countries.[19] While Canada's

---

[16] For instance, generic applicants will not receive marketing approval until all listed patents have expired or a generic manufacturer challenges the validity of the patents via a Notice of Allegation (NOA). If the generic manufacturer issues an NOA, the originator has forth-five days to apply for judicial review and request an "order of prohibition" preventing the Minister from issuing the NOC until the expiration of the patent expiry. This act triggers an automatic injunction of twenty-four months. See Patented Medicines (Notice of Compliance) Regulations SOR/1993–133, (Can) at §5(1)(a), (b), §5(3)(a) and §6(1).

[17] From the 1920s until the introduction of amendments in 1987 and 1993, Canada operated a compulsory license scheme for pharmaceuticals (among other products) that eventually fixed royalty rates at 4 percent of the net selling price. See, e.g., Patent Act, S.C. 1923, c. 23, s. 17. For further information, see Margaret Smith, "Patent Protection for Pharmaceutical Products" (November 1993) Report prepared for the Government of Canada, http://publications.gc.ca/Collection-R/LoPBdP/BP/bp354-e.htm; Christopher Scott Harrison, "Protection of Pharmaceuticals as Foreign Policy: The Canada-U.S. Trade Agreement and Bill C-22 versus the North American Free Trade Agreement and Bill C-91" (Spring 2001) 26 *North Carolina Journal of International Law & Commercial Regulation* 457, 507 (note 282); Milan Chromecek, "The Amended Canadian Patent Act: General Amendments and Pharmaceutical Patents Compulsory Licensing Provisions" (1987) 11 *Fordham International Law Journal* 504, 527–28.

[18] Generic manufacturers also benefited from the establishment of provincial programs to reimburse the cost of medicines for certain groups of individuals and legislation that required the purchase of generic-equivalent medicines where available. See Smith, above n. 17.

[19] Harrison, above n. 17, 547. See generally Thomas K. Fulda and Paul F. Dickens III, "Controlling the Cost of Drugs: The Canadian Experience" (1979) 1(2) *Health Care Finance Review* 55. It should be noted that Canada fundamentally altered the scheme in 1987 to

pharmaceutical patent regime had to be revised in light of the international obligations undertaken in the TRIPS Agreement – in that rules discriminating on the basis of field of technology and country of invention/manufacture needed to be revised – it was not required to introduce patent linkage. That requirement came from a commitment in the NAFTA.

It is therefore important to look at a number of jurisdictional-specific factors when evaluating the merits of patent linkage, including the policy intent that underpins the potential implementation of patent linkage, public health and economic policy, clarity of the relevant laws and regulations as well as the potential for judicial interpretation and other developments to influence or change the balance of competing health-related interests.[20] Such factors apply equally when evaluating the success of existing regimes or desirability of patent linkage for jurisdictions where patent linkage does not currently exist.

7.2.3   Patent Linkage in Hong Kong[21]

Hong Kong does not provide for patent linkage. In this regard, the authorities responsible for the granting of patents (Hong Kong Intellectual Property Department) are separate from the authorities responsible for the distribution and supply of pharmaceutical products (Hong Kong Pharmacy and Poisons Board). Moreover, the Drug Office of the Department of Health does not maintain a registrar of patented pharmaceuticals nor does it require applications for marketing approval to declare noninfringement of third parties' patent rights. In fact, the Department of Health's "Guidance Notes on Registration of Pharmaceutical Products/Substances" explicitly states that "the Pharmacy and

---

introduce, inter alia, a ten-year period of protection against compulsory licenses to import a generic medicine and seven years' protection against a compulsory license when the generic medicine would be manufactured in Canada. See Bill C-22 (1987) 35–36 Eliz. 2, ch. 41 (1987) amending the Patent Act, R.S.C. ch. P-4 (1970). See also Chromecek, above n. 17, 526–34; Brian W. Gray, "New Changes to the Patent System" (1988) 43 *Food Drug Cosmetic Law Journal* 641, 645–46. The changes came in the form of Bill C-91 (June 1992), which became law in February 1993.

[20] Bouchard et al., above n. 6, 8.

[21] Parts of the remainder of this section are drawn from Bryan Mercurio and Daria Kim, "Patently Lacking: An Analysis and Call for Systemic Review of Pharmaceutical Law and Policy – A Case Study of Hong Kong" (2014) 9(1) *Asian Journal of WTO & International Health Law and Policy* 63, 94–101.

Poisons Board does not take the factor of 'patent right' into consideration while deciding on an application for registration of a pharmaceutical product/substance."[22]

Hong Kong has considered and decided against the adoption of patent linkage on a number of occasions.[23] In some instances, the government's rejection of patent linkage is strongly worded:

> The Administration does not consider that registration of pharmaceutical products should be linked to the issue of patent. The drug registration system is established for protection of public health. As there is already a well-established patent protection system in Hong Kong, the drug registration system should focus on the safety, efficacy and quality aspects. In this regard, it is noted that . . . patent linkage could delay the process of drug registration purely because of patent reasons, and hence affect the availability of drugs.
>
> From the patent protection perspective, the proposed patent linkage would in effect give an extra patent protection for pharmaceutical products vis-à-vis other products which are equally protected under our Patents Ordinance. We see no strong reasons to provide for this given that the drug registration system has not deprived patent holders of any protection under the Patents Ordinance.[24]

---

[22] See "The Guidance Notes on Registration of Pharmaceutical Products/Substances," Hong Kong SAR Department of Health (February 2017), at 14, www.drugoffice.gov.hk/eps/do/en/doc/guidelines_forms/guid.pdf, accessed 22 February 2017.

[23] Discussion has always been triggered by industry associations and lobby groups. See, e.g., "Concerns and Proposals from the Hong Kong Association of the Pharmaceutical Industry," Business Facilitation Advisory Committee (BFAC Paper 2/06, 14 February 2006), http://theme.gov.hk/en/theme/bf/pdf/1bfacpaper2-06.pdf, accessed 22 February 2017; the American Chamber of Commerce in Hong Kong and HKAPI, "Position Paper on Pharmaceutical Patent Linkage" (2004), www.amcham.org.hk/images/stories/PositionPapers/patent%20linkage-2004.pdf; the Hong Kong Association of the Pharmaceutical Industry, "Position Paper on the Review of the Patent System in Hong Kong" (2012), www.hkapi.hk/positionpapers.asp; American Chamber of Commerce in Hong Kong, Intellectual Property and Pharmaceutical Committees, "Submission on the Consultation Paper on the Review of the Patent System in Hong Kong," 13 January 2012, www.cedb.gov.hk/citb/doc/en/submissions_list/070.pdf; all links accessed 13 March 2017. See also *Official Record of Proceedings*, Hong Kong SAR Legislative Council 10320–2 (2007), www.legco.gov.hk/yr06-07/english/counmtg/hansard/cm0711-translate-e.pdf; Hong Kong SAR Commerce and Economic Development Bureau, Intellectual Property Department, "The Review of the Patent System in Hong Kong: Consultation Paper" (October 2011), www.ipd.gov.hk/eng/pub_press/press_releases/2011/paper_20111004_e.pdf.

[24] See Second Meeting of the Business Facilitation Advisory Committee, "Agenda Item 2: Administration's Response to the Concerns and Proposals from the Hong Kong Association of the Pharmaceutical Industry" (BFAC Paper 3/06, 26 June 2006), www.info.gov.hk/fso/bfac/eng/pdf/2bfacpaper3-06.pdf, accessed 22 February 2017.

Despite such statements, the branded pharmaceutical industry continues to push for patent linkage through the courts. One strategy that has been used is to claim that while the application for marketing approval is not in itself an infringement, the fact that the applicant will have had to "work" or "use" the patent in formulating the application is an infringement. As the law regarding experimental use is vaguely drafted and legislation lacks an explicit "Bolar" provision,[25] this argument has at times found favor with the courts. Another strategy that has found some success is arguing that an application for marketing approval during the period of patent protection indicates an intention to bring the drug to market – which would indeed result in an infringement. The patent holder will thus ask the court to require a declaration (under penalty of contempt of court) from the applicant that it will not to bring the drug to market until the expiration of the patent, the effect of which is to remove the ability of the applicant to challenge the validity of the patent through use.

A more direct attempt to introduce patent linkage through the courts was made in *Abbott v. Pharmareg*,[26] where the court extended the period of patent protection beyond twenty years through an injunction[27] and in doing so "linked" the period of injunction to the period of time taken to obtain regulatory approval. The dispute arose over a process patent for using the substance sibutramine in the manufacturing of a drug to treat obesity. In 2009, the court agreed with Abbott that the importation, stockpiling and sale of Obirax (a product that also contained sibutramine)

---

[25] For more discussion of the Bolar provision, see Chapter 5.

[26] A similar attempt occurred in India, where Bristol-Myers Squibb secured an ex parte injunction; see *Bristol-Myers Squibb Company & Ors v. Dr BPS Reddy & Ors*, High Court of Delhi (19 December 2008) prohibiting the Drug Comptroller General of India (DCGI) from granting marketing approval for a generic version of Sprycel (dasatinib, used to treat chronic myeloid leukemia) before being overturned in *Bayer Corporation and Ors v. Cipla of India (UCI) and Ors*, High Court of Delhi (18 August 2009). The court cited several reasons for its decision: (i) the differing objectives between the Drugs Act (public health/safety) and Patents Act (private monopoly right), and the DCGI's lack of expertise in adjudging patent validity; (ii) that it is not within the DCGI's legislative mandate to determine patent status and validity; (iii) the negative health effects of reading patent linkage into the legislation, including on existing exceptions to patent rights and access to medicines; and (iv) the reticence in extending the boundaries of patents in the absence of clear parliamentary intent.

[27] The decisions are: (1) the decision of the Court of First Instance of March 27, 2009, *Abbott Gmbh & Co. Kg & Abbott Laboratories Limited v. Pharmareg Consulting Company Limited & Yin's Trading Company Limited*, HCA 166/2009; and (2) the decision of the Hong Kong High Court in *Abbott Gmbh & Co. Kg & Anor v. Pharmareg Consulting Company Limited & Ors*, HKCU 88, 8 January 2010.

infringed the patent and granted a pretrial injunction for the period until the patent expired (that is, until 21 November 2009).[28]

Shortly before the expiration of the patent, Abbott sought an extension of the interlocutory injunction for an additional nine months beyond the expiry of the patent claiming that: "[s]ince the defendants have imported and used the infringing Obirax capsules to apply for registration...and the application process took nine months, such acts constituted infringement of the Hong Kong Patent."[29] In so doing, Abbott claimed the infringers derived an unfair benefit and were able to "steal a headstart by importing or causing to be imported into Hong Kong OBIRAX thus allowing it to register same with the Department of Health even before the Hong Kong Patent had expired."[30] Thus, despite the clear statements from the government in 2006 and 2007 that the law does not link marketing approval to the patent status of the pharmaceutical, Abbott requested in 2010 that registration while a patent was in place amounted to an unfair abuse of the system.

While the 2010 court extended the injunction, it did not consider whether using the patent in preparation for an application for marketing approval or even if the act of application for marketing approval itself amounted to patent infringement.[31] Likewise, the 2009 decision only considered patent infringement by making, importing and stockpiling Obirax, but not its use for the purpose of obtaining marketing approval. Despite neither decision authoritatively rejecting the existence of patent linkage in Hong Kong, neither did the decisions create such a link. Thus, the situation remains somewhat unclear and uncertainly will persist until the government provides clear guidelines and legislative direction.

---

[28] See *Abbott v. Pharmareg*, HCA 166/2009, above n. 27, paras. 41–65. The defendants questioned whether the patent at issue for the second medical use met the novelty requirement, but the court ultimately confirmed the "permissibility" of the "Swiss type" claim for a subsequent second medical use of sibutramine. See ibid., para. 37. See also *Abbott v. Pharmareg*, HKCU 88 (2010) above n. 27, para. 40(4).

[29] *Abbott v. Pharmareg*, HKCU 88 (2010) above n. 27, para. 20. The complainants relied on the decisions in *Dyson Appliances Ltd v. Hoover Ltd* (No. 2) [2001] RPC 544 at 558–68 and in *Generics BV v. Smith Kline & French Laboratories Ltd.* [1997] RPC 801 for the proposition that the court will grant an injunction that extends beyond the patent expiration date in order to prevent an infringer from unfairly benefiting from any advantage sought to be obtained from acts of infringement committed during the term of the patent. Ibid., para. 19.

[30] Ibid., para. 14.

[31] The judge in the 2010 case stated: "[I] am of the view that it would not be proper for the court at this interlocutory stage to make any decision as the merits or otherwise of the case." Ibid., para. 48.

7.3   Assessing the Merits and Options

The issues involving patent linkage are many, but revolve around two larger questions: first, whether patent linkage should be adopted, and second, if so, what form of patent linkage should be adopted.

7.3.1   Should Patent Linkage Be Adopted?

There are many reasons to oppose the adoption of patent linkage. Chief among them is that it delays the introduction of generic medicines onto the marketplace. Such delays bring about economic rents to the industry but do so at the expense of the government and consumer, both of whom are forced to pay higher prices for pharmaceuticals beyond the normal patent period. Patent linkage has been found to delay the entry of generic competition by three to five years in some markets,[32] whereas the European Commission found delays of generic competition to the market in the EU of only seven months.[33] Importantly, the European Commission also found the extended delay in generic competition occurs even when litigation determines the patent is invalid, which in many jurisdictions happens in the majority of instances.[34]

Another reason to oppose patent linkage is that the potential economic and health benefits advocates claim it brings are questionable. On the contrary, studies in the United States and elsewhere often find patent linkage encourages firms to engage in anticompetitive behavior.[35] One Canadian study led by Bouchard concludes that "rent-seeking behavior by brand-name pharmaceutical firms to leverage loopholes in the regime is passed on in the form of continued monopoly costs to the public."[36]

Moreover, while it is true that originators deserve and society relies on their ability to innovate, the simple fact is that there is no evidence that patent linkage boosts innovation. As pointed out throughout this book, the reality is that the branded-pharmaceutical industry is using multiple tools to delay generic competition in the marketplace, including by focusing on incremental inventions and marginally useful second use

---

[32] Bouchard et al., above n. 6, 30.   [33] EC Final Report, above n. 14, 8.
[34] Ibid.   [35] See above n. 14.
[36] Ron A. Bouchard, "I'm Still Your Baby: Canada's Continuing Support of U.S. Linkage Regulations for Pharmaceuticals" 15 (2011) *Marquette Intellectual Property Law Review* 71, 114. See also Sawicka and Bouchard, above n. 14; Bouchard et al., above n. 4; Bouchard et al., above n. 5.

patents. Thus, far from stimulating innovation it appears that TRIPS-Plus provisions such as patent linkage discourage innovation while at the same time encourage market distortions and gamesmanship in an effort to maintain monopoly rights.

Yet another reason to oppose patent linkage is that it changes the nature of the regulatory regime by reversing the burden of proof. With patent linkage it is the generic applicant who must prove that it does not infringe on a patent, not for the owner of the private right to enforce the patent once infringement has occurred. This transforms a private property right that would normally depend on the owners' willingness and desire to enforce into a public right that will be enforced by a governmental authority, a significant departure from traditional IP norms. That IPRs are private rights, not rights that are enforced by government, is often lost, if not obfuscated, by the branded pharmaceutical industry. For instance, AstraZeneca stated in the context of Canadian law that patent linkage – including presumably the need for an automatic injunction – was needed to "prevent infringement" from occurring and attempted to reiterate its point by stating that in Canada it was difficult to obtain an interlocutory injunction after the product has been placed on the market. These statements are an astonishing reversal of the traditional view of IP protection and enforcement and a brazen attempt at institutionalizing the burden shift to generic applicants and governmental authorities.

The "prevention of infringement" severely curtails the scope of activities of generic manufacturers and completely removes the right and opportunity for generic manufacturers to willingly and knowingly take the calculated risk of making and placing a product on the market without authorization from the patent owner either in the belief that the patent is invalid (and thus unenforceable) or because they have found a way to circumvent the claims set out in the patent. Such action is one of the cornerstones of the patent system, whereby a competitor can bring the product to market and, if sued for patent infringement, directly challenge the validity of the patent. Taking away this right of action, without a corresponding move making it easier to challenge a patent by administrative means, transforms the challengeable presumption of validity of the patent into a much more secure property right.

Finally, there does not appear to be any need for patent linkage in Hong Kong. With generic manufacturers usually not applying for marketing approval until well after the expiration of the patents on pharmaceuticals, it is unsurprising that a study conducted by Hollis and

Grootendorst found that the average period of market exclusivity for the branded drug in Hong Kong is greater than that in the United States, Canada and other markets.[37] This information is valuable for the branded pharmaceutical industry, which has consistently lobbied the government for the introduction of patent linkage. Such efforts may be unnecessary, and political capital and resources are better directed to other issues. Of course, the economic losses to the public health system as a result of initiating patent linkage would also be more limited than elsewhere, as patent linkage would only delay marketing approval of generics applied for during the patent period and not affect the majority of generic entrants who only seek approval following the expiration of the patent term.

Hong Kong has thus far resisted the trend to adopt patent linkage. This should be maintained for the reasons outlined above. Moreover, given the judicial challenges outlined above, Hong Kong should strengthen the wording of the relevant regulations to ensure and make even clearer that an application for marketing approval does not amount to a patent infringement. This will send a strong signal that patent linkage is not part of the laws of Hong Kong.

7.3.2   If so, What Model?

While essentially all forms of patent linkage could possibly delay the introduction of generic competition into the marketplace, the differences between and among regimes matter. Some forms are particularly onerous, however, while others more balanced. But all of the regimes are based on the original US template. This seems oddly misplaced, as the policy intent and context of patent linkage in the United States may (and likely would) not be appropriate in another jurisdiction.

The policy intent in the United States was to stimulate the development of innovative drugs while at the same time facilitate the timely entry of generic competition to the marketplace. This purpose has been confirmed in the jurisprudence[38] and also encompassed in a statement by Senator Orrin Hatch when the Hatch-Waxman Act came into force: "The public

---

[37] Aidan Hollis and Paul Grootendorst, "The Price of Exclusivity: The Economics of Patent Extensions and Data Protection," in Bryan Mercurio and Daria Kim (eds.), *Contemporary Issues in Pharmaceutical Patent Law: Setting the Framework and Exploring Policy Options* (Routledge, 2017).

[38] See, e.g., *Mylan Pharmaceutical v. Bristol-Myers Squibb.* 268 F.3 1323, at 1326.

receives the best of both worlds – cheaper drugs today and better drugs tomorrow."[39]

In 1993, Canada relied on essentially the same justification for introducing patent linkage.[40] Likewise, throughout the AUSFTA negotiations patent linkage was promoted to Australians as necessary in order to stimulate investment into pharmaceutical R&D.[41] Using the same justification for every jurisdiction seems rather bizarre – the formula used to encourage innovation and the development of drugs, or even to adequately secure an appropriate level of pharmaceutical patent enforcement or facilitate the entry of generic competition into the market, differs in every jurisdiction. Simply stated, what is missing from the sweeping justification for patent linkage is the appropriate comparator, or baseline legislation, from which each proposed measure should be judged. For instance, the pre-1984 law in the United States treated test data as a trade secret and clearly hampered the entry of generic competition into the market by providing a de facto extension of monopoly sales. The bargain reached to provide additional forms of protection in exchange for providing an easier pathway for generics to enter the market seemed appropriate to the United States.

In contrast, Canada historically encouraged generic competition and local production through a compulsory licensing regime for pharmaceuticals. Far from facilitating the timely entry of generic competition into the market, patent linkage has harmed the once-thriving domestic generic industry and led to an increase in the price of drugs.[42] Moreover, with Canada's limited domestic market (with a population of slightly more than 30 million) it is unlikely that patent linkage has increased innovation or R&D in the pharmaceutical sector. While the specifics of legislation in Australia, Mexico, South Korea and elsewhere differ, the broader point

---

[39] Congressional Record – Senate at 23764 (10 August 1984), as cited in Bouchard et al., above n. 6, 10.

[40] This can be seen in several reports and Regulatory Impact Analysis Statements. See, e.g., *Canada Gazette* vol. 140, no. 24, 17 June 2006: "The Government's pharmaceutical patent policy seeks to balance effective patent enforcement over new and innovative drugs with the timely market entry of their lower priced generic competitors." See also Bouchard et al., above n. 6, 10–11 at note 48.

[41] See, e.g., Thomas A. Faunce and Joel Lexchin, "'Linkage' Pharmaceutical Evergreening in Australia and Canada" (2007) *Australia and New Zealand Health Policy* 8.

[42] Brett Skinner, "Generic Drugopoly: Why Non-Patented Prescription Drugs Cost More in Canada Than in the United States and Europe" (2004) 82 *Public Policy Sources (Fraser Institute)* 1; Joel Lexchin, "Intellectual Property Rights and the Canadian Pharmaceutical Marketplace: Where Do We Go from Here?" (2005) 35 *International Journal of Health Services* 237, 243; Bouchard et al., above n. 6, 11.

is that the baselines in these jurisdictions were more similar to Canada than the United States and therefore it is unlikely that patent linkage has stimulated R&D and innovation or even promoted quicker or easier entry of generic competition. Simply stated, the policy justification for patent linkage in the United States is not relevant to jurisdictions with different baselines.

That differences between jurisdictions matter is often lost on governments.[43] With the cost of litigation high in every country, it is questionable whether patent linkage is beneficial to most nations. More specifically, patent linkage (in addition to other laws and regulations that attempt to balance enhanced protections for the rights holder with encouraging generic entry into the market) may work in larger markets – and in particular the United States, with approximately 40 percent of the worldwide market – where the value of entry into the marketplace is high. In smaller jurisdictions, the benefits of entry into the market are more limited, and the costs of litigating a patent claim mean the benefits are marginal or negative, even with exclusivity on offer for the first generic entrant (as offered in the United States and Korea). In such jurisdictions, the net result of patent linkage is to delay generic entry into the market, with higher overall costs to the healthcare system.

What this means is that jurisdictions seeking to adopt patent linkage should be careful in planning and operationalizing the regime. Decisions taken at this stage will determine the ultimate effect of patent linkage on the health system. For instance, which "patent(s)" should be "linked" – in other words, should the regime link only the first/"main" patent or should multiple patents be linked (and placed on the register if a registration system is in place)? Another pertinent question is what type of patent should qualify for linkage? These issues may be technical but are fundamental to the scope of patent linkage. To date governments have responded in very different ways, seemingly without any empirical data or justification for their decisions.

Governments do not seem to recognize the importance of the issue as it relates to health and economics – the allowance of multiple patents for inventions beyond the chemical entity and follow-on patents could lead to

---

[43] For instance, Singapore's Medicines Act, 1975, Section 12A, is strikingly similar both procedurally and substantively to that of the United States, even including the thirty-month automatic injunction period. Singapore does not, however, maintain a patent register nor does it provide an incentive to generics to challenge the validity of the patent with a period of exclusivity granted to the first successful generic challenger.

patent holders gaming the system so as to delay the introduction of generic competition. Legislators in the United States recognized the potential negative effects of multiple patents, but nevertheless allowed multiple patents to be registered in the belief that delay to generic entry would be limited.[44] This belief seems mistaken, as the Federal Trade Commission in 2002 found significant evidence of gaming to delay market entry of generic competition.[45] In hindsight, it is not difficult to see how this occurred. In the United States (and Canada), courts have struggled to determine the appropriate threshold for what is a patent relevant to the marketed drug, and therefore eligible for registration, and when forced to do so have taken a broad approach to the term "relevance."[46] Meanwhile, marketing authorities (such as the FDA) are not experts in patent law and likewise take a broad approach to listing. The result is multiple patents registered for each drug.[47] More worrying is the trend of pharmaceutical companies to produce a large amount of follow-on drugs, each with their own registerable patents, which have the effect of delaying entry of generic competition.[48] For these reasons, allowing only the "main" patent(s) to be registered/linked is perhaps the single most important decision a jurisdiction can take to prevent the balance being tilted too far in favor of the originator and against entry of generic competition.[49]

Limiting linkage to the "main" patent(s) is also a critical factor in determining the suitability of a patent register. With pharmaceutical patents being complex in nature, and with dozens of patents of some high-value drugs, it is questionable whether health authorities are qualified to determine the applicability of a patent to the product of a generic applicant. With courts even having difficulty in distinguishing true innovation worthy of patent protection from nonpatentable discoveries, it seems

---

[44] See House Report No. 98-857(I) [H.R.(I), at 8–30.
[45] Federal Trade Commission, above n. 14.
[46] See, e.g., *Mylan Pharmaceuticals v. Bristol-Myers Squibb Co.* 268 F.3d 1323. In Canada, see *AstraZeneca v. Apotex, Minister of Health* 2004 FC 1277, https://goo.gl/6fuIJc, accessed 13 March 2017.
[47] Bouchard et al., above n. 6, 18; Bouchard et al., above n. 4; Hemphill and Lemley, above n. 14.
[48] This point has been analyzed at length in the literature. See, e.g., Bouchard et al., above n. 6, 18; Bouchard, above n. 4.
[49] See Hore, above n. 14; Avery, above n. 14. Alternatively, the Korean approach does not simply list all claimed patents but instead reviews the substance of the "Patent Listing Applications" to ensure that the relationship between the patent claims and approved product is legitimate. Such an approach could be a worthwhile model for others to follow in order to stem the flow of listings and litigation.

unrealistic to expect the health and marketing authorities to authenticate the claims of the patentee. Hence, most jurisdictions maintaining a register simply list all patents asserted by the original applicant. But such a practice has been susceptible to gaming by the branded industry, which constantly adds new patents and engages in "evergreening" so as to forestall competition. For this reason, some public health advocates heavily criticize the patent register.[50]

On the other hand, while a system that does not maintain a patent register eases the burden on the authority responsible for granting marketing approval, it does make the verification process more difficult for the generic applicant. A report commissioned by the Australian government recommended the addition of a "transparency register" that would include all patents owned by, or licensed to, the originator and relevant to the relevant drug so as to provide certainty for the generic applicant (who can better identify which patents are registered) and limit infringement proceedings to a finite number of patents per product (i.e., those registered).[51] In this regard, the use of a patent register would discourage excessive litigation, not only against generic applicants, but also against the marketing authorities, so long as the patent owner was precluded from litigating over patents not listed in the register. The intention behind the call for the creation of a register is therefore one of reducing costs and increasing transparency and certainty to generic companies seeking to apply for marketing approval, not a way to increase evergreening and delay the introduction of generics onto the market.[52]

The Korean regime offers an innovative safeguard and perhaps can serve as a model for others. While Korea makes use of a patent register called the "Green List" whereby patent holders can list patents pertaining to the substance, formulation, composition or medical use that

---

[50] Brook Baker, "Ending Drug Registration Apartheid – Taming Data Exclusivity and Patent/Registration Linkage" (2008) 34 *American Journal of Law and Medicine* 302, 307; Bouchard et al., above n. 4, 174. See, contra, Commonwealth of Australia, "Pharmaceutical Patents Review Report 2013," 149–54 (recommending the addition of a "transparency" register in order to ease the burden on generic manufacturers in searching for relevant patents on pharmaceutical products).

[51] Commonwealth of Australia, "Pharmaceutical Patents Review Report 2013," at 154.

[52] For instance, the report did not support several features common in other linkage regimes, including "the introduction of the features … that provide for an automatic stay on generic applications for regulatory approval, should an originator commence court proceedings, nor those that prevent generic manufacturers from undertaking all the steps necessary to prepare to enter the market upon expiry of the relevant patent, which includes obtaining regulatory approval." Ibid., 152–53.

are "directly relevant" to the approved medical product,[53] patents must be listed on the Green List *before* the granting of regulatory approval. In this way, the system does not allow patent holders to add patents to the register in an attempt to forestall generic marketing approval or facilitate infringement claims.[54] The Korean regime also adds an additional layer of protection in that its authorities vet applications instead of simply listing all patents identified by the originator. More specifically, the Korean Ministry of Food and Drug Safety reviews the substance of the "Patent Listing Applications" to ensure the relationship between the patent claims and approved product are legitimate and has the authority to change, narrow, edit and delist patent claims for failing to meet the requisite standard.[55] While this increases complexity, it also serves to improve the quality of the register and limit litigation expenses. In contrast, a register that simply lists all patents identified by the originator and also allows litigation involving patents not listed in the register casts doubt on the usefulness of the register and begs the question of its purpose.

Another issue is whether and to what extent the right holder should be granted an automatic injunction on the initiation of infringement litigation. While automatic injunctions feature in US, Canadian and Singaporean regulations, they do not appear in other jurisdictions.[56] Unsurprisingly, automatic injunctions have been shown to increase both the number of patents per high-value product and litigation. More specifically, pharmaceutical companies regularly abuse the registration process by listing a substantial number of patents not entirely related to the drug in the Orange Book, or even listing additional patents subsequent to an ANDA application from a generic company. Furthermore, the evidence points not only to increased litigation following the introduction of patent linkage, but also to an increase in the time it takes a generic to come to market.[57] To this end, the EC Pharmaceutical Sector Final Report found

---

[53] Enforcement Regulations of Korea Pharmaceutical Affairs Act, Decree No. 162 (18 October 2012), Article 30*ter*, para. 3.

[54] Ibid., at Article 30*ter.*

[55] Ibid., at Article 24, Paragraph 10; Article 30*ter*, para. 5. The Korean scheme also applies to biologic medicines, whereas in the United States biologics are separately regulated.

[56] For instance, in Canada the mere assertion of the originator that its patent is valid triggers an automatic injunction for a period of twenty-four months, or until the court has determined the issues (i.e., whether the generic applicant is "justified") or the patent expired, whichever is earliest. Patented Medicines (Notice of Compliance) Regulations SOR/1993–133, (Can) at 7.

[57] The Federal Court of Canada summarized the situation as follows: "by merely commencing the proceeding, the applicant obtains what is tantamount to an interlocutory injunction

that the mere threat of automatic injunctions sends a strong chilling effect to generic competitors, with data "illustrat[ing] the strength of the link between patent-related exchanges and patent litigation."[58]

The Korean and Australian regimes may be model approaches in that both limit the anticompetitive effects of the injunction. For instance, Korea does not issue automatic injunctions but rather will grant injunctions only where there is a "need to prevent significant damage." Where granted, injunctions are limited to a twelve-month period from the date of notice (as opposed to thirty months in the United States).[59] Moreover, and importantly, the injunction applies to generic *sales*, not to the granting of marketing approval. Likewise, Australia does provide for automatic injunctions but requires a patent holder seeking an interlocutory injunction to prevent the marketing of the generic pharmaceutical product to first notify the Australian Attorney-General (who shall be deemed a party in the proceedings) and obtain leave from a court.[60] Where the application for an interlocutory injunction is unsuccessful, the court has the authority to order the originator to pay compensation to the applicant as well as to the federal and/or state/territory government in order to recoup losses to the Pharmaceutical Benefits Scheme (the government system for purchasing and distributing subsidized prescription medicines to Australians). Moreover, Australia has adopted rather progressive "anti-evergreening" measures that attempt to safeguard the system by providing that following a certification by a generic manufacturer the patent holder must certify that any infringement proceedings it initiates are being commenced in good faith, have reasonable prospects of success and will be conducted without unreasonable delay, with penalties for a false or misleading certification of up to AU$10 million.[61]

---

for up to 30 months without having satisfied any of the criteria a court would require before enjoining issuance of an NOC." *Bayer AG v. Canada (Minister of National Health and Welfare)* (1993), 163 N.R. 183, at 189. See also *Eli Lilly & Company v. Apotex Inc.*, 1997 CanLII 6216 (FCA); *Merck Frosst Canada Inc. v. Apotex Inc.*, [1997] 2 FCR 561, 1997 CanLII 4806 (FCA). In the United States, issues can be resolved in one step and without the threat of damages. This is not the case in Canada, where summary proceedings under linkage regulations are often followed by infringement litigation. But automatic injunctions are not solely to blame for the increased delays. Perhaps more damaging to consumers are settlements between branded and generic firms that delay the introduction of generics into the market.

[58] EC Final Report, above n. 14, para. 575.

[59] Korea Food and Drug Administration, Implementation Plan of Patent-Drug Approval Linkage (30 October 2007).

[60] Australia's Therapeutic Goods Act 1989 (Cth), Section 26D.

[61] See ibid., Section 26C. The term "reasonable prospects of success" is defined in s26C(4) as follows: "(a) the second person had reasonable grounds in all the circumstances known to

Yet another choice is whether to encourage generics to challenge patent validity by providing them incentives to do so. The United States provides such an inducement in the form of a 180-day period of exclusivity to the first generic to successfully challenge the validity of a patent.[62] This serves to stimulate generic competition and effectively balances the automatic injunction provided to originators.[63] Unlike the United States, most adherents to patent linkage do not balance the automatic injunction with any market-based incentives to generics. This may not matter, however, as the high cost of litigation may not warrant the potential returns on offer for generic applicants. Simply stated, few markets would be large enough to serve as an incentive for a generic to challenge a patent – and this is certainly the case in Hong Kong, where most generic manufacturers do not even apply for marketing approval until well after the expiration of the patents of the originator drug. For this reason, most do not provide the inducement to encourage generics to bring claims – yet the lack of this inducement coupled with an automatic injunction changes the balance originally struck in the US legislation in a manner that is against competition. Such is the case in Canada, which offers a twenty-four-month injunction without the corresponding benefit to generics.

Australia's regulations could serve as a useful model to others seeking to balance the rights of the patent holder with larger societal benefits. Australia does not provide for automatic injunctions but instead requires the originator to seek an injunction through a court order, with penalties for failing to act in good faith.[64]

Another, more systemic, issue is how patent linkage fits with experimental use provisions, particularly where a Bolar or regulatory review exception is written into legislation that expressly allows a generic to

---

the second person, or which ought reasonably to have been known to the second person (in addition to the fact of grant of the patent), for believing that he or she would be entitled to be granted final relief by the court against the person referred to in paragraph (1)(a) for infringement by that person of the patent; and (b) the second person had reasonable grounds in all the circumstances known to the second person, or which ought reasonably to have been known to the second person (in addition to the fact of grant of the patent), for believing that each of the claims, in respect of which infringement is alleged, is valid; and (c) the proceedings are not otherwise vexatious or unreasonably pursued."

[62] By contrast, Korea provides for a twelve-month period of exclusivity to the first generic company to successfully challenge the validity of a patent if litigation commences *before* filing for marketing approval. See Korean FDA, above n. 59.

[63] There is, however, some evidence to suggest that the exclusivity period is not working as designed. See Federal Trade Commission, above n. 14.

[64] See also the approach taken by Korea, above nn. 53–55.

"use" the patented pharmaceutical for the purpose of preparing an application for marketing approval. In *Canada – Pharmaceutical Patents*, a WTO panel held that such practice fit within the perimeters of the exception clause (Article 30) of the TRIPS Agreement.[65] To some commentators, linkage acts as a barrier to countries wishing to resort to the regulatory exception to Article 30. This may be an overstatement, as even in most patent linkage regimes a regulatory review exception allows a generic manufacturer to prepare and submit an application for marketing approval during the patent term; even if such application cannot be approved until the expiration of the patent, it can be approved immediately upon the expiration of the patent, and thus generic drugs would come to market several months before they would if no regulatory review exception was in place.

That being the case, many jurisdictions suffer from having vaguely worded and opaque regulatory review exceptions. For instance, Section 75(b) of the Hong Kong Patents Ordinance reads: "The rights conferred by a patent shall not extend to acts done for experimental purposes relating to the subject-matter of the relevant patented invention." The lack of clarity and precision in the language could be interpreted narrowly or broadly and in this sense it is unclear whether, for instance, the term "experimental purposes" covers conducting tests using a patented subject matter as part of an application for the pharmaceutical regulatory approval. Thus, and despite the fact that a regulatory review exception is entirely consistent with the TRIPS Agreement, it remains unclear whether such conduct is consistent with Hong Kong patent law.[66] The vagueness and undetermined nature of legislation such as this illuminates the need for patent linkage to be introduced in conjunction with a clearer and more tailored research exemption that specifically includes patent use to facilitate an application for regulatory review in order to minimize delays to the introduction of generic competition on expiration of the patent.

Even though the EU does not maintain a patent linkage regime, its Bolar exception can serve as a model in providing generic manufacturers with

---

[65] *Canada – Patent Protection of Pharmaceutical Products*, WT/DS114/R, at 7.84 (17 March 2000).

[66] This is a common problem, as the incorporation of Bolar provisions varies widely. See Christoph de Coster, Julia Bödeker and Paul England, "Not All Bolar Exemptions Are the Same," TaylorWessing Synapse (September 2013), www.taylorwessing.com/synapse/september13.html, accessed 5 March 2017; Darren Smyth, "More on Amendments to Bolar Provisions – This Time in Ireland," *IPKat* blog, 11 August 2014, http://ipkitten.blogspot.hk/2014/08/more-on-amendments-to-bolar-provisions.html, accessed 5 March 2017.

the comfort that "[c]onducting the necessary studies and trials with a view to the application [for marketing approval] and the consequential practical requirements shall not be regarded as contrary to patent rights or to supplementary protection certificates for medicinal products."[67] Such a statement would explicitly allow generic manufacturers to "use" the patent in conducting the necessary studies, tests and trials before making an application for marketing approval and, in certain jurisdictions, challenging the validity of the patent via certification (e.g., paragraph 4 certification in the US).

As importantly, care must be taken to ensure that patent linkage does not conflict with or impede compulsory licensing provisions and the right of countries to take measures to protect public health. This would seem to necessitate legislation that suspends patent linkage in the event that the government issues a compulsory license (for either domestic use or export under the waiver of Article 31 of the TRIPS Agreement).[68] Failing to legislate in such a manner could result in a situation where an importer or local manufacturer cannot obtain marketing approval to sell the drug subject to the compulsory license in the jurisdiction. Somewhat surprisingly, such legislative protections are virtually unknown to this author in any jurisdiction.[69]

---

[67] See, e.g., European Directive 2004/27/EC (amending Directive 2001/83/EC) on the EU code relating to medicinal products for human use. The scope of the clause, however, remains unclear "due to the use of ambiguous, vague and broad terminology [and] diverging implementation in the various EU Member States." See European Generic Medicines Association, above n. 15, at 23–24. One important area of divergent interpretation is whether the Bolar exception extends to the filing of an application for price and reimbursement listings. In one case, a Swedish court refused to find the Swedish Medical Products Agency liable for contributory infringement for its determination that a generic medicine (risperidone) was interchangeable with Risperdal, holding that the Medical Products Agency cannot determine the validity of patent rights and can only decide whether the medical demands for interchangeability have been met. See European Generic Medicines Association, above n. 15 at 24–25. In this regard, the "EC Pharmaceutical Sector Preliminary Report" stated: "As long as these activities are strictly necessary to prepare for [a marketing approval] application, they are not deemed to infringe patents rights ... in view of the so-called Bolar provision [which] creates a safe harbor for certain tests and studies while the reference product is still patent-protected so as to enable the generic producer to apply for marketing authorisation once the eight-year period of data exclusivity granted to the [patent] holder ... has elapsed." See "EC Preliminary Report," above n. 15, 260.

[68] WTO General Council, "Implementation of Paragraph 6 of the Doha Declaration on the TRIPS Agreement and Public Health," Decision of the General Council of 30 August 2003, WT/L/540 and Corr.1, 1 September 2003, www.wto.org/english/tratop_e/trips_e/implem_para6_e.htm, accessed 13 March 2017.

[69] Of course, a manufacturer will in most countries not need marketing approval to produce a generic for export as the drug will not be released onto the domestic market.

A final issue to note is how to essentially engage in legal transplantation without oversights or mistakes. The legal transplantation process is not always entirely smooth. Most notably, Singapore faced issues regarding the cause of action in litigation. More specifically, while the US Patent Code statutorily provides that an ANDA submission is an infringement, Singapore simply added Section 12A to the Medicines Act in lieu of introducing an amendment to the Singapore Patents Act for the filing of an application for marketing approval as a new cause of action. This led to some confusion, and required the court in *AstraZeneca v. Sanofi-Aventis* to get slightly creative in holding that Section 12A of the Singapore Medicines Act, read together with the accompanying regulations, constitutes a cause of action separate and independent from a patent infringement action under the Patents Act.[70]

In the case, Sanofi-Aventis applied to the Health Sciences Authority under Section 12A of the Singapore Medicines Act for marketing/licensing approval to import a cholesterol-reducing drug into Singapore despite the fact that at least one patent on the drug was held by AstraZeneca. Sanofi-Aventis served a Notice to Proprietor of Patent on AstraZeneca stating the reasons why it did not believe its drug infringed AstraZeneca's patent. AstraZeneca duly commenced an action against Sanofi for a declaration of patent infringement if Sanofi were to import the products into Singapore. Sanofi-Aventis responded by seeking to strike out AstraZeneca's action for a declaration of infringement on the ground that the action was frivolous, vexatious or an abuse of process of the court, since AstraZeneca failed to allege any instance of a past act of infringement in its claim. The court agreed with AstraZeneca that the responsive action is infringement not pursuant not to the Patents Act, but rather to Section 12A of the Medicines Act, which when read with other regulations forms a separate cause of action for which a patent holder can seek a declaration of infringement.[71] Thus, the court did not agree with Sanofi-Aventis that Section 12A of the Medicines Act merely provides notification

---

[70] *AstraZeneca AB (SE) v. Sanofi-Aventis Singapore Pte Ltd* [2012] SGHC 16, www .singaporelaw.sg/sglaw/laws-of-singapore/case-law/free-law/high-court-judgments/ 14771-astrazeneca-ab-se-v-sanofi-aventis-singapore-pte-ltd-2012-sghc-16, accessed 13 March 2017.

[71] Ibid., at 35 (stating that "section 12A of the Medicines Act, read with its accompanying subsidiary legislation, contemplates a cause of action separate and independent from a patent infringement action under the Patents Act"). In so doing, the court rejected the arguments from Sanofi-Aventis (1) that Section 12A did not provide for a cause of action separate and independent from a patent infringement action under the Patents Act, and (2) correspondingly, that the Patents Act only deals with actual infringements and there is no separate mechanism provided for threatened infringements.

to inform the patent holder of an application for marketing/licensing approval relating to a patented product, but does not provide the patent holder with a right or cause of action to commence infringement proceedings.

The merits of patent linkage for most jurisdictions remain questionable – this is especially so for countries without any significant pharmaceutical industry. In every case, countries considering the adoption of patent linkage should take these general principles and "best practices" guidelines into consideration:

- Patent linkage should not forestall the development of generic competition or unduly delay an application for marketing approval.
- Patent linkage should not prohibit a generic manufacturer from challenging the validity of a pharmaceutical patent. Likewise, the grant of marketing approval should not be a defense to any action for infringement. Where patent linkage does delay the registration of a generic product, marketing approval should take effect on the day the patent expires or is invalidated.
- Patent linkage should apply only to patents involving the primary active ingredient(s) and not to compositions, dosage, new use and process patents.
- When a country uses a patent register, patent claims attempting to halt generic marketing approval should be limited to patents listed on the register at the time of the application for marketing approval.
- Regulations should not allow for automatic injunctions following a claim for patent infringement, but rather should only be granted after the plaintiff has made a prima facie case that the patent in question is valid. In any event, requiring a mandatory notice provision whereby a generic applicant must inform the patent holder of its application should provide enough time to allow the latter to determine whether it should initiate an infringement proceeding (as opposed to presuming the validity of the patent).
- Where automatic injunctions are granted, an exclusivity prize should exist for the first generic to successfully challenge the validity of the patent.
- As a matter of expediency, efficiency and legal harmonization, all claims involving marketing approval and patent infringement should be heard in a single forum, so far as possible.
- Attempts to prevent or delay generic competition through payments and other inducements from the innovator company should be illegal, whether through competition law or otherwise.

7.4 Conclusion

This chapter reviewed the historical development of patent linkage, questioned the necessity and desirability of patent linkage and highlighted the fact that the context, contours and effects of patent linkage differ between jurisdictions.

Patent linkage is not required by the international IP framework. Jurisdictions that choose to adopt patent linkage do so voluntarily, even if it is included as an FTA obligation. While patent linkage regimes have presumably all been designed to suit the particulars of the differing jurisdictions, there is little evidence that any of the systems reduces costs, increases access to medicines or promotes innovation. Perhaps the most worrying part of patent linkage is that despite almost all the empirical evidence suggesting it has negative health and economic effects on a country, only one country is considering its removal and more countries are adopting it as law. As more countries adopt patent linkage, empirical evidence on the effect of the various forms of patent linkage should also grow. If used wisely, such evidence can form the basis of a tardy but informed debate on the benefits and detriments of patent linkage.

To this end, Hong Kong and other governments must think carefully before adopting a regime of patent linkage, and ensure its introduction follows a systemic review that takes into account policy priorities and objectives and fully accounts for all potential costs. This is, of course, what occurred when the United States introduced patent linkage in 1984 as part of a broad law aimed at balancing promotion of innovation and safeguarding public interests, including through the early introduction of generic competition in the marketplace.

Any review of patent linkage would necessitate an evaluation not only of the economic benefits/costs and potential models and choices (e.g., a patent registry, automatic injunctions, exclusive marketing periods for the first generic to challenge, penalties for frivolous claims, etc.), but also of the basic framework, including how patent linkage intersects with other patent and relevant regulatory laws. Foremost among such issues is the relationship between patent linkage and the regulatory review exception. In Hong Kong and a number of other jurisdictions, the regulatory review exception is vaguely worded and ill-defined. Introduction of patent linkage without a more precisely worded research exemption could create disharmony within the law, as would provisions that conflict with or impede compulsory licensing.

If Hong Kong does consider the adoption of patent linkage – or, more likely, agrees to do so in an FTA – the patent linkage regimes in Australia and South Korea should serve as a model. Both regimes adopted patent linkage as part of FTAs with the United States but tailored the regime to their own needs – and while it is premature to call these systems a success, at first instance the systems appear to have more effectively balanced the interests of the branded industry, generic interests and consumer interests than other jurisdictions. Unfortunately, these countries are in the minority. Most regimes adopt patent linkage on the basis of no evidence and implement a version that closely resembles the US regime.

Hong Kong should resist temptation to adopt patent linkage, but if does it should learn from the experiences of others and ensure better and more precise drafting to negate some of the more undesirable aspects of patent linkage.

8

Conclusion

Pharmaceutical patent law is a controversial and seemingly unsettled area of international IP law. The TRIPS Agreement is just the starting point and complexity is added with every new FTA and addition of sui generis and related rights. The branded pharmaceutical industry has been successful in lobbying governments to legislate for and include in FTAs a maximalist IP agenda that extends the rights and better protects branded drugs from competition on the marketplace. In some respects, provisions that guarantee a certain period of market exclusivity are justified as the process of discovering, inventing and bringing drugs to market is expensive and not without substantial risk. One would hope that even the most ardent NGOs promoting access to medicines would admit that absent an incentive to create, the pipeline of new drugs would cease.[1] At the same time, one must be mindful of the fragile IP balance between inventors and the broader interests of users/society. Moreover, one must also be mindful that one size does not fit all and that these interests can vary between and among jurisdictions. Contextualizing framework agreements and making adequate and appropriate use of the flexibilities provided in the international agreements are crucial for the proper functioning and administration of a pharmaceutical patent system.

This book primarily discusses this balance as it applies to Hong Kong. Hong Kong is not unlike most other nations in many respects – it does not host branded R&D activities or a large and competitive generic industry; it has an aging population; and health costs are rising at a rate faster than the GDP. Of importance to Hong Kong is the place of the rule of law, which the jurisdiction views as its comparative advantage over others in the region. These issues were explored in some detail in Chapter 2, as

---

[1] WTO, WIPO and WHO Promoting Access to Medical Technologies and Innovation: Intersections between Public Health, Intellectual Property and Trade 32 (2012) (concluding that the concepts of access to affordable medicine and medical innovation are "intrinsically intertwined").

was the curious, piecemeal and rather stunted approach Hong Kong has taken to the regulation of pharmaceutical patents and related industrial developmental issues. This chapter provided the background and context necessary in order to formulate a framework of objectives and priorities for Hong Kong. The chapter also develops an argument for an integrated approach that would help ensure that legal and policy measures target specific practical needs and are applied in a balanced and holistic way and that decision-making is based on empirical data and other evidence that reflects the benefits as well as social costs associated with the regulations and legislation. Pharmaceutical patent law and healthcare policy can no longer be viewed and treated as separate entities, and determinations and decisions must be country-specific and made only after clear governmental objectives have been set.

Having reviewed the situation, Chapter 2 concludes with the recommendation that Hong Kong must integrate the law and policy in a more systemic way and set out objectives and priorities for the system that reflect the need to provide the populace with high-quality healthcare and affordable and safe medicines, but without ignoring the burden that rising healthcare costs are placing on the territory's budget. Without large-scale manufacturing and R&D activities in Hong Kong and such activities unlikely to increase in the future, there are no industrial policy concerns to compete for attention. Thus, the only sensible option for Hong Kong is to clearly identify access to medicines and cost containment as priorities and construct the pharmaceutical patent system accordingly. Simply stated, Hong Kong must formulate a policy that maximizes public welfare and minimizes unnecessary spending in order to preserve the long-term welfare of the health system in the territory. Of course, and again, it must do so in a way that is territory-specific and without offending its international obligations or risking its reputation as a center of rule of law and strong IP protection.

The preceding chapters then demonstrated how Hong Kong could benefit from taking a holistic approach to pharmaceutical patent law and policy. Taking an issue-by-issue approach, the book methodically reviews the most important areas of pharmaceutical patent law with a view to making jurisdiction-specific recommendations for Hong Kong. Each chapter reviewed the international framework of WTO and subsequent advances made in FTAs before looking closer at how key jurisdictions have implemented the rules in their domestic laws.

Chapter 3 focused on patentability standards, and more particularly on the obligation under Article 27.1 of the TRIPS Agreement to grant patents on inventions, whether products or processes, provided that they are new, involve an inventive step and are capable of industrial application. As demonstrated in the chapter, each of the criteria leaves ample room for tailoring to meet the needs and objectives of a particular jurisdiction with the TRIPS Agreement not providing any guidance as to the meaning and scope of the terms. The chapter also closely examined second use medical patents in this regard given their prominence in modern pharmaceutical development and controversial nature. Patentability standards are of particular importance as the jurisdiction transitions to an examination system. In line with the objectives set out in Chapter 2, the chapter recommended that Hong Kong adopt strict patentability standards that fully respect prevailing international standards (including the granting of second medical use patents) but guard against overprotection and interests that run counter to those of the territory. The specific recommendations made, if adopted, will assist Hong Kong in establishing a fair, predictable and efficient system based on a holistic view of health and other local priorities.

Chapter 4 discussed the emerging standard of patent term extension (PTE). Designed to provide for a minimal period of market exclusivity for a pharmaceutical product and thereby encourage continued R&D and innovation in the field, most developed markets grant PTEs for either unnecessary delays in the granting of a patent or marketing approval of the drug. Hong Kong does not currently grant PTEs, but the international trend is clear and the jurisdiction will very likely consider its adoption in the near future. For Hong Kong, however, it must be clear why it would adopt PTE; the reason for many – that it will lead to greater innovation – is not directly applicable to Hong Kong. With no pharmaceutical R&D, PTE will not directly lead to innovation or sector development in Hong Kong. Of course, as every other economy Hong Kong will indirectly benefit from the advancement of medical science and development of new drugs. More directly, PTE would prolong the period of monopoly sales and therefore increase the costs of drugs, to the detriment of consumers and pharmaceutical spending for the territory. The winner would be the pharmaceutical companies, which would receive a windfall with the extended period of monopoly sales. If and when Hong Kong does decide to implement PTE, it would be well advised to look at the experience of other jurisdictions as a guide. The chapter considered a variety of policy options that would shape the contours of the PTE system so that Hong Kong would pay its share for successful and innovative R&D but at the same time recommended the adoption of several principles and safeguards to ensure that the public interest was protected against overprotection.

Chapter 5 discussed the important topic of exceptions, with particular focus on the experimental use exception and compulsory licensing. In regard to the former, the chapter finds that Hong Kong could benefit from a broader, more tailored approach that takes account of its position as a pharmaceutical importer with little to no branded operations currently operating in the territory. This is particularly the case with the regulatory review exception, which operates to explicitly allow a generic to "use" a patent to apply for marketing approval without the threat of an infringement claim. In regard to compulsory licensing, the current law in Hong Kong takes an extremely broad approach, and since the jurisdiction is unlikely to issue a compulsory license on pharmaceutical absent a public health emergency or crisis, it may wish to consider narrowing the scope of the law so as to avoid unnecessarily offending pharmaceutical interests or tarnishing its well-earned reputation as a regional leader in the protection of IPRs.

The topic of Chapter 6 was test data exclusivity, a sui generis right akin to an IPR that rewards the creation of standardized and better data as a benefit to society. Like PTE, test data exclusivity is designed to ensure a minimum period of market exclusivity for a successful pharmaceutical product – which would apply even if the originator of the data receives no patent for the product. This encourages the production of useful data where the receipt of a patent is unlikely or nonexistent. The alternative, of providing no protection, would mean either that a third party can "free ride" and immediately use the originator's data to produce a rival medicine or that the originator does not conduct the tests, much to society's detriment. While test data protection is the subject of Article 39(3) of the TRIPS Agreement, there is no consensus as to its meaning. Most countries do not read the provision as prohibiting domestic regulatory authorities from registering generic drugs based on the data submitted by the originator. That restraint, however, is included in numerous FTAs, including the HK-EFTA FTA, which demands eight years' protection. This is unfortunate, as test data protection in Hong Kong and other small jurisdictions seems out of line with the purpose of the right – that is, to encourage and reward the generation of test data – given the market size is too insignificant to influence or determine the decision to conduct trials and other data-generating activities. While the author would have recommended that Hong Kong not adopt test data protection, it is too late. That said, the chapter recommends Hong Kong take several legislative steps to safeguard the healthcare system and limit the potential negative effects of test data exclusivity.

Chapter 7 discussed the controversial issue of patent linkage. After reviewing the historical development of patent linkage, the chapter questioned the necessity and desirability of patent linkage and highlighted the fact that the context, contours and effects of patent linkage differ between jurisdictions. While patent linkage may have made sense in the US context, its application in other jurisdictions is highly questionable. Patent linkage certainly does not make sense in the Hong Kong context, where generic manufacturers usually wait until the expiration of the patents on a branded drug prior to applying for marketing approval and where market exclusivity for the branded drugs is already greater than that in the United States, Canada and other markets. If Hong Kong were to consider its adoption, careful consideration must be given to ensure the system takes into account policy priorities and objectives and does not unduly burden the health system and access to affordable medicines. Unlike most jurisdictions, which seemingly follow the US approach without much thought, Australia and South Korea offer models that apply patent linkage but at the same time effectively balance the enhanced protection with societal interests and could be used as models should Hong Kong consider the adoption of patent linkage.

The main objective of the book is to reveal Hong Kong's scattered approach to pharmaceutical patent law and policy law and recommend that a more holistic approach be taken in order to increase coordination between the law and the broader objectives and priorities that should guide health and pharmaceutical policy. In the absence of clear government policies, aims and objectives, this book constructed objectives and priorities for Hong Kong in this regard, and on that basis took an issue-based approach to demonstrate failure of the government to develop appropriate laws for the jurisdiction. In each chapter, shortcomings are revealed and recommendations are made to better coordinate and align with the constructed objectives and priorities. In order to improve efficiency, reduce costs and better provide for the citizens, Hong Kong would be wise to initiate a wholesale review of the system. This book and the underlying research can serve as a starting point for such a review.

INDEX

For EU product safety concerns, contact us at Calle de José Abascal, 56–1°,
28003 Madrid, Spain or eugpsr@cambridge.org.